PARIS : Place de la Concorde.

MEMORABLE SCENES

IN

FRENCH HISTORY:

FROM

THE ERA OF CARDINAL RICHELIEU,

TO

THE PRESENT TIME.

EMBRACING

THE PROMINENT EVENTS OF THE LAST THREE CENTURIES,

WITH

INCIDENTS IN THE LIVES

OF CARDINAL RICHELIEU, LOUIS XV. LOUIS XVI. MARIA ANTIONETTE, LOUIS XVII. MIRABEAU, ROBESPIERRE, NAPOLEON I. MARIA LOUISA, NAPOLEON II. AND NAPOLEON III. ETC.

BY

SAMUEL M. SMUCKER,

AUTHOR OF "COURT AND REIGN OF CATHARINE II." "EMPEROR NICHOLAS I." LIFE OF "ALEXANDER HAMILTON," "ARCTIC EXPLORATIONS AND DISCOVERIES," "HISTORY OF THE MORMONS," ETC., ETC.

NEW YORK:
MILLER, ORTON & CO., 25 PARK ROW.
1857.

Entered according to Act of Congress, in the year one thousand eight hundred and fifty-seven,
BY MILLER, ORTON & CO.,
In the Clerk's Office of the District Court of the Northern District of New York.

PREFACE.

The career of conquest, suffering, and glory which France has run in modern times is without a parallel in history. She may never have deserved, and she may not now deserve, the title and dignity of being the greatest of nations. Other communities may have been more powerful, more populous, more opulent, and more worthy of admiration and esteem, than she. They may have made greater discoveries in science; they may have effected more important reforms in politics and religion; they may have produced nobler achievements in the fine arts; they may have given birth to bards who have sung in loftier strains of poetry, and to philosophers who have descended to profounder depths of speculation. But yet, if the career of France were blotted out from the history of our world, it would produce a greater chasm and a more sensible loss, than would be felt by the elimination of the records of any other nation.

Hence it is, that the peculiar interest which French history possesses has led to the production of innumerable publications on the subject; yet it is probable that no class of descriptive works command the same degree of general interest as those which refer to French history. There is a superior charm connected with the events which have occurred in France during the last two centuries, which seems to be inexhaustible, to be ever fresh and new. The great French nation groaning under the tyranny of an ancient, illustrious, but pernicious dynasty; struggling desperately for the possession of political liberty—a thing then unknown in Europe; overwhelmed by the bloody surges of a mighty revolution; then passing in the vain search for peace and security from one transient form of government to another, till at length it lay unresistingly beneath the giant grasp of the triumphant Corsican; then crushed by a hostile continent in arms, and cast adrift again on the wide and stormy sea of political adventure; and once more, after many strange vicissitudes, resting as it now does, in stately and resplendent repose beneath the heir to the name and fortunes of the "Child of Destiny;"—such are the imposing scenes presented in modern times by the checkered history of France.

In the following pages I have endeavored to describe some of these Memorable Scenes. I have avoided as much as possible the beaten track generally pursued by writers on these subjects; and by exploring the recesses of old and musty tomes, not always accessible to the reader, to reproduce some scenes and narrate some events which have long been buried from general observation by the literary rubbish which surrounded them. I have given prominence to such events and to such epochs in French history as seemed to me to possess the greatest interest and importance; yet as to the propriety of the selections made, there must necessarily exist, among readers of different tastes, a great diversity of opinion.

S. M. S.

CONTENTS.

INTRODUCTION.

BRIEF SURVEY OF FRENCH HISTORY.

CHAPTER I.

FRANCE UNDER THE ADMINISTRATION OF RICHELIEU.

CHAPTER II.

MORALS AND MANNERS BEFORE THE REVOLUTION.

CHAPTER III.

OPENING SCENES OF THE FIRST REVOLUTION.

CHAPTER IV.

TERRIBLE POWER OF ROBESPIERRE AND THE JACOBINS.

CHAPTER V.

LOUIS XVI. AT THE BAR OF THE NATIONAL CONVENTION.

CHAPTER VI.

THE DOWNNALL OF THE ANCIENT MONARCHY.

CHAPTER VII.

DEATH OF THE ROYAL MARTYRS, LOUIS XVI. AND XVII.

CHAPTER VIII.

THE FALL OF ROBESPIERRE AND THE MOUNTAIN.

CHAPTER IX.

NAPOLEON'S EXPEDITION TO EGYPT.

CHAPTER X.

MARIA LOUISA, AND THE COURT OF ST. CLOUD.

CHAPTER XI.

EXPEDITION OF NAPOLEON IN RUSSIA.

CHAPTER XII.

NAPOLEON DURING THE HUNDRED DAYS.

CHAPTER XIII.

EXILE OF NAPOLEON AT ST. HELENA.

CHAPTER XIV.

NAPOLEON III. EMPEROR OF THE FRENCH.

MEMORABLE SCENES.

INTRODUCTION.

A BRIEF SURVEY OF FRENCH HISTORY.

THE triumphant arms of Julius Cæsar vanquished the inhabitants of the beautiful and fertile clime of ancient Gaul, about fifty years before the birth of Christ; and with their subjugation to the Roman yoke they also acquired a degree of civilization and historical importance which they never before possessed, but which, from that remote period until the present, have continued to increase with the progress of ages.

In the year 420 the Franks, a free and warlike race who dwelt in the vicinity of the Rhine and the Weser, made an irruption into Gaul; strove to subdue the still prevalent power of Rome, and to wrest the scepter of the country from her grasp. This first attempt proved unsuccessful; but in 451 the Franks finally conquered the inhabitants of Gaul, after defeating the formidable armies of Attila, the king of the Huns, at the bloody battle of Chalons. Meroveus, the leader of the victorious Franks, then established his capital on the spot now occupied by Paris. He fixed his power permanently in the land of the vanquished Gauls; and he became the founder of an illustrious dynasty of princes, since known in history as that of the Merovinian kings.

Under Clovis the Great, the power of Imperial Rome was entirely and permanently banished from the Frank territory. He defeated the Roman general Syagrius, in 486, at the great battle of Soissons. That monarch also determined to enlarge his territory. His character was warlike and cruel; but he was not undeserving of the praise of a great conqueror. He subdued the inhabitants of Bretagne, the Alemanni on the Rhine, and the Visigoths who inhabited the fertile region which lay between the Pyrennees and the Garonne. Having been successful in all his ambitious aims, he rested from the anxious toils of war, and became a christian, in accordance with the fashion of those times; and in fulfillment of the vow which he had made, to worship the God of his wife Clotilda, if in the end he was victorious over all his foes. He was baptized with great pomp and ceremony by St. Remi, at Rheims, in the year 496. He was there anointed with the miraculous oil, reputed to have been sent down from heaven by means of a dove. From the period of the conversion of Clovis the Great, France became numbered among the catalogue of christian nations.

At the death of Clovis, his royal patrimony was divided between his four sons. Childebert, to whose share fell the kingdoms of Paris, Orleans and Soissons, is considered as the successor of Clovis. Clotaire II., an indolent and voluptuous prince, threw the whole burden of empire on the shoulders of his ministers. To these *Maires du Palais* he intrusted absolute power. The consequence was that, after possessing the substance of authority during several generations, these officers ambitiously aimed, also, at the acquisition of its name and titles. They made themselves independent of the sovereign; and seized the kingdoms of Austrasia, of Neustria, and of Burgundy. In these provinces they ruled with the title and prerogatives of independent kings. The most eminent of this line of usurpers was Pepin. His son Charles Martel, increased by his warlike exploits the power and celebrity of his race. His son *Pepin Le Bref*, founded the illustrious Carlovingian dynasty in 751. Under the reign of his successor, the peerless Charlemagne, the empire of the Franks attained its meridian splendor. He was a great conqueror, a wise legislator, and a revered saint. His empire, obtained partly by inheritance, partly by conquest, and partly by treaty, extended from the Ebro to the Elbe and the Danube; from the Northern sea to the Mediterranean and the Adriatic; including France, Germany, part of Spain, Hungary and Bohemia, some provinces of Dalmatia, and Italy, as far as the confines of Naples. Out of the disjointed wrecks of the falling empire of ancient Rome Charlemagne constructed a consolidated cluster of dominions, equal in magnitude and power to that possessed by Augustus himself.

The vast monarchy of Charlemagne descended to his son, Louis le Debonnaire; but its unwieldy fabric fell to pieces, as soon as it passed into his feeble and trembling grasp. By the treaty of Verdun in 843, the crowns of France, Germany, and Italy were wisely separated from each other; and the youngest son of Louis, Charles the Bald, became the first monarch of the separate and independent kingdom of France.

This second dynasty continued on the throne during a hundred years; but this was an ignoble period of French history, and its most important incidents consisted in fierce and bitter struggles which took place between the kings, and their turbulent and refractory nobles.

In 987 Hugh Capet ascended the throne, and became the founder of the third, or Capetian dynasty, which has in succeeding ages inherited the possession of an insecure crown. But the evils of the feudal system, which then existed in all their excess in France, distracted the nation for many generations with bloody and destructive wars. The power of some of these petty princes and feudal lords may be inferred from the fact that, in the twelfth century, one of them possessed the sovereignty of sixteen of the present departments of France. Another possessed that of seven. A third held six. The whole south of France belonged to a number of feudal lords; and throughout the kingdom the audacious power and independence which they arrayed against the supremacy of the sovereign, indicated that the authority of the latter was held by a very insecure tenure.

The influence of the feudal nobility was at length broken by the energetic measures adopted by Louis IX. The introduction of written laws and statutes by that monarch; the use of letters of nobility by Philip II.; and the establishment of representatives of the people in a deliberative assembly, by Philip IV., all tended to diminish the supremacy of feudalism throughout the nation.

In 1420 France was invaded by Henry V., king of England. He induced the imbecile Charles VI. to appoint him his heir, and to give him his daughter Catherine in marriage. But Charles himself survived the English aspirant, and at his own death the crown descended to the infant son of Henry V., to the exclusion of the dauphin, who had assumed the title of Charles VII. A bloody civil war was the result of this ambitious rivalry; but victory was at length won to the standards of the dauphin; the English were banished from the territory of France, except in the fortified cities of Calais and Guienne; and the name and services of *Joan of Arc* were rendered immortal in the annals of heroism, patriotism, and virtue.

After the accession of Charles VII., all the institutions of France, and the measures of the government, tended toward the establishment of the regal power. He first among the monarchs of France, maintained a standing army. He adroitly increased, by purchase and by forfeiture, the extent of the crown lands, until they included a not inconsiderable portion of the French territory. He first undertook to impose taxes without the consent of the states-general, or the concurrence of the feudal lords.

Under the stern scepter of Louis XI. despotism in France became more cruel and more absolute than it had ever been before. He became an eminent example of tyranny and deceit.* At the death of Charles VIII. the crown passed from the possession of the Valois branch of the house of Capet; and by the accession of Louis XII. in 1498, the Orleans division of that illustrious family ascended the throne. With Francis I., in 1515, the *second* house of the Valois Capetians resumed the sovereignty of France. During this period, one of the darkest in the annals of history, the nation was convulsed and scourged with endless wars, both political and religious. France

* His favorite maxim was: *Dissimuler c'est régner.*

was deluged with human blood. The persecutions which the Protestants, or Huguenots, were compelled to endure, have forever stained the history of the nation, with ineffaceable infamy and disgrace.

These cruelties at length culminated on the memorable and bloody eve of St. Bartholomew; when thousands of the best and bravest citizens of France were massacred under the direction of Charles IX. and his sanguinary mother, Catherine de Medici.

Henry IV. was the first *Bourbon* prince who ascended the throne of the Capets. His auspicious reign began in 1589. He put an end to the religious wars which, for so many disastrous years, had desolated France. He proclaimed the celebrated and beneficent edict of Nantes, which guaranteed to the Protestants the full exercise and enjoyment of their religion. The period of his reign introduces us to that more memorable era in French history, when greater men and more absorbing incidents appear upon the scene; and demand a more minute survey of the remarkable qualities which they exhibited, and of the important and permanent results which they produced.

CHAPTER I.

FRANCE UNDER THE ADMINISTRATION OF CARDINAL RICHELIEU.

THE illustrious name of Richelieu is intimately connected with the power and glory of the French monarchy. Before his accession to his high place, France had been degraded from the honorable eminence which she occupied at the death of Henry IV., to poverty, imbecility, and contempt. The vast treasures which that monarch had accumulated, and had left in his coffers at the period of his decease, had been lavishly squandered during the regency of his widow, Mary de Medici. The court and the nation had become impoverished. The fierce contests which raged between the princes of the royal family and the nobles; the insatiable rapacity of the courtiers; and the ambitious and jealous caprices of the queen-regent, had thrown France into a lamentable state of prostration and misery. The monarchy possessed no firm basis of power. Endless dissensions distracted the councils of the ministers, unprincipled aspirants after power and wealth crowded all the avenues to the throne, and harassed those who held the feeble reins of government, with plots, intrigues, and cabals. The favorites of the court, and even nobles of high and honorable birth, exhibited the most grasping and unblushing cupidity. They created new offices and franchises. They levied tolls on the public highways and on private edifices. They devised new taxes and imposts.

All France, indeed, seemed to have been given up to pillage and plunder; while the multitude of the offenders appeared to secure the immunity of each.

The strong mind of Richelieu discerned the intricate and inveterate nature of those evils. His powerful arm at length fell with a crushing blow on the tottering fabric of the feudal system in France, and swept it away. On the ruins of that system, and interwoven with the ascending and magnificent proportions of the structure of kingly power which he reared, he also created the leading features and outlines of the gorgeous edifice of modern French civilization. In truth, his intellectual character was as great as his influence was powerful. He was as inflexible as he was sagacious. He was as persevering as he was daring. He was as vindictive and revengeful as he was ambitious. He was as unscrupulous and unprincipled as he was fertile in resources. He remained as undismayed in the midst of dangerous conspiracies and deadly plots against his life and power, as he was comprehensive in his plans of conquest, and zealous for the aggrandizement of his own glory, and the glory of his king, which he cherished with a love second only to that which he entertained for himself. His remarkable career forms a great epoch in French history. It stands forth prominently, as one of the collossal beacon-lights which remain towering and glittering through the gloom of the past; and in the wide waste of by-gone ages, no period can be named which looms up with more solemn and impressive grandeur to our view, than his. It was he who made France the most important country in Europe, during the period of his ministry. He rendered the court of Louis

XIII. the great focus of political power and interest throughout that continent. And when he died, he had prepared the way for the gorgeous reign of Louis XIV. which succeeded; during which, the splendor of the French monarchy attained its unsurpassed, and even its unequaled, zenith.

Armand du Plessis Richelieu, was born of a noble family, at Paris, in 1585. At an early period his attention was directed toward the army, but afterward to the church, as the most propitious theater of his future career. In pursuance of this latter expectation, he became a student of the Sorbonne, in 1607, where he completed the usual course of ecclesiastical study. He then entered the priesthood. During this early period of his life he was remarkable for his intelligence, his wit, and his gallantry. Neither his prudence nor his religious profession prevented him from indulging in licentious adventures, to the excessive and shameful degree fashionable at that period, among all classes in France. But these excesses did not prevent his rapid promotion in the church, for partly through the influence of his family, and partly through his own successful and skillful intrigues, he was consecrated bishop of Luçon, at the earliest period of his age permitted by the requirements of the canon law; and he thus took his place among the ecclesiastical, as well as among the secular princes of the realm.

Henry IV. had married Mary de Medici, the daughter of Francis II., grand-duke of Tuscany. This princess was destined to experience the most singular and unparalleled extremes of fortune. She was possessed of great personal beauty, and strong talents for political intrigue. But neither her beauty nor her talents could bind to her the fickle heart of her husband. She became the mother of two princes, one of whom afterward ascended the throne under the name of Louis XIII. Fearful of her aspiring nature, her husband had never allowed the ceremony of her coronation to take place. At length, however, during an interval of confidence and good feeling between them, Henry IV. consented to the celebration of that event. Accordingly, on the 13th of May, 1610, Mary de Medici was solemnly crowned queen of France; and on the 14th, Henry fell a victim to the dagger of the assassin Ravaillac! His death was very naturally attributed, by those best acquainted with the court secrets of that dismal and dangerous period, to the vindictive, ambitious and revengeful spirit of the Italian queen.

This princess immediately became regent of France, and her power, despotic, whimsical, and pernicious as it was, continued undiminished during the minority of her son. The court and the administration were constantly split up into desperate and dangerous factions, and France seemed rapidly to be approaching to the verge of ruin. The eyes of the queen-regent were at length opened to the perilous state of the kingdom; and she ordered and proclaimed the assembling of the states-general, for the purpose of aiding the sovereign in the correction and removal of the existing evils. This was the last time that this body was convoked in France, until it was summoned to meet by the unfortunate Louis XVI., amid the rolling of the thunder which presaged the approaching storms of the first great revolution. It was in this convocation of the states-general, thus summoned by Mary de Medici, that the illustrious Richelieu first appears upon the public political stage of France.

On this occasion Richelieu acted as speaker for the ecclesiastical order. In the assembly, the three orders contended fiercely for their respective interests; and their jealous conflicts rendered their deliberations utterly useless to the state. The *tiers etat* contended, among other things, that a decree should be passed, to the effect that kings could in no case be deposed for heresy. They desired that the sovereign should be declared entirely free from the spiritual power. This proposition Richelieu opposed with great eloquence and subtlety. At that period of his career, he was on terms of amity with Mary de Medici, who was a bigoted Catholic. She ruled her son, the dauphin. The priests ruled her. And Richelieu, being still identified with the ecclesiastical order, ruled the priests. Hence his interests dictated his policy on this, as on all other occasions. The dissensions, however, which divided the three orders, soon became so fierce that Mary de Medici dissolved their assemblage, before their deliberations had produced any results, either favorable or unfavorable to her power.

In 1616 Louis XIII. was married to the Spanish Infanta. This princess is better known in history under the name of Anne of Austria. On the occurrence of this event, the old ministry of the regency, consisting of the president, Jeannòn Villeroi, and the chancellor, Silleri, were dismissed. A new administration was formed in place of the *barbons*, or dotards, who had been removed; at the head of which was placed the prince de Condé. Into that ministry Richelieu was also admitted; and thus, for the first time, he came directly in contact with the machinery of state. Nor was it long before he made his powerful mind felt in the deliberations of the ministers, and in the measures adopted by the government. It was Condé's purpose to retain the supreme power by weakening that of Mary de Medici with her son. A long and bitter conflict ensued; during which Richelieu apparently took the part of the queen-mother. At first the influence of the latter was triumphant; Condé was dismissed from his post and imprisoned in the Bastille. Concini, the Italian confidant and favorite of the queen-mother, assumed his place and his power. But soon, with the vacillation so usual in the history of ministers, and of governments, the tide of regal favor turned, Concini was degraded and assassinated; and the old ministry, with Villeroi at their head, returned to the possession of power. The queen-mother was then, for the first time, exiled from the court by the command of her son. She fixed her residence at Blois; and Richelieu, who had adopted the resolution to conciliate both parties, and thus, at length, to rise upon the strength of both, accompanied her. His object was, that while he seemed to share with Mary de Medici in the ignominy of her banishment, he might act as a spy upon her movements, worm himself into her councils, and then betray them to the king. He found a favorable field for the execution of this purpose, in the restless and insatiable spirit of intrigue, which was the great characteristic, the bane, and the disgrace of Mary de Medici. It was the shrewd purpose of Richelieu, after hostilities between the royal combatants had reached a certain point, to step in as conciliator between them; render important services to both; and be rewarded by them with the highest post of influence and honor in the state.

The event fulfilled the expectations thus entertained by the crafty courtier. Mary de Medici escaped from Blois, through the agency of the duke d'Epernon, the governor of Metz; and by him and his attendants she was conducted to Angoulême. The king, Louis XIII., on hearing of her escape from the place assigned her for her residence, was at first disposed to take severe and vindictive measures. But Richelieu found means of suggesting gentler purposes to the royal son of so willful and determined a mother; and as soon as it was resolved to take the latter alternative, Richelieu offered his services as negotiator. The king ceded to Mary de Medici the government of Anjou; and three cities were also given up to her as hostages for the future conduct of the king. Condé was restored to his former confidence and honor in the ministry. The queen-mother returned to Paris, and was reconciled to her son. All the grounds of hostility and jealousy which had distracted the royal family for five years, were apparently buried in oblivion; and Richelieu received the reward of his exertions, in the confidence and esteem of both parties. It was after effecting this memorable reconciliation between the king and his mother, that Richelieu was elevated to the post of prime minister of France. It was then, also, that he received the promise of the cardinal's hat, which was soon obtained for him at Rome, through the joint influence and agency of the sovereign and his mother.

At length, then, we behold the crafty, ambitious, and sagacious churchman, elevated to the dizzy and dangerous eminence to which he had boldly aspired; and from this moment commenced one of the most extraordinary administrations which has ever illustrated the history of nations. This event occurred in the year 1624. During the space of eighteen years afterward, Richelieu continued to be the leading, the most imposing, and the central figure in the history of Europe; the arbiter of the fate of millions of men, and the absolute governor of the hearts and fortunes of mighty kings and princes.

Previous to the elevation of Richelieu to the post of prime minister, Louis XIII. had governed France with a feeble and trembling hand. The secret deliberations of the royal councils were usually well known, almost before the termination of the sittings at which they had taken place. Richelieu at once seized the reins of government with a firm and powerful grasp, and rendered himself, until the day of his death, absolutely indispensable to his feeble master, whom he inspired with a sentiment of fear and respect, not unmingled with jealous, yet impotent hatred. So absolute did the crafty cardinal soon become, that it was with very considerable truth that, in speaking of the direction of the government, he declared that the proper form for him to use in reference to it, was *Ego, et Rex meus.*

Such successful ambition, it might readily be supposed, would soon raise around the minister indignant and powerful rivals, who would attempt by every possible means to diminish his influence, to precipitate him from his high eminence, and to compass his ruin. Not the least convincing evidence of the consummate abilities of Richelieu, is to be found in the success with which he discovered, discomfited, crushed, and punished the most skillful combinations which were ever formed against him. At the head of one of the most dangerous of these, was Gaston, the duke of Orleans, and brother of the king. During the visit of the duke of Buckingham to France, to negotiate a marriage between the future king of England, then prince of Wales, and Henrietta, the king's sister, the insufferable arrogance of the English embassador had offended and disgusted the French minister. A deadly hostility between these able men was the consequence; nor was that hostility diminished when Richelieu saw that Buckingham even dared to intrigue with Anne of Austria, his master's queen, for whom he himself indulged an improper fondness. The object of the conspiracy against Richelieu, which followed, was intended to dethrone Louis XIII., to place his brother, the duke of Orleans, on the throne, to remove Richelieu from power, and to inflict retributive punishment on him and his adherents, for all the indignities which they had haughtily imposed on their rivals. Richelieu detected this conspiracy, and communicated it to the king, and to the queen-mother. Immediately Colonel Ornam, one of the conspirators, the governor and confidant of the duke of Orleans, was arrested by the orders of the minister, and thrown into the Bastille. He languished there in the deepest and darkest dungeon of that fortress until his death. Count Chalais, another of the conspirators, together with the count de Soissons, the duke de Vendome, his brother the grand prior Vendome, Barabas, the able Scaglia, his associates and confederates, each severely felt the dreadful effects of the triumphant vengeance of Richelieu. Even the duke of Orleans himself, who had proposed to marry the wife of Louis XIII., in the event of his deposition and death, was compelled to purchase his immunity by marrying Mademoiselle de Montpensier; and by abandoning all his friends to his powerful and vindictive foe. At the instance of the latter, even the queen herself was summoned before the council and severely reprimanded by the sovereign, for the acquiescence which she was supposed to have given to the projects of the conspirators. Scores of noblemen of distinguished birth and powerful connections, were buried beneath the turrets of the Bastille, as the penalty for having been implicated in this first plot against the minister, and a guard of musketeers was thenceforth assigned him, for the future preservation of his personal security.

The city and fortress of La Rochelle had long been the strong-hold of Protestant or Huguenot discontent in France. It had successfully resisted, either by force of arms or by bribery, every attempt which had been made by the predecessors of Louis XIII. to capture it. Richelieu resolved to accomplish what had surpassed the abilities of kings and ministers before him. The princess de Rohan, a person eminent for her high birth, her heroism, and her devotion to the Protestant cause, commanded the city and its defenders. Richelieu sent a numerous army, under the orders of Marshal Schomberg, to besiege the works. The duke of Buckingham, who, after his return to England, never forgot nor forgave the indignities which were inflicted on him by the cardinal during his late sojourn in France, prepared to assist the Rochellois with an English fleet. The latter were themselves extremely determined and enthusiastic in their resistance to the attacks of the army of the king of France. They chose a new burgess at this crisis, and when he was inducted into office, he presented a poniard to the magistrates and said: "I accept the office of burgess, only on condition that this poinard shall be plunged into the heart of the first traitor who shall dare to speak of surrender; and against myself, if I ever propose capitulation!"

Richelieu but laughed at the vaunting fortitude of the heroes of Rochelle. He built a gigantic mole into the sea, fourteen hundred feet in length, which effectually prevented the approach of the besieging ships, and of the succors from England. Louis XIII. sojourned in person in the French camp; and just as the duke of Buckingham was about to embark on the last squadron of the fleet which left England, he was assassinated by an emmissary of the cardinal, named Felton, an Englishman. At length, after one of the most memorable sieges on record, which continued with fluctuating fortunes during a whole year, Rochelle capitulated. The city was stripped of all its privileges; the works were manned with the victorious troops of the king; and the triumph of the cardinal in this uncertain and difficult enterprise, was absolute and complete. His exultation and the growth of his power were in proportion augmented.

Previous to this period in the history of this remarkable man, he had uniformly acted on the sagacious principle of courting the good will of Mary de Medici, the queen-mother. His sagacity had readily taught him that his master, the king, possessing by nature a soft and pliant disposition, would, until he arrived at a certain age, remain in a great measure subject to the influence of his mother. Therefore, until Louis XIII. arrived at that age, Richelieu flattered and courted his mother, and through her, he ruled her son the more absolutely. But after the king had reached the period of which we now speak, the maternal influence over him became weakened, and he was taught by the crafty cardinal that he was at length old enough to throw off those leading-strings which once had controlled him, and to think and act for himself. The object of the prelate in giving this advice, was to diminish the number of his own royal masters, and servants; so that, instead of being compelled to serve and govern two, he might only serve and govern one. This was the origin of that most remarkable and malignant conflict, which about the year 1628, began between Richelieu and Mary de Medici, a conflict which lasted during the remainder of their lives with unabated intensity; which involved the royal family in constant broils and disgraceful tempests; which finally drove the unfortunate queen-mother from home and country; which imbittered her days with the keenest suffering and mortification; and which at last compelled her to die in a foreign country, in solitude, poverty, and misery, such as finds no parallel in the chequered page of human vicissitude.

Mary de Medici was a remarkable woman; and one every way difficult to govern or control. Partly from long habit, and partly from her natural disposition, she felt an irresistible temptation to interfere in affairs of state, and to influence her son, the king. During the minority of the latter, she exercised that influence over him by right, as queen-regent. After the majority of the king, she claimed to exercise the same supremacy by courtesy, as queen-mother. In either case, her assumptions would have been repugnant to the insatiable ambition of Richelieu; and hence arose the deadly and life-long struggle between them. Nor had Richelieu an easy task to perform in crushing the spirit, and destroying the influence of Mary. She was a woman of warm and often generous impulses. She possessed great resolution of purpose, and determination of will. She was free from the vices of hypocrisy and deceit. She neither possessed, nor pretended to the possession of, any skill in the subtle arts of deception and diplomacy; and it is certainly very high praise for her that, though she was a woman of warm temperament, though she was a native of ardent Italy, and though she lived in the most licentious and dissolute court in Europe, no breath of scandal has ever dared to impeach her stainless virtue. She was also constant in her friendships. But on the contrary, the character of Mary de Medici was tarnished by many great and glaring blemishes. She was so obstinate that reason rarely effected any change in her first-formed purposes. She was vindictive and revengeful in the extreme. She could not endure either reproof or opposition, with the least show of seemly grace; and when her rivals or opponents had once incurred her hatred, she rarely or never forgave. Hence her whole life, after the rise of the stern and unrelenting Richelieu to power, was one continual scene of mortification, of indignant conflict, and of impotent resistance to his supremacy. And while her qualities were admirably adapted to call forth the hostile powers of the cardinal, they were also such as to lay her open to his insidious and wily nature, and to give him every advantage over her movements, and over her destiny.

The first notorious outburst of passion and jealousy between these celebrated rivals, was in reference to the second marriage of Gaston, the duke of Orleans, the brother of Louis XIII. This marriage had become a matter of great importance, inasmuch as Anne of Austria, the wife of the king, had for many years remained childless, and because the health of Louis XIII. was precarious. In case of his death without issue, Gaston would ascend the vacant throne. The duke of Mantua desired that his daughter should become the future queen. But Mary de Medici had entered with all the unconquerable ardor and resolution of her nature, into the project of obtaining for her son an alliance with one of her own relatives, Anne de Medici. The duke of Orleans really felt an attachment for the daughter of the duke of Mantua. The intriguing mind of Richelieu could not, of course, remain idle during the progress of this important rivalry. The duke of Orleans applied for advice to the king. The king applied for counsel to Richelieu. And Richelieu, to prevent the further growth of the power and influence of Mary de Medici, advised the king to permit his brother to marry the princess of Mantua. Meanwhile, the queen-mother expressed her hostile and contemptuous feelings toward the *protegé* of the cardinal, in the most public an insulting manner; and the consequence was, the existence of the most bitter and implacable enmity between all the parties concerned in the conflict. And it was apparent that, to whomsoever the unlucky duke would eventually be married, a deadly hatred would be entertained by the disappointed faction toward the successful aspirant, and toward all those who had contributed to her triumph.

During the hostilities carried on in 1630, by Louis XIII. against the duke of Savoy, the king remained with his army in the field, attended by the cardinal. Peace being concluded—the terms of which being greatly in favor of France—the king and cardinal resumed their journey toward Paris, in August of that year. At Lyons the king became ill, and serious apprehensions were entertained that his end approached. The wife and mother of the king were also present with him; and while the apparent danger of the monarch continued, they plotted with intense and malignant activity, to accomplish the ruin of the cardinal the moment the king should expire. But Louis, contrary to their wishes, recovered. His disease was nothing more than an imposthume in the stomach, which eventually broke, and the matter being discharged, the king recovered more than his usual health. But during this interval of suspense, the two queens, the two Marillacs, the one the keeper of the seals, and the other the marshal, Vautier, the first physician to the queen, the princess de Conti, the duchess d'Elbouef, the countess de Fargis, and some others, had formed a powerful cabal against the cardinal, which the unexpected recovery of the king for the present baffled.

The king and his suite returned to Paris, but the suppressed volcano still burned with intense, though hidden fury. The cardinal had been informed, by his secret agents, of all that had transpired. While the king lay sick at Lyons, his apprehensions had been aroused, and he began to take measures for his safety, in the event of the king's death. Among other things, he requested Marshal Bassompierre to grant him the use of the Swiss guards as an escort, until he should have arrived in Langeudoc, at a retreat which he had there chosen. The marshal refused; and in the sequel, was made a memorable victim of the cardinal's insatiable revenge.

On their arrival in Paris the hostility of the cardinal and Mary de Medici broke out afresh. Louis repaired in person to the palace of the Luxembourg, in which the queen-mother resided, for the purpose of effecting a reconciliation. He ordered the cardinal to be in attendance, in an adjoining apartment. Mary de Medici broke forth in transports of rage and abuse against her powerful and wily enemy, as soon as the interview began. The king in vain attempted to appease her. Hoping that the presence of the cardinal might, perhaps, have that effect, he ordered him to enter the room. As soon as he appeared, she poured a torrent of abuse upon him. She stigmatized him as a villain, an ungrateful, malignant wretch. She called him the disturber of the public peace. She declared that he had usurped the power of the king, and that he made the whole court and nation subservient to his selfish and unprincipled ambition. Rising from her seat, she approached the cardinal, who remained standing in an humble attitude during this extraordinary scene, and pointing her finger at him, she exclaimed to the king, in a transport of rage—"There is the man who would willingly deprive you of your crown, to place it on the head of the count de Soissons, who is to marry his niece, La Combalet!"

Overcome by the intensity of her emotions, the unhappy queen-mother sank into her chair, and burst into tears. The wily cardinal, who knew best how to act under these extraordinary circumstances, remained silent. The king spoke for him, as he intended that he should. He declared that the cardinal had been a faithful and able servant to him; but at the same time, he ordered him to retire. The king was left alone with his mother. The latter then resumed her endeavors to effect the ruin of her foe. She appealed to every possible consideration which ought to influence the monarch. She was his mother; she had borne him under her bosom; she had brought him into the world; he carried in his veins her blood; she loved him only as a mother could love; and yet "that cursed caitiff, the cardinal," had treated her with every indignity; had destroyed her influence over his mind, and her credit in the court; he had ruined her happiness; and the sight of his daily triumph over her imbittered her whole existence. At the same time, he was nothing but a selfish adventurer. He cared not a straw for the king, save as the instrument of his ambition, and his revenge. He oppressed the people, the nobility, and the court. He united all riches, honors, dignities, in himself. Could a dutiful son hesitate a moment how to choose between his own mother, and such a wretch? The voice of reason and of religion dictated but one course, and that course was, to put an end at once and forever to the disgraceful and malignant tyranny of the cardinal.

The violence of the conduct of the queen-mother defeated its own purposes. The king was disgusted, rather than won. He retired, determined upon the very opposite course demanded by his mother. In truth, Louis XIII. was a weak and unprincipled creature, over whose feeble mind Richelieu had acquired an absolute dominion. All he cared for was his own security and ease; and to the possession of these, the talents and services of the cardinal were indispensably necessary. The king had but little discernment; yet that little was just enough to enable him to see that there was no one who could fill the place of Richelieu; and hence he determined that nothing should displace or degrade him.

But at that moment, these purposes of the king were unknown to both of the hostile parties. When he left the presence of the king and queen-mother, Richelieu himself expected his disgrace. He hastened to his palace, and commenced immmediately to pack up his papers, to burn the most dangerous of them, and to secure his plate and jewels. He intended to retire to Brouage, of which place he was the governor, in order to escape the vengeance of his numerous and powerful enemies.

During this short interval, a singular scene was presented at the palace of the Luxembourg, the residence of the queen-mother. Mary de Medici seemed certain of her triumph. Her exultation was beyond all bounds. Soon the welcome news flew through the whole court circle, that the powerful, the feared, the hated cardinal was about to fall from his dizzy eminence, and to meet that ruin which he had inflicted on so many others. The drawing-rooms of the queen-mother were crowded with the happy and exulting multitude of her friends. Plans of vengeance and humiliation were devised, to render the fall of the cardinal more mortifying and complete; and congratulations were offered to the queen-mother, and to all her favorites, that now, at last, the era of their triumph had arrived.

While this gay and premature scene was passing at the Luxembourg, on November 11th, 1630; and while Richelieu was hastily preparing to escape from the impending ruin, the king repaired to Versailles. There he threw himself on his bed, and declared to his favorite, St. Simon, that he felt as if he were inwardly on fire; and that the violence of his mother had so disconcerted him that he could find rest nowhere. After a short interval his feeble mind reverted to its usual prop, the cardinal, and he sent for him to come immediately to his presence. Richelieu instantly complied with this welcome order. He threw himself at the king's feet, and thanked him as the best, the most constant, the most indulgent master that ever the sun had shone upon. The monarch assured him of his continued favor, and told him to dismiss his fears. Richelieu at the same time adroitly said, that he could not accept the honor of remaining near the person of the king, for fear of being the cause of a scandalous separation between a mother and her son. He would seek some solitude where he could weep over the fact, that he had been compelled to seem an ingrate to his benefactress, the queen-mother, in consequence of his paramount devotion to the more important interests of her son. He kissed the king's feet and then rose. Louis then again commanded him to remain in his office of prime minister, and even divulged the names of those who, in addition to his mother, had been most active in making unfavorable representations to him against the cardinal.

The triumph of Richelieu over this powerful cabal soon

became known; and in a day, the saloons of the Luxembourg became a perfect solitude. Of all the crowds of courtiers who, a few hours before had congratulated Mary de Medici upon her supposed triumph, not one was there to be seen! The queen-mother discovered, when too late, how impregnable the power of Richelieu had become; and from that moment he determined to effect her ruin, and the ruin of all who in any way had taken sides with her against him. This transitory triumph of the queen-mother and her friends, has been justly termed in all succeeding time *la journeé des Dupes*—the day of the dupes!

The vengeance of the cardinal was terrible, and the gratification of it became one of the great aims of his subsequent life. The Marillacs, Montmorenci, the princess de Conti, Marshal Bassompierre, and many others, were ruined as victims to his insatiable revenge. Some expired upon the wheel of torture, or on the scaffold. Others were imprisoned in the Bastille, and spent many years in solitary and cheerless confinement. Among the latter was the case of Marshal Bassompierre. This man was one of the most accomplished, distinguished, and fascinating courtiers and generals of that period. He had become celebrated for his victories, when commanding the French armies; and he had acquitted himself with high honor in several embassies of great importance which had been intrusted to him. Nor was he less celebrated in the gentler arts of love. It is a circumstance which serves to illustrate the state of morals prevalent in the court of which a prelate and a churchman was the acknowledged head, that Bassompierre, immediately before his arrest, and in apprehension of that event, on the 24th of February, 1631, burnt more than *six thousand love-letters* which he had received from different ladies, and which would have compromised the honor of the most distinguished families in the kingdom! Bassompierre was confined in the Bastille for twelve years; nor was he released until the strong hand of death had put an end to the vengeance, together with the life, of the implacable cardinal.*

But his fiercest persecutions were reserved for the unfortunate Mary de Medici. Richelieu now determined on nothing less than her entire banishment from France, her degradation, impoverishment, and ruin. He first induced the king to visit the city of Compeigne, accompanied by his mother. The object of this trick will soon be apparent. After a short residence there, the king and his suite suddenly returned to Paris, without informing Mary de Medici of his purpose. When she prepared to follow him, she found the gates of the city shut upon her. She was a prisoner within its walls! Her mental sufferings, at the infliction of this indignity to a princess of her temper, may be imagined, but they cannot be described. After a few weeks of detention there, she succeeded in making her escape; and after some vicissitudes, she fled to Flanders, feeling that she should never be secure from the deadly hatred and violence of the cardinal, as long as she remained within the French territory.

The subsequent vicissitudes of the life of Mary de Medici, her sufferings, and her fate, almost exceed the exag-

* *See* Memoires du Marechal de Bassompierre, contenans l'Histoire du sa vie, et de ce qui s'est fait de plus remarquable a la cour de France pendant quelques annees. Amsterdam, 4 vols, 1723.

gerations of romance. She successively visited Holland and England. Her own daughter Henrietta sat upon the throne of the Stuarts, and yet she was powerless to secure the return of her mother to France. The omnipotent cardinal sternly forbade it. She herself wrote to her son Louis XIII., but Richelieu himself dictated a cold, and almost an insulting refusal. Even her property in France was confiscated by the orders of Richelieu; and Mary de Medici became dependent upon the charity of her friends for her subsistence. Louis XIII. in one of his letters to her declared, "that he had every wish to serve his mother, but that he could not send her any money, because he had no doubt her evil councillors would make a bad use of it."

At length, in the year 1637, Mary de Medici was even driven from England, through the intrigues of the cardinal; and she took her last refuge in the ancient city of Cologne. There, in a small house in which, sixty years before, the immortal Rubens had been born, an old shoemaker and his wife then resided. They occupied the rooms on the first floor. The second and third stories were let to lodgers. And in the garret of that house dwelt Mary de Medici, and her single remaining attendant, her serving man, Mascali. The apartment was poorly furnished, and the utmost poverty was exhibited by everything around them. On the 10th day of January, 1641, the ex-queen was sick; and that once noble form, which had formerly graced the most brilliant throne in Europe, by the side of the chivalrous Henry IV., lay shivering from cold and hunger, on a hard and humble bed. Mascali went out to procure, if possible, some food, to give sustenance to the famished woman. At length, after a short absence, he returned to the garret, with a bowl of gruel obtained from the shoemaker on the first floor. The ex-queen greedily received it; and the next day she felt better. She thought, as she looked out from the window of the garret, over the wide and uneven waste of snowy roofs around her, that as the sun shone so brightly, she would venture to take a short walk. By Mascali's help, she descended safely the steep and narrow stair-case, and passed out into the street. She had not gone far before she was suddenly accosted by a nobleman, in courtly dress. It was her ancient friend, the duke of Guise, who had also been banished from France by Richelieu; and who detected the features of his former sovereign and friend, amid the humble and faded weeds in which she was then arrayed. He bowed instantly very low; and taking off his hat, he addressed her in terms of the profoundest sympathy and respect. The next day he sent a note to her humble lodgings. It declared that, out of the wreck of all his former fortunes, he had only two hundred *louis d'ors* remaining; and that he enclosed one hundred of them for the use of her majesty.

This sum of money supported Mary de Medici for two years, in that garret in Cologne. At length even these were exhausted, and no alleviation had come to the misfortunes of the exile. On the 12th of February, 1642, a low, moaning sound of pain issued from that hard and humble couch. The faithful Mascali entered the garret, exclaiming "Nothing! nothing!" He had gone forth to procure food, and had obtained none. The moaning sound continued. It was then again winter; and the apartment was cold and cheerless. Mascali collected the rags together which the apartment contained, and endeavored to warm the dying queen. At this moment the rumbling sound of carriage wheels was heard stopping at the door of that humble house. A heavy man is heard toiling up the steep stair-case. At length a knock resounds at the door. Mascali opens it. Fabro Chigi, who afterward became pope under the name of Alexander VII., entered the apartment, to impart to the sufferer the last succors of religion. He had just discovered the presence of the ex-queen of France in Cologne, and had hastened to her bedside. It was too late to afford physical relief; and he endeavored to impart to her spiritual comfort. Among other things, he is said to have urged her to forgive her enemies, as she was soon to appear before God in judgment. She feebly acquiesced. He then uttered the name of Richelieu, and said that even he must also be forgiven. The frame of the dying queen seemed to be instantly convulsed with a pang of anguish. She turned her dark eyes reproachfully toward the priest; moved away from him convulsively in the bed; exclaimed, in the long-disused language of her sunny and happy youth: "*E troppo!" that is too much!* and then expired. Chigi is said to have afterward confessed, that he had indeed required too much for human nature to perform.

There, in poverty and from actual starvation, in a garret in Cologne, Mary de Medici, the most illustrious victim of the implacable and unscrupulous Richelieu, ended her memorable and unfortunate career. Such was the fate of one who was the wife of Henry IV., the mother of the then reigning sovereign of France, the mother of

Isabella, queen of Spain, of Henrietta, queen of England, of Christina, duchess of Savoy, of Gaston, duke of Orleans, and a direct descendant of that immortal house of Florence, which had produced Lorenzo the Magnificent, Pope Leo X., Pope Clement VII., and many other illustrious princes.

Having banished the mother of the king from France, Richelieu found it necessary to commence hostilities against his next most powerful enemy, the king's brother, the duke of Orleans. After much persecution the latter, who was a frivolous and vindictive prince, determined to invade France with a hostile army, and punish the cardinal and all his enemies. He ravaged Burgundy and Auvergne, and burnt Dijon. Richelieu sent an army against the duke, under the command of Marshals Schomberg and La Force. The duke of Montmorenci, a patriotic and distinguished nobleman, who hated the cardinal in consequence of his unscrupulous ambition and cruelty, joined the duke of Orleans. He was the highest noble in the realm, next to the royal family. At Castelnaudary, a battle was fought between the rival factions and their troops, which resulted in the defeat of the rebel troops, in consequence of the baseness and cowardice of the duke of Orleans himself. This defeat placed the duke of Montmorenci in the power of the triumphant cardinal. The captive duke was tried and condemned to death on the charge of treason. Great efforts were made by some of the most distinguished princes of the realm, to induce the king to pardon him. The most urgent intercessions and affecting appeals were used in his behalf. He was executed in spite of them all. The omnipotent Richelieu had determined that Montmorenci should perish! Through the agency of the cardinal, the duke of Orleans was again reconciled to his brother, the king; a reconciliation which lasted until all the money which the duke obtained was spent upon his mistresses, and in gaming.

When the stirring events of the Thirty Years' War began to convulse Europe, Richelieu adopted the policy of fortifying France by treaties with foreign states, but resolved not to take any active part in the conflict. Accordingly, he formed alliances with Sweden, with Holland, with the prince of the Netherlands, with the duke of Saxe-Weimar, with the Swiss, and with the dukes of Savoy and Parma. It never had been the policy of this able minister to encourage the carrying on of foreign and aggressive wars by the armies and generals of France. He either did not believe the character of Louis XIII. possessed of sufficient strength to induce him to follow out such a policy, or else he found his own power and supremacy in the state more easily secured and preserved, by confining the attention of the king to internal events, and to the contests, intrigues, and factions of the court.

Even the successor of St. Peter at Rome, Pius V., having had the misfortune to offend the cardinal, did not escape his all-powerful vengeance. Richelieu sent the Marshal d'Etrees, whom the pope most cordially hated, as his ambassador to Rome; and gave him peremptory orders to treat the sovereign pontiff with such marked indignities as to give him extreme mortification. The ambassador executed his mission so effectually that his rudeness and insults so deeply wounded the pope, that it hastened, and even occasioned his death.

It was at this period of triumph that the cardinal besought Louis XIII. to permit him to bestow a gift upon him, in some humble measure indicative of his profound sense of the obligations under which he considered himself to his royal master. The king consented, and Richelieu presented to him the magnificent assemblage of buildings then called Le Palais Cardinal, afterward known to an infamous celebrity under the name of the Palais Royal. To this munificent gift Richelieu added his Chapelle de Diamants, his chased silver buffet, and his great diamond. Gifts like these serve to show the vast amount of wealth which Richelieu had secured during his career of successful ambition; and they prove the insatiable rapacity with which he had improved his opportunities of acquisition.

It was a portion of the crafty scheme of Richelieu, to retain his vast influence over the king, by diminishing the credit not only of the queen-mother, and of his brother, the duke of Orleans, but also that of his wife, Anne of Austria. Hence he endeavored to keep up in the mind of Louis, a dislike for his queen, and as she had remained so long childless, it was a matter of importance to him to continue, and if possible to increase, the alienation which existed between the royal pair; for as soon as it would become known that Anne of Austria was about to present an heir to the throne, her influence over her husband, and her consideration in the state, would have been vastly augmented.

But in this particular case, the purposes of the wily and selfish prelate were foiled in a most singular and unexpected manner.

The temperament of Louis XIII. was particularly cold; and the only attachments which he ever seemed to have formed for the female sex, were of a purely Platonic character. Among the circle of the female acquaintances of the king, there was no one more attractive and pleasing in her person and intellect, than the virtuous, amiable, and accomplished Mademoiselle Lafayette. The king, in passing through Paris on his way from Versailles to St. Maur, stopped at the convent of the *Filles de St. Marie*, in order to spend several hours in the society of this lady, who had taken refuge in that retreat from the persecutions of Richelieu, who was jealous of the king's regard for her. During his conversation with her, a furious storm arose, which rendered it impossible for the king either to proceed to St. Maur, or to return to Versailles. The tempest continued with unabated violence until night approached. It became a question of importance then, where the king should lodge during the night. It would be unseemly for him to remain in the convent. It would be unsafe for him to repair, without his usual guards, to any public or private residence. He had for many years never slept in the apartment or dwelling of the queen, who resided in the palace of the Louvre, in Paris. The king was greatly agitated. This was one of the most desperate emergencies of his life, and he, without the aid of the cardinal, was utterly confounded. At length Mademoiselle Lafayette benevolently suggested, that it would be best for the king, under these circumstances, to repair to the residence of the queen, where he would be not only secure, but also would be waited upon in such a manner as to render him comfortable. Overborne by the necessities of the case, rather than induced by any regard for his wife, the king at length consented. Word was instantly sent to the Louvre, that Louis would lodge at that palace during the night; supper was ordered to suit his taste; the neglected queen received him kindly; and nine months after that stormy night Louis XIV., who reigned over France for more than seventy years, was born!

A relative of Mademoiselle Lafayette was a person of too much importance in himself, and too intimately connected with the career of Richelieu, to be passed by without notice. This person was the celebrated Father Joseph. In some respects the character of this man was superior to that of Richelieu, in others, it was inferior. He possessed a degree of firmness, and stoical indifference to the vicissitudes of fortune, of which Richelieu was destitute; for the latter was ever suspicious and fearful of impending danger and disgrace. Joseph did not possess the profound, far-reaching craftiness of Richelieu. He was confounded by the long and tangled details of a great intrigue, in the unravelment and direction of which his master found his greatest glory and delight. But the craft of Father Joseph was that petty, superficial cunning, which characterizes feeble, though supple and hypocritical or treacherous minds. Joseph was, in a word, the imp, the inferior devil of the great Beelzebub who so absolutely ruled him, the king, and France. Possessing the utmost respect for the talents of his master, admiring his principles, and applauding his projects, as far as he comprehended their nature and their intended effects, he was in every sense a servant and assistant to Richelieu of inestimable value.

And yet, the cardinal entertained no more real or sincere regard for Father Joseph, than he did for any one else. After some years of devoted service to his master, Joseph thought that it was high time for him to receive some splendid and substantial remuneration. His ambition did not allow him to be satisfied with anything less than a cardinal's hat, or at least, with the archbishopric of Rheims. The absurdity of such aspirations might have been apparent to any one from the fact, that an elevation so high would have rendered Joseph a rival of his master, and would have put an end forever to his dependence and subserviency. Richelieu readily found abundant pretexts for delaying the accomplishment of these wishes of his most trusted servant. He indeed offered him the bishopric of Mans, as a commencement of his elevation. But Joseph refused; and redoubled his importunities for a cardinal's hat. Richelieu, to appease his eagerness, instructed his ambassador at the papal court to commence negotiations on the subject; but at the same time he took such secret measures as effectually thwarted the furtherance of the project.

There are not wanting persons who contend that Father Joseph was a man of great capacity. Grotius, for instance, declares that he sketched all the outlines of Richelieu's measures, and that the latter put the finishing touch to them. It is certain, that the monk was admitted to all the great state secrets of his master; that he was deputed to negotiate with kings, princes, and the highest potentates of Europe. One of his greatest merits in the estimation of Richelieu was his utter and daring unscrupulousness, which never hesitated at the perpetration of the most desperate and outrageous measures. Thus he once sent an officer with an important message into Germany, the particulars of which, however, were so severe and cruel, that the officer supposed that there must have been an error in his instructions. He returned for more explicit directions, and found Father Joseph celebrating mass. Being pressed for time, he approached the priest and whispered, "Suppose these people defend themselves, what must I do?" Suspending for a moment his sacred functions, Joseph turned aside, and whispered to the officer, "*Qu'on tue tout*"—*Kill them all!* and then proceeded to finish the mass.

At length, when the importunities of Father Joseph for the cardinal's hat became so urgent as to be inconvenient, he was seized with a mortal disease, and opportunely died. Some have asserted that he was poisoned by the orders of Richelieu. There is no evidence of the truth of this charge, except that the unscrupulous ambition of the cardinal would have led him thus to rid himself of a man who was becoming a dangerous and an aspiring rival. But such evidence can hardly be regarded as satisfactory and conclusive. Whatever may have been the real fact in the case, Richelieu kept up the utmost show of tender friendship toward him to the last, and even had him removed, shortly previous to his death, to his own palace at Ruel. While Father Joseph was lying on his death-bed, Richelieu entered his apartment, and wishing to give him the geatest encouragement in his power, in harmony with the character of his servant, he exclaimed, "Courage! Father Joseph, courage! Our troops have taken Brisach!" The monk died in December, 1638, and Richelieu exclaimed, when he was informed of his death, "I have lost my right arm." He pretended to shed tears over his grave; which display of sensibility induced the simple Louis XIII. to say: "I have lost one of my best subjects, and Monsieur le Cardinal his confidant and intimate friend."

The last conspiracy against the authority of the cardinal, which he was called upon to confront, and which he eventually crushed, was that of the king's favorite Cinq-Mars. This person had been introduced to the favor of the king by Richelieu himself, who readily discovered that Louis yearned for the society of some agreeable and harmless person, as a relief from the serious and solemn intricacies of state and of council which occupied the larger portion of his time. Cinq-Mars was a handsome young man, of amiable and pleasing temper, of very moderate abilities, and admirably suited to the purpose for which he was intended. He at once rose high in the confidence and friendship of the shallow king, and remained at the same time, the subservient tool of Richelieu.

At this period the young courtier was secretly attached to a beautiful and fascinating mistress at Paris, named Marion de l'Orme. It was the habit of Cinq-Mars to hasten to her residence, the instant the king retired to bed, and to return thence in the morning early enough to await the monarch at his rising. Sometimes, however, he was too late for this purpose, and in those instances as soon as Louis inquired for the favorite, he was informed that he had not yet risen.

Marion de l'Orme belonged to that celebrated class of women, whose character and career form some of the most interesting yet mournful pages of history. She was the intimate friend of the notorious Ninon de l'Enclos; and like her, she was extremely beautiful, accomplished, and perfidious. She possessed a large share of refined wit and intelligence; was luxurious and expensive in her habits of living; and regarded the indulgence of her voluptuous tastes as the highest end and blessing of existence. Her fascinations enslaved the minds, as well as the passions, of her admirers; and so potent were her charms that they had even subjugated the crafty Richelieu himself. At one period the illustrious churchman had been an ardent and humble suppliant for her favors. It is not singular, therefore, that the peerless beauty, the fascinating wit, and the attractive grace of this modern Aspasia, were able to detain in the soft dalliance of her gilded boudoir, this handsome but feeble-minded favorite of the king, long after the sterner dictates of policy and of interest would have admonished him to be gone. And when, to her own attractions, there were added, as was sometimes the case, those of the equally fascinating Ninon; when, during the late hours of the night these two remarkable women, and their lovers, banqueted in the splendid apartments of Marion, beguiling the time with the piquant scandals of the court; while Ninon pensively sang her softest, sweetest love-ditty, and Marion gayly narrated her most pleasing anecdote; while the choicest viands of the earth combined with charming wit, brilliant repartee, and winning flattery, satiated their physical and intellectual appetites; when such mingled banquets as these, at which a Pericles, an Apicius, even a Napoleon, would not have disdained to assist, regaled the senses of the fortunate favorites, it is not strange that the considerations of prudence often gave way before syren voices of such seductive, though fatal melody.

When kings and ministers elevate men of moderate fortunes to such high eminence, they naturally expect them to be obedient, and subservient to their wishes. The untimely absences of Cinq-Mars excited the indignation of Louis; and when the real cause of them became known, that cause aroused the indignation of the jealous Richelieu. Yet, after a little petting and scolding, the dispute was adjusted; but only to break out afterward again with intenser and more fatal fury.

The king in his free and confidential conversations with his favorite, disclosed all that occupied his thoughts, but at the same time, he forbade Cinq-Mars to divulge certain things to the cardinal. The latter had been in the habit of learning many things through the subserviency of Cinq-Mars; and he soon discovered that, for some reason, his protegé not only became less communicative, but that, in proportion as he became the depositary of the king's secrets, in that proportion he became arrogant toward the minister. At length, he even went so far as to conspire for the assassination of the cardinal. He endeavored to attach the duke of Orleans and the duke de Bouillon to his conspiracy. Meanwhile, his own arrogance even toward the king, became almost insufferable. He asserted publicly, that he did not spend as much of his time as he did formerly in the cabinet of the king, because his breath was so offensive that he really could not endure to go near him! Just at this period, Richelieu became sick at Norbonne, and Cinq-Mars delayed the assassination, in the confident expectation that the minister would die, without the necessity of his intervention. This fatal error, and the delay to which it led, was the cause of his own ruin.

The cardinal unexpectedly recovered. He employed the first moments of his convalescence, in devising the means whereby to destroy Cinq-Mars. Accident opportunely came to his aid, and he obtained from an unknown hand, a packet containing a copy of the secret treaty which the duke of Orleans and Cinq-Mars had entered into with the king of Spain; a treaty in which important rights of France were ceded to that country, without the knowledge and consent of the king, or his minister. Richelieu immediately sent this document to the king, as proof of the treason of Cinq-Mars; and the former favorite was immediately arrested at Norbonne. The king appointed a commission to try the conspirators—Cinq-Mars, De Thou, and the duke de Bouillon. The two former were condemned to death for treason; and Richelieu, fearful lest the imbecile sovereign should relent and pardon them before the completion of their sentence, ordered them to be executed on the same day. During the trial, Cinq-Mars maintained an obstinate and contemptuous silence; but when the soft and ambitious voluptuary was being led to the torture-room, his fortitude gave way, and he freely and openly confessed everything. On the scaffold he acted with more intrepidity, and one of the last acts of this ill-fated young courtier was, to send with his jeweled portrait, a message of tenderness to the fair Marion de l'Orme.

Three months after the accomplishment of this great

triumph, the mighty cardinal expired. He had reached the height of human glory; he had trampled all his foes beneath his feet; he had governed France for nearly twenty years with unparalleled splendor and success; he had heaped up vast treasures which no man scarcely could number; he had filled all Europe with the renown and the terror of his name; and now he was about to fall beneath the invincible power of the common enemy and conqueror of all. His disease was a dangerous and painful abscess on the breast. The imbecile king whom he had so long ruled with such absolute. sway, attended him during his last sickness, and even administered his medicines with his own hand. He at length confessed to M. de Lescot, bishop of Chartres, and received absolution. On the 4th of December, 1642, he became much worse, and his end was evidently approaching. Being then asked whether he forgave all his enemies, he replied with his customary craft, "that he never had any, except the enemies of France; and that he acted toward them as he implored Divine Justice to act toward him!" He also added, "that he embraced the articles of the Catholic creed with a perfect faith; and that if he had a hundred thousand lives to give, he would sacrifice them all for the faith and for the church?" With such monstrous lies on his dying lips, did this great hypocrite, tyrant, and assassin quit the scene of his innumerable crimes, and approach the presence of his impartial Judge!

Richelieu expired in the fifty-eighth year of his age, and in the eighteenth of his ministry. When Louis XIII., the imbecile wretch over whom he had ruled, was informed of his death, he exclaimed coldly, there is a great politician dead; and in this single speech, he embodied more wisdom than all the utterances of his whole life before.

As to the personal character of this celebrated man, we are convinced that there can be but one honest opinion entertained by those who have carefully examined his history. It will be admitted by every one, that his talents as a statesman, his sagacity, his penetration, the fertility of his resources, his firmness, and the consistency of the policy which he pursued, were all unrivaled and unquestioned. That he introduced order, vigor, and regularity into the administration is equally clear. That he rendered France, her armies, her court, and her king, respected and even feared throughout Europe, is indisputable. That he was one of those great, commanding, towering geniuses which visit the world at rare and long intervals, and leave behind them indelible and eternal foot-marks on the shores of time, for after ages to wonder at and to admire, will be admitted. But on the contrary, it is equally clear, that he was one of the most selfish, one of the most unscrupulous, one of the most cruel and unprincipled of mankind. His only god was himself. He despised his king, and only used him as the pliable instrument of his own aggrandizement. And to his insane worship of that god, he sacrificed the noblest and best blood of France. His revenge for supposed hostility or insults, was more implacable and insatiable than that of any other great man, whose deeds adorn and disgrace the page of history. It was with great truth that the illustrious Grotius wrote of him, after his death, an epitaph in which he declared among other things, that "in this was he wretched, that he made all men so; being as well the torment, as the ornament of his times."*

The announcement of his death was the sudden signal for exultations in various quarters of the habitable globe. At that moment the dark and chilly dungeous of the Bastille resounded with the frantic screams of joy, which were uttered by his many victims; from the illustrious Bassompeirre down to the obscure Dessault, who wrote a letter to the cardinal, when on his death-bed, full of scathing, and not unjust or undeserved invective. The innumerable fugitives in foreign climes, who had fled their country to escape his wrath, congratulated each other; and exulted over his death as if Satan himself had at last been crushed by the omnipotent and retributive arm of God. The French court whom he had so long overawed, and the French people whom he had so cruelly oppressed, rejoiced with one common joy that the great curse of mankind had at last, after so many years of patient endurance and suffering on their part, and of pernicious supremacy on his, descended to the eternal silence and darkness of the grave.

It is said, that not a human being in France mourned the cardinal's death, except his king, and his own favorites. To these he bequeathed munificent legacies. He gave the king, in addition to the presents made him during his lifetime, the sum of fifteen hundred thousand livres. He bequeathed his splendid library to the uni-

* "Hoc tamen uno miser, quod omnes fecit,
Tam saeculi sui tormentum, quam ornamentum."
And he adds afterward, very appropriately:
"Quo migravit sacramentum est!"

versity of the Sorbonne, which he had established. But all his untold wealth he had, during the latter years of his administration, cruelly extorted from the people; and he had several times almost driven them to despair by the extent and rigor of his exactions. In a word, this great and gifted man was the most complete embodiment of selfish and unscrupulous mental power, which the world has even seen; and while his whole life was spent in elevating himself, by depressing the power of the French nobles, under the plea of strengthening the prerogatives and supremacy of the king, he degraded, depressed, and ruined the people, whose interests and whose rights he treated with contempt, and habitually trampled under foot.

And yet, the crafty cardinal, during his triumphant career, met with many mortifications. He attempted the composition of tragedy, and produced an impotent and unfortunate play, named Mirame; on the representation of which he expended three hundred thousand crowns. He was irritated beyond measure at the failure of this performance; and some of those who indulged their wit upon its absurdities, expiated their offense by many long years of captivity in the Bastille. Richelieu himself confessed that the six feet of earth, as he termed the king's cabinet, gave him more trouble than all the rest of Europe combined. He was tormented with endless suspicions of conspiracies and plots against his life and supremacy. He was even harassed with jealousy against those who excelled him in the only thing in which he failed, the dramatic art; and the great Corneille himself suffered under the penalties of his hatred. And it is unquestionably true, that had not

Louis XIII. been one of the most imbecile and contemptible of kings; had he not been devoid of all mental dignity, energy, and penetration, it would have been impossible for even the crafty Richelieu to have retained so long, the splendid and gorgeous, but baleful eminence, from whose heights he so greatly astonished the world, and so deeply cursed his country.

CHAPTER II.

MORALS AND MANNERS OF THE COURT OF VERSAILLES BEFORE THE FIRST FRENCH REVOLUTION.

THE regency of Anne of Austria, the supremacy of Mazarin, and the reign of Louis XIV., ensued upon the death of the impotent royal puppet who had been so adroitly governed by Richelieu. The long reign of Louis XIV., glittering with a false, delusive splendor, which emanated from a colossal throne erected upon the ruins of the nation's liberty and prosperity, dragged the French court and people nearer than before to the yawning abyss of ruin. At length Louis XV. assumed the scepter; and if France, heaving with the tremendous struggles of her great revolutions, presents a striking and impressive subject of reflection, the character of her court, and the condition of her people immediately previous to those memorable scenes, are not less monstrous, nor less pregnant with interest.

During the protracted reign of Louis XIV., France had been the worst governed kingdom in Europe, even in that dark age of princely corruption, tyranny, and oppression. To be a noble, or a member of the court, seemed to have given an immunity in almost every vicious excess. It was during the unparalleled darkness of that period that the greatest outrages were perpetrated by a voluptuous and pampered nobility, upon the most valuable and precious rights of a frivolous and complacent nation. The eyes of the French people seem to have been strangely blinded, and their resentment disarmed by having beheld the false and delusive splendors of the reign of Louis XIV.; than whom a more sensual, voluptuous, though magnificent sovereign, never adorned or disgraced a throne.

During this period, both the person and the prerogatives of the king were regarded with a sacred and superstitious awe, as being elevated far above the reach of popular scrutiny, censure, or indignation. While the French people admired the grandeur of their monarch, and the brilliancy of his court; while they cherished the renown conferred upon the nation, by the celebrity of French nobles, statesmen, generals, and titled and mitred debauchees; they forgot, in a great measure, the outrages constantly perpetrated by those persons upon their own most valuable privileges, under the color of the royal prerogative, and the immemorial rights and immunities of princes. At that period, the French nation were still disposed to believe that all the tyrannical acts of their sovereign were committed under the influence of evil counsel; and in the same loyal and charitable spirit, they continued to hope and believe that whatever he did which was virtuous and commendable, was the result of the inherent benevolence and excellence of his own character. This delusion continued, in a great degree, to exert its protective and conservative influence during the reign of Louis XV.; and postponed for a time that dreadful catastrophe which, during the reign of his successor, swept away king, throne, and sovereignty into one terrible and universal ruin.

The fruitful source of countless evils to France during the reign of Louis XV., was the influence and administration of the duke of Choiseul, minister of foreign affairs. This talented but unprincipled statesman was an Austrian by education and feeling. He had been French minister at the court of Vienna; had there become the favorite and confidant of Maria Theresa; and was secretly attached to Austrian interests and policy. On his return to France, he obtained in conjunction with Madame Pompadour, the king's mistress, complete control over the weak and pliant mind of the sovereign.

Choiseul was strong in the protection of Madame Pompadour, whom Maria Theresa had permanently attached to her own interests, by flattering her vanity with compliments and presents. Choiseul supported the authority of the parliament, whose protector he styled himself. He became the declared enemy of the Jesuits, and succeeded eventually in suppressing the order throughout the French dominions. His character, was bold, thoughtful, cunning, and sagacious. He possessed much firmness and resolution. He was steadfast and consistent in his plans. In a word, though his name and administration have become almost oblivious to posterity, being eclipsed by the greater brilliancy and magnitude of succeeding events; yet he was in no respects inferior in ability to statesmen of more enduring fame—to Mazarin, to De Ritz, or to Richelieu.

It was through the influence of this man, united with that of Madame Pompadour, that in 1758 Louis entered into a treaty with Austria, which greatly aggravated the already existing evils in France; which, in fact, made the latter country a mere province and dependency of Austria; and which, by binding the French king to furnish money and troops to Austria whenever called upon, rendered Louis XV. the tool and subject of Joseph II.

It had always been the wise policy of the preceding sovereigns and statesmen of France, to weaken the supremacy of Austria as far as possible. For this end had Henry IV., Richelieu, Mazarin, Louis XIV., and Belle-Isle, labored and negotiated. All the results of their labors had been lost by the baneful influence which the duke of Choiseul exercised over the weak and timid mind of his sovereign.

Among the various measures projected and accomplished by this minister, was the suppression of the Jesuits in France. This wonderful order of men, whose lives, whose talents, and whose energies are all devoted to the defense and propagation of absolutism both in church and in state, have ever been from the hour of their establishment, the most powerful supporters of despotic thrones and empires. In all lands and in every quarter of the globe, their efficiency has been found to be immense, and their attachment unwavering, to the interests of the throne and the altar. It matters not to them how tyrannical a sovereign may be, or how absolute his authority; it is enough for him to be an enemy to human freedom and a friend of their faith; and he will find the secret and the public support of the disciples of Loyola of infinitely more value than a powerful army; than an extensive and vigilant police; than a full and inexhaustible treasury. To them all crimes, all expedients, and all measures, are alike in their merit, or in their enormity, provided they are favorable to the great and unchangeable end of all their exertions, and of their very being—the retarding of human progress, the suppression of human liberty, and the establishment of despotisms. They have, on many important and critical occasions, secretly, but successfully, rolled back the advancing tide of revolution, which threatened to submerge beneath its waves the trembling thrones of affrighted monarchs. Men wondered at the sudden and mysterious change which took place in the current of events; and while they beheld the clear proofs of the existence of *some* hidden and powerful agent; so perfect and consummate was the concealment, that they were utterly unable to designate *what* that influence was, whose wondrous effects they clearly beheld. That concealed, insidious, and powerful agency was often the unrivaled and stupendous order of the Jesuits.

Yet, strange to say, this was the very body of men whom the infatuated minister of Louis XV. so unwisely, for the interests of his master, suppressed. This event took place in 1762. No sooner had the energy and protection of this society been withdrawn; no sooner had the Jesuits ceased to support the throne by the influence which they exerted; by their secret instructions in the confessional; by their powerful discourses from the pulpit; by their learned prelections in the university, and lecture-room; and by the profound works which they elaborated from the press; than the foundations of the French monarchy began to loosen and give way. Together with the support of the Jesuits, the attachment of the clerical orders, in a great measure, was lost to the throne. For it was the policy of the duke of Choiseul, while he was abasing the Jesuits, to elevate the new philosophy of Voltaire and Rousseau, to the high dignity and influence which had been previously enjoyed by the churchmen. The suppression of the Jesuits was in a great measure regarded as the triumph of the philosophers; as an attack upon the priesthood; as a disgrace intended for religion and the church.

While this blow was directed by the ministers of Louis XV. against the great representative of morality, order, and religion in the nation, those unfortunate results followed which might naturally have been expected. France became one wide land of revelry, irreligion, and profligacy. The court became the scene of the most excessive and infamous debaucheries. The French people ever prone to imitate those above them in rank and power, copied the fashionable improprieties of the court, without possessing that elegant refinement which, in the vices of the great, takes away half their offensiveness. Then commenced that scene of corruption so memorable in the history of nations. Mankind have read with horror, or at least with astonishment, the records of the voluptuous excesses and splendid pleasures of ancient Corinth—a city beautifully situated on the isthmus of that name, where a vast temple of Venus had been erected in a style of magnificence unsurpassed, even in the countries of Xerxes or the Parthenon, whose towering form glittered invitingly from afar, beneath the azure sky of that fair land of genius and of song. But Corinth, filled as she was with the most beautiful and voluptuous courtesans of all climes, and crowded with the most opulent and lavish debauchees of all countries; Corinth, in whose great temple the countless priestesses of the impure goddess celebrated her rites without any censure of law or public opinion to restrain them;—the deeds of Corinth were purity and innocence, compared with the excesses which then characterized the brilliant and cultivated capital of France. Men have thought that Rome under Nero or Caligula, had reached the worst extremes of human corruption. But in the age and reigns of Louis XIV. and XV., the world was taught to believe that the race of Poppeas and Messalinas, of ancient date and celebrity, had not yet passed away; but that the lapse of centuries had even added to the intensity of their passions, and to the refinement of their vices. Not all the instances of ancient or modern immorality which have excited the wonder and disgust of mankind, have presented so vast and so astounding an instance of individual and national corruption, as that displayed by the court and people of France, at the period under consideration.

The court itself was under the absolute dominion of women; at the head of whom in influence, in beauty, and in infamy, was the king's mistress, Madame de Pompadour; a name as badly celebrated in modern, as was Aspasia or Thais in ancient times.

This lady, whose real name was Poissan, first attracted the attention of Louis, when hunting in the forest of Senart. She was of humble birth; but her amazing beauty and grace at once fixed the admiration of the amorous monarch. In 1744, at a masked ball, he declared to her his passion, and she immediately became the king's acknowledged mistress. Her complexion was very fair. Her figure, arms, and hands were remarkably beautiful.

Louis first provided apartments for her at Versailles. He presented her at different times with six estates, besides so vast a quantity of furniture and valuables that, after her death, the sale of them occupied twelve months.

She was introduced at court with great *eclat*, and was soon created marchioness de Pompadour. Knowing the king's aversion to business, she resolved to relieve him of that burthen, and to assume the reins of government herself. She appointed some of the ministers, and dismissed others. Her talents for administration were respectable; though her chief hold upon the affections of the monarch was her beauty, and her ability to amuse and divert an indolent king, whose time hung heavily upon his hands. She sometimes received the monarch in the garb of a milk-maid; and the mighty sovereign of a great nation was charmed and ruled, more by the frivolities of this giddy, though fascinating woman, than by all the sages and statesmen of France combined. In all the royal residences she erected theaters, in which she herself performed; and she liberally rewarded Voltaire and Rousseau, for literary productions which they wrote at her request, and for her amusement.

The superior talents of Madame Pompadour are admitted by all who are impartial in their estimate of her character. Maria Theresa herself complimented her judgment, and did not disdain to ask her advice. She even corresponded with the favorite, and honored her with the epithet of *aime et bonne cousine.* She brought about the treaty, in a great measure, in connection with the duke of Choiseul, which united France to Austria, and proved the most powerful blow to the authority and influence of Frederick the Great, during the seven years' war.

Amiable and complacent as was this remarkable woman to those who flattered and fawned upon her, she was terrible in her vengeance upon those who indulged their wit or sarcasm at her expense. The gloomy cells of the Bastille, with all their horrid scenes of suffering and of despair, were generally the life-long portion of those who were so unfortunate as to incur her displeasure. A few flattering verses addressed to her by the Abbe Bernis, made him a cardinal. Some years afterward, hearing that he had spoken of her with disrespect, her resentment was furious, and he was disgraced, impoverished, and exiled. Latude, a young French officer, wounded her vanity, perhaps even unintentionally. The consequence was, that the miseries of the Bastille were his reward for the long and hopeless period of thirty-five years.

It was to her corrupt ingenuity that France was indebted for the invention of the infamous and renowned *Para-aux-Cerfs*. This establishment was situated near the forest of Satory, at Versailles; and in it she assembled a number of young ladies, remarkable for their beauty and their immorality, to divert the transient affections of the indolent and imbecile king. By means of this voluptuous establishment, corruption was introduced into many of the first families of the kingdom; and Louis XV. became the Sardanapalus of modern times; the most debauched man of his age. He spent a hundred millions of francs on the beauties of this establishment; and that, too, at a time when the revenues of his kingdom were greatly embarassed and oppressed. It became the center and hot-bed of vice, where its refinements were studied, and its worse excesses were boldly practiced and approved.

While these things were going on at court, public disorders were increasing throughout the kingdom. There were troubles in the church; troubles among the magistracy; and troubles among the people. In 1757 an abortive attempt was made by Damiens to assassinate the king. When Madame Pompadour heard of this catastrophe, she was compelled to leave the palace; and remained an exile from it, as long as the danger of the king threatened to be fatal. Upon his recovery she returned again, and reässerted her former influence with redoubled power. At length, in 1764, she expired, at the palace at Versailles. For several years her health had been declining, and her end was not unexpected. She died at the age of forty-two. For twenty years she had exercised an unbounded and baneful influence, over the mind of the imbecile monarch, as well as over the destinies of France. She was to blame, in a great degree, for the many evils in church and in state, which gradually brought on the final catastrophe of the revolution, and overturned all in one common ruin. Her influence was probably more absolute and complete, than that of any mistress who ever ruled a king. While a few of her favorites enjoyed the benefits of her successful love and triumphant ambition, there were thousands who writhed under the fury of her capricious resentment; and all France was made to mourn the evils entailed upon the nation, by her infamous lust, and her extravagant licentiousness.

Upon the death of Madame Pompadour, the queen endeavored to win back Louis XV. to a course of virtue, and of attention to his family, and his subjects. For a very short time she seemed likely to succeed. But her attempt was vain. The king soon relapsed again into his usual habits of indolence and lust; and by coming under the influence of another mistress not less dissolute or fascinating than her predecessor, he rendered the evils which already afflicted France, still more ruinous and intolerable. This woman was the celebrated Madame Du Barry.

Of her, a French writer truly says: "She was a child as beautiful as Love, but had served an apprenticeship to debauchery in all the brothels of the *Rue St. Honoré.*" This young woman was the daughter of a farmer in Vaucouliers, and was born in 1746. Her parents died shortly after her birth; and she was thus thrown upon the world. She came to push her fortune at Paris, and entered the employment of a dressmaker. In that brilliant capital, she soon fell a victim to the countless temptations which beset the path of the young and the beautiful. She gradually descended from one degree of vice to another, until her splendid and unrivaled charms were paraded for public prostitution, in the most celebrated brothels of the capital.

Madame Du Barry is reported to have commenced her vicious career at the early age of twelve. After having been regularly thrown upon the town as we have said, she met the Count Du Barry, a licentious young man from Thoulouse, a frequenter of the houses of ill-fame in the capital, and already distiuguished by the unenviable name of *le roué.* He procured her favors for the young noblemen of the court, and particularly for

Lebel, the principal clerk of the department of foreign affairs, with whom she at last lived publicly as his mistress. He at length placed her at the head of a gaming establishment in Paris, which, in consequence of her notorious beauty soon became celebrated. It was from this position that she was transferred to the royal bed.

It is said that Lebel had been the principal agent of Madame Pompadour, in establishing the *parc-aux-cerfs.* When he had determined to introduce Madam Du Barry to the king, it became necessary to provide her with a respectable name, as her own was ignoble and unknown. Marshal Richelieu, who was also concerned in the intrigue, persuaded the Count Du Barry to consent to a formal marriage with the complaisant young lady; and thus to stain the honorable name of his ancestors with the infamy of this connection. She was then introduced to the monarch as the Countess Du Barry; and so satisfactory to the king were his first interviews with this practiced and fascinating courtesan, that he immediately acknowledged her as his mistress, and proceeded to surround her with more than the usual splendors and luxuries which were attendant upon that disgraceful dignity.

The imagination of Louis, as well as his body, was worn out by a long and excessive career of debauchery. The elegant and refined blandishments of Mesdames Tournelle and Pompadour, could no longer have gratified him; and he found a new excitement and fascination in the shameless embraces and abandoned excesses of this young girl. She treated him as the accomplished prostitutes of the Palais Royal usually treated the old and worn-out rakes of the metropolis. This was something novel and interesting to Louis; and hence the violent infatuation which seized him in reference to his new mistress; which continued with unabated vehemence, till the hour of his death.

The prodigality of Madame Du Barry was ruinous to France. She always used gold plate, and possessed a cup of that metal of enormous size and value, presented her by the doting king. Her carriage cost fifty-two thousand francs. On the day of her *fête*, Louis gave her a bouquet of diamonds, valued at three hundred thousand francs; and a dressing table of massive gold, surmounted by two golden cupids, holding a crown enriched with diamonds, and so ingeniously arranged, that she could not look on the mirror without seeing herself crowned. When she lost immense sums at play, she gave drafts at sight upon the court banker, Beaujon; which he paid with greater regularity than the expenses of the government. During the life of Louis XV., it is ascertained that she drew in this and in other ways, eighteen millions of francs from the royal treasury. This was the manner in which the exhausted revenues of the kingdom were expended, immediately previous to the outbreak of that revolution which wreaked such terrible vengeance on the innocent inheritor of the name, the crown, and the obloquy of the Capets; and while these abuses do not wholly excuse the infamous excesses of that revolution, they certainly go a great way to palliate their enormity. And yet, Madam Du Barry was a pattern of amiability, of generosity, and of benevolence. All confessed their admiration of her great beauty, charity, and good nature.

To divert the ennui of the aged monarch, Madam

Du Barry imitated the expedient of Madam Pompadour; and allowed, in the recesses of the palace, disgraceful scenes of licentiousness to occur between the young courtiers and their mistresses, whom they were permitted to introduce for that purpose. The king conducted her in turn to all the royal palaces; and at each of them, he gave splendid and expensive entertainments in her honor. Had it not been for the opposition of the duke de Choiseul, and his sister, the duchess de Grammont, it is probable that Louis XV. would have married his mistress, in the excess of his attachment, and of his imbecility. Though she failed in accomplishing this ambitious purpose, yet her unfading and peerless beauty retained its potent influence over the monarch, till the day of his death. When attacked by the small pox he sent for her; affectionately embraced her; covered her with kisses; and vehemently declared that his greatest grief in dying, was the loss of such unrivaled and angelic charms!

Such were the pursuits and the attachments of the sovereign of France, whose reign immediately preceded that of the outbreak of the first revolution.

After perusing this short description of the character of the French king and court, the reader will not be surprised to learn the consequences which naturally resulted from such prolific and powerful causes. They are, indeed, without a parallel in the chequered history of nations.

As was the sovereign, so were all the officers of the kingdom, appointed by him, and by his ministers. In the administration of justice throughout the whole realm, there was no longer even the semblance of impartiality or honesty. A liberal bribe, the favors of a beautiful wife, or the caresses of a fascinating mistress, could always sway the decision of a judge. Personal freedom was universally insecure, for *lettres-de-cachet*, without accusation or trial, were issued without even the authority of the king, to gratify the malice and caprice of his courtiers. The servants of the crown, and the officers of the army, drew immense salaries, such as would scarcely now be credited. These expenses exhausted the resources of the treasury. The most important deliberations and measures of the government were decided in the arms of mistresses; and the whims of thoughtless courtesans determined the fate, and ruined the interests, of thousands of citizens. The most important interests of agriculture were destroyed by the outrageous game-laws which existed. Wild boars and deer were allowed to run at large through the most richly cultivated districts, and to destroy the most valuable crops. It was forbidden to hoe and weed, lest the young partridges should be disturbed. It was forbidden to mow hay, lest their eggs should be destroyed. When these infamous laws were broken, and the culprits were arraigned for trial, the most outrageous corruption and oppression were practiced, which were sure in the end to ruin the defendants, and cast them penniless upon the world. People were compelled to have their grain ground at the landlord's mill, and to make their wine at his press. The feudal services required by the landed gentry were outrageous and incredible. The taxes were immense, and burdensome beyond endurance. The aristocracy, in connection with the clergy, possessed three-fourths of the soil of France. Yet they, for the most part, refused to reside upon their estates;

but spent their revenues amid the dissipations of Paris; while their agents increased the evil by the perpetration of additional outrages, to promote their own separate interests. The condition of the peasantry of France at this period, was miserable beyond all description. Their houses were unfurnished and cheerless. Their apparel was ragged and filthy. Their toil was endless and unprofitable. They saw no possible alleviation of their present sufferings; no reasonable hope of future deliverance.

In the church, the corruption was two-fold. First, it was impossible for talent and virtue, if of inferior rank, to rise to the higher dignities of the profession. These were all appropriated by the titled and profligate members of aristocratic families. The state of morals was corrupt in the extreme, among both the higher and the lower orders of the clergy. To be an archbishop, or an abbé, was equivalent to being suspected as a person of licentious and dissolute habits. Religion and its ministers passed into universal contempt; nor could the eminent virtues of a few, redeem the profession from the degradation produced by the notorious vices of the many.

The disrespect into which religion and its representatives had fallen, was augmented by another powerful cause. The period had dawned upon France which was to witness the triumph of infidelity. These were the halcyon days of unbelief and ridicule; the hour of triumph to Voltaire, to Rousseau, and the Encyclopedists.

As soon as a nation becomes devoid of all religious reverence and feeling, the hour of its ruin is not far off. *Some* religion of some sort, is necessary to the well-being of every social compact—of every organized community.

This fact is illustrated by the history of nations. The absence of all religion has ruined many of them. The presence and power of even a heathen faith, which taught the existence and the supremacy of the gods and man's accountability to them, has preserved others in permanent prosperity. This was the true secret of the power and duration of the Grecian and Roman republics. The ancient Greek, being of imaginative and cultivated mind, in the absence of all revealed instruction on the subject of religion invoked the aid of his powerful intellect, and of his brilliant imagination; and the result was that gorgeous, beautiful, and imposing array of deities, who inhabited the golden palaces of Olympus, and reveled amid the voluptuous scenes of Elysium. To the Greek, or the Roman, every peal of thunder was the voice of angry Jove. On the battlefield, he thought he beheld the powerful achievements of some favorite and propitious god, scattering death among his foes. His splendid temples were adorned with exquisite sculptures and paintings, of those beautiful and heavenly forms with which his refined and glowing fancy had peopled the immortal seats of paradise. With such an array of gods before them, the Greeks and Romans felt or acknowledged their superior existence, their supremacy, and man's moral accountability to them. The consequence was, that they never commenced a battle without invoking the divine assistance; and they were liberal in their services and their sacrifices to what they believed to be the requirements of the true religion.

But so soon as France became, in effect, a nation of infidels, denying the existence of the Deity, his control over the affairs of men, and man's accountability to him, both here and hereafter—the nation became one vast and countless assemblage of debauchees, of adventurers, of unprincipled and reckless scoffers of religion, and even of decency. The few believers in the order of things which had just passed away, were stigmatized as superstitious; and every license in morals, in opinions, in church, and in state, began to be commended and praised under the specious title of Freedom; nor was there any conservative or corrective power, either in the existing church or state, capable of resisting the disorganizing effect of these widely-spread and radical evils.

In addition to all this, the finances of the kingdom, which had been much embarrassed during the reign of Louis XIV., became hopelessly deranged under the feeble and perverted administration of his successor. The annual deficit during the last years of this sovereign, amounted to *seven millions of pounds sterling.* This ruined state of things could not long continue. The nation was on the verge of total wreck. The *tiers-etat* were becoming desperate. The volcano under the throne was accumulating its pent-up fires. The superincumbent mass could not much longer suppress it, and a terrible and destructive explosion was about to break forth, dashing that throne and its appendages to atoms.

Louis XV. at length died, having taken the small pox from one of the girls of the *Parc-aux-Cerfs*, who had been infected with the disease only a few hours before, and was ignorant of her condition. He gave her in return the half-cured distemper under which he himself labored. His ignoble reign continued from its commencement in 1715, till his death in 1774, during the immense period of fifty-nine years. Before he expired, the two diseases had changed his body into a rotten carcass. He received the last sacraments from a poor and blind old priest, who alone would venture to undertake the task. He was then buried secretly by the night-men of Versailles. Such was the ignominious end of the last king of the elder Bourbon race who died in his bed!

Louis XVI. was born on the 22d of August, 1754. He was the grandson of Louis XV., and second son of the dauphin by his second wife, Maria Josephine, daughter of the elector of Saxony.

During his youth, his education was entrusted to the Countess Marsan, whose rare mental and moral qualifications, well fitted her for the important trust. This lady was governess in the royal family. In his younger years, and whilst surrounded by the most fashionable and dissolute court in the world, Louis was always remarkable for the seriousness of his deportment, for the propriety of his conduct, for the morality and purity of his actions. He seemed to be strangely indifferent to all the brilliant seductions which encompassed him. The attractive dissipations, the beautiful women, the luxurious banquets, and the gay festivities which laid their seductive splendors at his feet, all appeared alike indifferent to him.

Three prominent features marked his youthful character; his integrity, his indecision, and his weakness. He seems to have had but little vigor or energy of mind; and was unable to think and determine for himself. And yet, he was not devoid of mental qualities. His memory was extraordinary, and he retained with great accuracy, the information which he had acquired with great facility. His knowledge of languages was extensive; and he was successful in mastering all those branches of learning to which he applied himself. He even possessed considerable literary taste; and republished and edited an edition of Fenelon's Telemachus. He also executed translations of portions of Gibbon's great work on the Decline and Fall of the Roman Empire. It may be said of him that he was a moral, and even a religious prince; nor was the intense spirit of scandal which characterized his age and country, able to discover any breach of virtue, or even of modesty, which could be laid to his charge. There was one peculiar eccentricity with which he indulged himself, as harmless as it was peculiar. He was fond of the labors of a *locksmith.* He caused an apartment in the palace to be fitted up with the apparatus of a smith; and thither he often retired, to indulge himself with his favorite exercise. The melodious music of the dance, in sweet cadence and harmony with which so many graceful feet moved in the gilded halls of Versailles, was often interrupted by the alternating echo of the anvil and the furnace, resounding beneath the sturdy hand of the laborious monarch. The only vice ever laid to the charge of this prince, was the use of wine, which he sometimes carried to a more than reasonable extent. It was in this unobtrusive and harmless manner, that the youth of Louis XVI. passed away; furnishing no presage of that stormy and disastrous destiny, which was so soon to be his portion.

The dauphin, father of Louis XVI., was so partial to his son, that he excited the jealousy of his brothers, the count of Provence and the count d'Artois. This preference was the result of the peculiarly amiable and serious disposition of Louis, who at that time was known by the name of the duke de Berry. Madam Adelaide, who was particularly attached to him, endeavored to correct his excessive timidity, and said to him, "Speak at your ease, Berry; exclaim, bawl out, make a noise like your brother Artois. Dash and break to pieces my china; make yourself talked about." But all these chiding reproofs were of no avail. The duke de Berry became every day more silent and thoughtful.

While the prince repulsed flatterers, and did not disguise his contempt for them, he took an interest in the miseries of the unfortunate. He took great pleasure in observing the labors of workmen employed at the palace and the gardens. He would frequently assist them in raising a heavy stone or beam. He became very expert in making locks; and obtained the title of the "Good Vulcan" from the royal family, on account of the blackness of his hands when working at this favorite amusement.

At the death of Louis XV. the French nation were so weary of his long and almost endless reign, that Louis XVI. was universally hailed by the remarkable epithet of "Louis the Desired." He had himself declared, previous to the death of his predecessor, and as a reproof of the depravity of the old court, that he desired to be called after his accession, by the name of "*Louis the Severe.*" He discovered no taste at any time for violent or noisy pleasures. He hated balls, gaming, shows, and pageants of all sorts. He detested libertinism. He was indeed a Lot, lonely and unheeded, amid the corruptions of the mighty Sodom by which he was surrounded. One only pride he seemed to have entertained, in connection with the exalted station of which he was the unwilling heir. This was the attachment which he felt to the glory of his house; and he dreaded everything which might tarnish its luster.

When Louis ascended the throne, in 1774, he was in his twentieth year, and had already been married four years. Though he had ever been exemplary in regard to women, and was strictly faithful to his wife, the French could not imagine it possible that a Bourbon and a king could long retain his virtue; and they prophesied that he would show the family trait, as all the rest had done, at the age of forty, when he became tired of the queen. His only amusement was the chase. His principal mental diversion was his geographical studies, and the examination of his charts, globes, and spheres. He was unusually dexterous in the art of washing these. His memory in geographical knowledge was prodigious. He possessed a good select library for his own use; containing rare and expensive works, which he frequently and carefully perused. Directly over this library, was the singular apartment appropriated to his amusements as a locksmith. Here he spent much time under the tuition of *Gamin*, a common mechanic of the day, who afterward betrayed him to the convention, and aided in accomplishing his destruction. He declares, that in their intercourse he treated Louis with the rudeness of a common apprentice; that the latter was fond of inspecting and making curious and ingenious locks; that he worked hard at the anvil, and the forge, and seemed to take delight in the vigor of his exercise; and that he would frequently conceal himself from the queen and court, and pass stolen hours with this locksmith, just as other men steal interviews with their mistresses!

Over this mechanical apartment, was a lofty platform covered with lead, on which the king, seated in an easy chair, and with an immense telescope, surveyed for hours the courts of Versailles, the roads to Paris, and the gardens and villas in the neighborhood. He had contracted an attachment to Duret, who waited on him in his private apartments; who sharpened his tools, wiped his anvil, pasted together his charts, and adapted his telescopes to the king's eyes.

As sovereign of France, Louis was excessively severe in the punishment of any improprieties in his courtiers, when he became convinced of their thorough depravity. These acts of rigor seemed to be momentary fits of resentment, excited by the turpitude of the criminal. The strong and determined will which devises and executes great measures of national policy, he never possessed. His memory was prodigious, as will appear from the following incident. He was one day presented with a long financial account for his examination, in which an item was erroneously introduced, which had been inserted in a similar account of the preceding year. "Here is a double entry," said he. "Bring me the account of last year, and I will show it to you." His recollection of the matter was accurate, and the error was corrected. But it was his misfortune, not his fault, that he did not possess the great administrative talents of a Richelieu, or a Cromwell. He was *good*, and that was nobler than to have been *great*.

When Louis XVI. ascended the throne his resolutions were admirable. He resolved to become a reformer and revolutionist; and he determined to remedy and correct every abuse under which the nation groaned, and the pampered court and aristocracy flourished. Had he been allowed to prosecute his plans, his crown and life might have been preserved; and the horrors of the revolution might have been rendered unnecessary.

But it was not to be his happy destiny to accomplish this honorable purpose. He was thwarted and prevented by so many causes, that his efforts were rendered utterly imbecile. These obstacles arose from his parliaments; from his ministers; and from his unfortunate connection with Maria Antoinette. This princess, who exerted so important an influence in reference to the destiny of Louis, and of France, now requires our more particular attention.

She was the daughter of Francis I. emperor of Germany, and Maria Theresa, the celebrated queen of Hungary. She inherited her mother's talents, her beauty, and her ambition. In 1770, at the tender age of fifteen, she was conducted to France as the affianced bride of Louis XVI., at that time the Dauphin. The marriage was celebrated at Versailles with great pomp and splendor. During the festivities which attended this important event, a calamity occurred, which threw a check on the general joy, and furnished a sad and terrible omen of the future disasters which attended that inauspicious marriage. A temporary scaffolding took fire, and amid the terror and confusion which ensued among the multitudes crowded into the temporary saloons, three hundred persons were either suffocated or burned to death.

During the first four years of the married life of these

princes, they seemed to be perfectly happy. Three years of this period passed away before the accession of Louis to the throne. Their mutual affection seemed intense; and as yet none of those political storms had burst forth which afterward raged so furiously around them. At this happy period, Maria Antoinette is described as possessing an angelic figure, a remarkably clear complexion, a brilliant color, regular features, and beautifully expressive eyes. She had the Austrian under lip. Her disposition was cheerful, happy, and confiding. She was indeed the subject of general adulation. The pulpit, the academy, the press, the almanacs, according to the chivalrous custom of that age, were filled with flattery of her charms, and of her virtues. The old spirit of the preceding reigns, which was accustomed to treat exalted rank and birth with chivalrous respect and delicacy, had not yet become extinct. The insane vulgarity of Jacobinism had not yet ventured to degrade and debase every person, and everything, which time and virtue had surrounded with the just reverence of mankind. The well-known rhapsody of Burke, in reference to Maria Antoinette at this period, deserves to be re-quoted, as necessary to give a fair idea of the happy position which she enjoyed at this propitious period. "It is now sixteen or seventeen years," says this eloquent writer, "since I saw the queen of France, then the dauphiness, at Versailles, and surely, never lighted on this orb, which she hardly seemed to touch, a more delightful vision. I saw her just above the horizon, decorating and cheering the elevated sphere she just began to move in, glittering like the morning star, full of life, and splendor, and joy! I thought ten thousand swords would have leaped from their scabbards, to avenge even a look that threatened her with insult. But the age of chivalry is gone. That of sophisters, economists, and calculators has succeeded, and the glory of Europe is extinguished forever." The kindness and generosity of her nature, which often induced her gracefully to stoop from her exalted station, to do acts of charity and condescension to the poor, won for her then, the enthusiastic applause of all gallant and chivalrous men, and of a respectful and generous people. Let us cite an instance. A stag which had been wounded in the chase, when the king was present, struck a poor peasant with his horns. The queen, on hearing of the incident, flew to his assistance, took his wife into her carriage, loaded her with kindness, and granted her a pension. This was but one of many similar incidents which occurred at this period.

The first mortification which Maria Antoinette was compelled to endure, at the court of Versailes, was the dismissal and disgrace of the duke of Choiseul, the minister of foreign affairs, and the unchangeable friend and partisan of Austrian interests. It was he who had brought about the marriage of Louis with Maria Antionette. It was he, who sought by every means to oppose the faction of Richelieu, and the mistress of Louis XV., Madam Du Barry, but that faction now proved too powerful for him, and caused his disgrace. Louis XVI. ever afterward mistrusted his wife, whenever the interests of Austria came in question. Maria Antionette hated Madam Du Barry, and was jealous of her; and the first act of severity of which she was guilty in France, after her accession to the throne, was the rude and unceremonious banishment of this favorite, the moment the old king was dead.

Such was the character of the queen at the period when she first shared the throne with Louis. The other members of the royal family occupied so important a position, and exerted so decided an influence on succeeding events and on the fate of Louis, that it is proper to dwell, at some length, upon their peculiarities and character.

The king had two brothers, the count of Provence, called, according to etiquette, *Monsieur*, and the count d'Artois; men as diametrically different from the king in dispositions, as two persons could possibly be. The count of Provence was an absolutist in principle; and was opposed to all measures of reform that could be proposed. He entertained the idea, that all the nations of Europe grew out of royalty as existing in the reigning monarchies; and that the house of Bourbon was the first and greatest of all the families on the earth. Yet he was vacillating and incoherent in his political ideas. He was opposed to the house of Austria, and to the intrigues of Maria Antoinette in its favor. He considered her as the scourge and the calamity of France. He possessed a deeply meditative cast of mind; was remarkable for the independence and originality of his ideas on the subject of government; and was, in a large degree, the most talented of the grandsons of Louis XV.

The count d'Artois, the second brother of the king, had inherited from nature a very different disposition. He was strongly inclined to pleasure; and his irregular and premature inclinations rendered the excesses of his youth outrageous. His licentiousness was unbounded, and universally censured, even by the least scrupulous of men on that subject—by the French nobility themselves. In the same degree that the king was virtuous, chaste, and moderate, he was impure, extravagant, and outrageous. He was also an inveterate gambler, and on one occasion he desired to entice the king to join him in this indulgence. "Will you stake a thousand double louis-d'ors," said the count to him one day. "I will play with you with all my heart," said the latter, "but I will stake no more than a crown. You are too rich to play with me." At another time, while Louis was making a journey, some repairs were ordered in the apartments he was to occupy. Hearing that these repairs cost thirty thousand francs, he was very indignant. Said he, "I might have made thirty families happy with that sum." Yet this was the man whom the revolutionists guillotined, as the representative of every vice!

But Louis XVI. seemed to be the only eminent example of virtue in his family. The duke of Orleans, the father of *Egalité*, had been married to Louisa Henrietta de Conti. The duchess of Orleans, during two years of her married life, was attached to her husband; too much so, indeed, if the reports are true, concerning the singular behavior of this couple at court, upon the beds of their friends when visiting, and even in the gardens. But the duchess soon became scandalous in her life. She prostituted herself without shame, or even selection, to the men of the court, and to persons of all ranks, from a prince of the blood, to her coachman Lefranc. Tired of sharing the pleasures of love with men whom she knew, she indulged her insatiable appetite by soliciting the embraces of strangers, in the old garden of the Palais Royal, in the evening. She gloried in the fact that she deserved the epithet of the modern Messalina.

After the death of this shameless woman, the duke of Orleans married Madam Montesson, a lady of rare beauty, intelligence, and virtue. This person he seems to have sincerely loved; and she was worthy of his affection. She reëstablished good order and decorum in his house; while a taste for the arts, and refined wit, took the place of the coarse licentiousness with which the duchess of Orleans had degraded it.

But the corruption and infamy of this remarkable family seem to have reached their climax in the person of the duke de Chartres, afterward termed *Egalité*. This prince was handsome in countenance and figure, and possessed a fair share of natural intelligence and talent. But his disposition was excessively depraved and corrupt. He is said to have entered upon a career of vice at the early age of sixteen years. Some of the persons employed in his education then initiated him into habits of prostitution. An abandoned though beautiful woman by the name of Deschamps, was introduced to him, who first corrupted his mind and morals, and led him into his first breaches of virtue. From the seductive arms of this woman, he soon passed into those of the most celebrated courtesans of the time—to those of Md'lle Michelon, and of Md'lle Duthé. Having himself become thoroughly corrupt, he next seduced the young prince of Lamballe, by means of the infamous women with whom he had become connected. It is said that he afterward poisoned this prince, in order that he might inherit the whole estate of the duke of Penthievre, whose only daughter he subsequently married. He was indeed *monstrum a vitiis nulla virtute redemptum.*

The ordinary excesses and refinements of lust were far from satisfying the depraved disposition of this remarkable man. Even after his marriage with the amiable and virtuous princess whom we have just named, he continued to lead the life of a libertine; to ramble through all the houses of debauchery in the capital, and to order the most extravagant and licentious suppers. The most abominable orgies alone were his delight. He erected in the neighborhood of Paris, a sumptuous temple of prostitution, where his favorites indulged themselves in the most abandoned profligacy. To this obscene temple were conducted, under the shades of night, the most celebrated, and the most fascinating prostitutes of the capital, sometimes to the number of one hundred and fifty. On their arrival, they found a splendid banquet prepared with hot wines and high seasoned food, of which the company were obliged to partake, quite naked. After his guests had reached the state of the Bacchanalians of antiquity, they fell down drunk into the arms of the friends and lacqueys of the duke. "One day," says a writer who was often a partner in these infamous revels, "I was in one of these parties of the duke of Chartres. We were all stark naked, as was our chief. We did full justice to the banquet; and when that was ended, the prince gave the well-known and desired signal. Instantly every one took his own pleasure, in his own way, and the prince, walking up and down amid this motley scene, laughed at the weaknesses, and ridiculed the passions of humanity." At other times, at this same cyprian temple, the prince took his diversions in a not less infamous way, by calling in the aid of the mechanical arts, and using the inventive faculties of the ablest mechanics. He had an apartment appropriated to, and filled with, various machines, which were devoted to the sports of love, in all their various attitudes. Even invisible machines, and naked figures in relief, were made obedient to the command of the abandoned revelers; inflamed their passions; and contributed, unconsciously, to their gratification. The most astounding part of all this was, that the duke of Chartres was not anxious to conceal these enormities from the light of day, or from the knowledge and censure of mankind. He rather aided in their circulation. He laid a wager, at Versailles, that he would return to the Palais Royal, quite naked, on horseback, at full gallop. The companions of his debaucheries were the first to blush at this horrid proposition, and they besought him at least to set out, not from Versailles, but from his stables. He refused even the latter amendment, and won the original bet. It was he who introduced among the French the passion of retaining in their service handsome jockeys, whom they picked up among the dregs of the Parisian population, to aid as obsequious instruments of their pleasures. He established an association of profligates, whose sole employment was to consult together for the purpose of devising some new abomination.

Such was the character of the principal representatives of the royal family of France, at the period of the outbreak of the revolution. The mighty and turbulent waters of that flood, were now beginning slowly to move to and fro. The agitation was, as yet, but gentle and insignificant. But erelong it became terrible and destructive. The unfavorable impression produced upon the French nation, by the unbridled licentiousness of some of the members of the house of Bourbon, produced a powerful effect in hastening on the revolution. The excited minds of the *tiers etat* did not distinguish between the vices of the many, and the redeeming virtues of the few. They supposed that as the royal family had been for generations the most corrupt race in Europe, so now also, they were all still possessed of the same character. With the undistinguishing and stupid fury which characterzies the rabble in all ages, they were about to harass, to torment, and to destroy the only innocent person whom, of all the royal family, they should most carefully and anxiously have protected. Louis XVI. should have been allowed to escape unhurt, from the ravages of a revolution which swept away the whole royal family. But on him they expended the bitterest vials of their wrath, and deprived him of throne, of happiness, and even of life itself, for no other imaginable reason, except that he unfortunately was born a Bourbon, and had been crowned a king!

CHAPTER III.

OPENING SCENES OF THE FIRST FRENCH REVOLUTION.

Let us contemplate Louis XVI. as he ascends the throne, and addresses himself to the difficult task of conducting the operations of a worn-out, embarrassed, and imbecile government. It may with truth be said, that his troubles had begun the very day on which he assumed his ill-fated scepter.

One of his first acts was to appoint M. Mauripas his prime minister. This old courtier had obtained the confidence of the king, by seeming never to contradict him. Whenever he wished to gain the monarch's signature contrary to his inclination, he never proposed the matter directly. He said something of interest respecting England, or Spain, or the emperor of Germany. He announced some particular success or disaster; and then, under pretense that the paper to be signed related to the subject of their conversation, he stole the signature of the confiding monarch.

Mauripas occupied an apartment in the palace near those of the sovereign; and thither the latter would frequently repair, to spend his time in the cheerful and diverting society of his minister. The salary, the style of living, and expenditure of Mauripas, were indeed sufficiently unostentatious. He possessed both sagacity and prudence; he was laborious in the performance of his duties; and as for the rest, he let the troubled world take whatever course it pleased. Such was not the man to guide the ship of state securely, in those troublous and tempestuous times.

The voice of the nation demanded that M. Turgot, an honest man, and a profound genius, should be called to the post held by Mauripas. Louis obeyed the popular will. Mauripas was dismissed, and Turgot was appointed. He had been a priest, a prior of the Sorbonne, and was at one time enthusiastic enough to say, that "all the blessings of the people were derived from the christian religion." He afterward asserted that christianity "was a work of useless superstition." Of him Malesherbes declared that he had the head of Bacon, with the heart of a L'Hospital; and that he labored to effect the results which the revolution afterward accomplished by more violent means. Louis XVI. at this period declared that "the only true friends of the people were himself and Turgot." But the minister was soon dismissed, in consequence of the opposition of the nobility, whose excesses he absurdly attempted to reform. The lower orders, delighted at the display of disinterestedness which he exhibited in distributing three hundred thousand livres among the poor of Paris, thought that prime ministers no longer lived, and intrigued, only for the gratification of their own avarice. They called Turgot by a name which certainly does infinite honor to his memory—"*the virtuous minister.*"

He was succeeded by M. Necker, a Genevan, whom public opinion once more designated to the king, as a suitable and popular minister. This man was the architect of his own fortune, and had amassed vast wealth by his abilities as a financier. He was a disciple of the school of Colbert. He had published several financial works, which contributed to the popular idea that he possessed talents eminently adapted to retrieve the falling fortunes of the king, and of the state.

Nor were these expectations disappointed. By his first measures Necker reëstablished order in the finances. He paid off the heavy debts contracted by the American war. He discovered unexpected financial resources. He revived public credit. But he could not remove the immense mountains of disabilities and sufferings which crushed the French people, without introducing extensive reforms, which touched the interests and the abuses of the higher orders. This he at length attempted to do, and the consequence was, that they obtained his removal, as they had done that of Turgot and Mauripas before him.

Louis next chose for his prime minister M. Calonne. This man was clever, fertile in resources, confident in his genius, and in his measures, making great promises, encouraging brilliant hopes, cheering the desponding, and laughing at the difficulties which surrounded the state. His vigorous measures for a time seemed likely to remove the most dangerous of the impending evils, and threw a brighter gleam of hope over the dark and clouded sky which then lowered on every side. To all the demands of the queen, he said: "If what your majesty asks is possible, it *is* done; if it is impossible, it *shall be* done." But nothing of real value could be accomplished without the consent of the privileged orders. The only way to remove the financial embarrassment of the nation was—not to impose new taxes on the people, for they would not endure it; nor to enlarge in any way the expenses of the government, for the treasury could not afford it; but to extend the taxes to a greater number of persons, that is, to the nobility and clergy, who, possessing one-half of the whole wealth of the kingdom, were still exempt from all taxation.

The year 1788 commenced with open hostilities between the misguided king, and his parliament. The parliament passed a decree, abolishing the *lettres-de-cachet;* and demanding the recall of exiled persons. The king canceled this decree. The parliament reëstablished it. The king then determined to attempt, in effect, the abolition of the parliaments, by taking away their power of judging without an appeal; by withdrawing their right to register laws and edicts; and thus to annihilate their political influence and importance.

The king next resolved upon a measure, which, while it shows his good intentions, also clearly illustrates how poorly men can foresee the end from the beginning, and how often the very measures which they adopt for their own advantage and protection, result in their ultimate injury and ruin. To conquer the opposition of the court to every wise measure of reform, Louis determined to appeal to the *tiers etat*, (the third estate,) and to summon a convocation of the "states-general." The consequence thus conferred by the king himself upon the popular voice, afterward became the engine of his destruction, when the people became perverted by the influence of their corrupt and frantic leaders.

The king ordained that the states-general should consist of one thousand members; that the representation should be in proportion to the population, and to the taxes paid in each *baillage;* and that the number of the deputies of the *tiers etat*, should be equal to that of the other two orders of the state combined.

This decree of the king at once threw France into an intense state of political commotion. Then arose that spirit of popular declamation and discussion, which soon became the general order of the day, and the disgrace of the nation. Immediately assemblies were collected everywhere throughout France, in which the most intemperate and excited minds raved on the subject of the existing abuses; on the outrages of the court and the nobility; and on the immortal blessings of liberty. Then arose that spirit of Jacobinism, so disgraceful in its character, and so ruinous in its effects to France. Nothing now began to be heard, but the howlings of insane demagogues, who, under pretense of inquiries into the state of the country, the necessary provisions of a new constitution, and the reforms which were to be effected, began to threaten the overthrow of all the existing institutions of society. They traduced the church. They cursed the priesthood. They denounced the aristocracy. They reviled the court. They threatened the popular vengeance on all dignities, civil, ecclesiastical, and even military. France must be disenthralled and redeemed. All the liberal professions must be abandoned. All the nobler arts of life, and the pursuits of literature and philosophy, must be renounced. All pensions must be abolished. All the prerogatives and appointments formerly appendant to the crown, must be suppressed. The most necessary taxes must be reduced. The minister of the king was burned in effigy. The masses were inflamed by the harangues at the popular clubs, and in the dens of the demagogues, by those desperate and ruined men, who, having nothing to lose by any change, however unfortunate, might perhaps gain by any event, however disastrous. The affrighted king already saw the arms which he had unwisely placed in the hands of the people turned to his own destruction, and that of his throne.

Even nature seemed to conspire, at this most unpropitious moment, to increase the general discontent, and redouble the unpopularity of the unhappy sovereign. On the 15th of July, 1789, a furious hail-storm, such as had never before visited the vine-clad hills of France, destroyed the produce of the earth. The consequence was, that the inhabitants of Paris were threatened with starvation, from the scarcity and the high prices of provisions. Riots occurred everywhere. Vast multitudes of vagabonds without any resources, or any regular pursuit, ranged abroad throughout France, and excited the popular frenzy. Some unfortunate speculations of the nobility in grain, by which they monopolized a large amount of it, increased the evil, and drove these wretches to madness. They threatened the palace of the king at Versailles. They convulsed Paris with their commotions. The bakers' shops were pillaged. A desperate and abandoned woman brought some damaged flour to the palace, forced herself into the presence of Maria Antoinette, exhibited the most insane fury, and even threatened violence to her person.

Such was everywhere the state of the nation, when the elections for the states-general took place. It may easily be imagined what scenes of violence, extravagance, and insanity would be presented by an excited populace, and especially by an excited *French* populace, under such peculiar circumstances. The elections everywhere were active, and in most places noisy and tumultuous.

The states-general were now about to assemble. It may be supposed that the newly chosen representatives of the people would be pledged by their previous career, and by their principles, to oppose the court, to denounce the king and the nobility, and to labor for the establishment of universal liberty and equality. Who composed this memorable assemblage? Provincial lawyers of no practice; literary men who had long starved on the humble pittance which men of letters generally receive in return for the produce of their brains; tradesmen who had failed in business, and who had no connections to retain them at home; play-actors, gamblers, and debauchees of every class and grade, for the first time found themselves incorporated into a deliberative assembly, by a great nation, invested with important powers and prerogatives, without any moral power to overawe or to moderate them. They resembled an assemblage of children placed in an apartment filled with the most delicate and valuable machinery, which they had the privilege of handling and altering; but which they were soon utterly to ruin and destroy.

The most important circumstance connected with these initiatory events, was the election of the *count de Mirabeau*. He had been already rejected by the nobility, the order to which he belonged. He was then supported by the *tiers etat.* He canvassed Provence, his native country; succeeded in being elected, as the fruit of infinite labors; and was enrolled among the immortal representatives of the people. At length the moment of the assembling of this extraordinary body had arrived. The opening scene of this most memorable epoch in modern history is about to take place. France is now to speak to all ages and to all countries, through her assembled representatives. The curtain is about to rise, and a drama to begin, the incidents of which present a strange mixture of sublimity and of terror.

It cannot be disguised that France and even Europe, looked on this assembly of the states-general with solemn awe and interest. The external forms which were observed were not unworthy of the occasion, and were calculated to heighten the effect produced. The opening session occurred on the 4th of May, 1789. A solemn procession took place to the ancient and majestic cathedral of Notre-Dame. There have been few spectacles more imposing to the eye, or more impressive to the senses, than that which then occurred. The place itself in which this august scene was enacted, was appropriate to the occasion, and inspired the mind with emotions of reverence and sublimity. It was the most ancient and the most illustrious temple in France. It was a Gothic cathedral, in which the majesty of human genius sat enthroned in its lofty aisles, its stupendous arches, and in the brilliant splendors of the high altar. It was the venerable edifice in which twenty kings, of generations long since passed away, had been crowned. It was the church which had echoed with the eloquent voice of Bossuet; whose lofty arches had resounded with the sublime pathos of Massillon. Those silent walls had witnessed the imposing ceremonies which attended the baptisms, the coronations, and the funerals of mighty sovereigns, long since crumbled to their kindred dust, of Henry IV., of Louis X., of Francis I., and of Louis XIV. The imposing procession was headed by the king and queen, immediately followed by the court. Next came the two higher orders, the nobility, splendidly dressed, glittering with gold and diamonds; and the superior clergy, attired in their magnificent vestments. Princes, peers, and generals were clothed in purple, and wore hats adorned with nodding plumes. The representatives of the people came next. They wore the plain black suits of genteel citizens; and it was observed by the keen eye of a contemporary, that though unassuming in their dress, their countenances seemed resolute, determined, and indicated the consciousness of untried power. It was remarked too, that the duke of Orleans, (*Egalité*,) though walking in the rear of the nobility, chose to loiter so far behind as to become mixed with the foremost deputies of the *tiers etat.* The streets were hung with tapestry belonging to the crown. The regiments of the French and Swiss guards formed a line from St. Louis to Notre-Dame. An immense concourse of citizens looked on in respectful silence. The windows were filled with spectators of all ages, and adorned by the presence of beautiful women. Bands of music placed at intervals, filled the air with martial and melodious sounds.

On the arrival of the procession at Notre-Dame, the three orders seated themselves on benches placed in the nave. The king and queen took their places beneath a canopy of purple, spangled with golden *fleurs-de-lis*. The royal family, and the great officers of the crown, occupied seats near the throne. Impressive and solemn music reverberated through the lofty arches of the ancient pile in which they were assembled, filling the countless multitude, which crowded every nook and avenue, with reverence and awe.

The ceremonies began by a sermon from the bishop of Nantz. His discourse was appropriate to the memorable occasion. "Religion," said he, "constitutes the greatest strength of empires. It alone confers stability upon thrones. It alone secures the prosperity of nations." Next followed a written address from the king. He recommended disinterestedness and prudence to the assembly; and declared the purity and benevolence of his own intentions. Barentin, the keeper of the great seal, then spoke. He was followed by Necker, the minister; who read a memorial on the state of the kingdom and the disorder of the finances. He declared that there was a deficiency in the treasury of fifty-six millions.

Had any observer who possessed the eye of omniscience, then surveyed that vast assembly, and been able to foresee the portentous future, what indescribable sensations would he not have experienced! He would have seen that king and queen, then radiant with splendor and majesty, cruelly executed on the scaffold, and covered with blood. He would have numbered out, among the deputies there assembled, the hundreds who, after passing through immense struggles, would end their days in despair and ignominy by the knife of the guillotine. He would there have seen amid that crowd a man, small in stature, nervous, and insignificant; who afterward obtained possession of a terrible power, and wielded it to the destruction and ruin of his native land and of his race—the restless, furious, and bloody Robespierre. Perhaps, too, among that mighty throng he might have discerned another looker-on, then equally insignificant in his person, and still more obscure in his position; but whose genius and grandeur in after years, overshadowed the world; who afterward himself secured and wore the very crown which on that imposing day adorned the head of the heir of the haughty Bourbons; and who at length, after being the hero of a hundred battles, died in solitude on a remote and rock-bound island of the ocean. He might there have seen the diminutive figure, the pale face, and the eagle eye of *Napoleon Bonaparte*, then poor and friendless; but indulging in high, dauntless, and aspiring hopes. And among the many fair women, who graced that scene with their fascinating smiles, he might have noted Madam Beauharnais, who was also reserved for a remarkable and memorable fate, exceeding in romance and interest that of any other woman of modern times; whose chaste and seductive charms afterward won the affections of the man of iron will, and stupendous genius, with whom she shared that throne. Such were the incidents connected with the first meeting of the states-general of France, under Louis XVI. Storms were lowering in the political heavens. But as yet there had been no violent outbreaks, no demonstrations of popular fury, which indicated the horrible extremes which were soon to ensue. So far, all had been decorous and dignified, such as became the sovereign and the representatives of a great ànd cultivated people, assembled under ancient forms, and with imposing ceremonies, to deliberate on measures promotive of the common good.

But difficulties and disturbances soon began to exist, between the *tiers etat*, who now arrogated to themselves the title of *Commons*—a name unheard of till then, in French history—and the other two orders, who constituted the states-general.

The commons assembled with a determination that the nobility and clergy should sit with them, in the same body; that they should proceed together to examine the credentials of the representatives of each order; and thus, in conjunction, should perform the task of legislation and reform.

The object of this arrangement was to give the commons the advantage of their superior numbers, in the votes to be cast. The other two orders discovered the trick, and refused to acquiesce in the arrangement. The latter remained in their own hall, determined not to yield. The commons sent frequent messages to the clergy and nobility, urging their acquiescence. They asked the clergy in the "*name of the God of Peace*," to submit to a measure which they thought necessary to the welfare and prosperity of the country. Bailly, the president of the commons, waited on the king to urge his interposition. The king declined interfering in the struggle between the several orders. Neither party seemed disposed to give way. Mirabeau, for the first time, then addressed the assembly, and displayed that impressive and powerful eloquence which on many subsequent and memorable occasions startled and aroused the nation, and eventually shook the throne to its center. He rose and said "that any plan of conciliation rejected by one party, could no longer be examined by another. A month was now passed and nothing had been done." The assembly then proceeded to a separate verification of credentials, and thus forever separated itself, in feeling, in interest, and in action, from the other great orders of the state.

The next question to be decided by the assembly was, the *name* to be used by the representatives of the people. Mounier suggested that of the "deliberative majority in the absence of the minority." A better cognomen still was that proposed by Mirabeau: "The representatives of the French people." The proposition of Legrand, was the one at last agreed upon, that of the *National Assembly.*

The nobility and clergy were now alarmed at the boldness and resolution exhibited by the *tiers etat.* They had not expected such a display on the part of people, who never before, in the history of the French nation, possessed the least right to exercise legislative and political authority. Necker, the minister, alone of those about the king was attached to the popular cause. But the court succeeded in resisting the plans of reconciliation which he laid before the monarch. At length the latter determined to hold a royal sitting, in which the deputies of the three orders were to assemble together, in the presence of the king. The meeting was held; but the freedom of speech was overawed by the presence of soldiery. The sitting had none of the dignity and grandeur of the preceding one, which had been held on the fourth of May. The king made an address, in which he used violent expressions, offensive to the commons. He delared the inviolability of all feudal rights, both the useful and the honorary. He even indulged in reproaches against the *tiers etat.* He commanded the separate sittings of the orders; thus aiming a blow at the favorite measure of the commons. He ordered their obedience and their acquiescence to such measures as he, his ministers, and his court should ordain.

In this instance, Louis XVI. exhibited the peculiar weakness of his character. He had nothing in view but the interests of his subjects. This he had clearly shown on various occasions. He was himself not a luxurious, not a tyrannical, not an extravagant, nor a lavish prince. He had not a single vice of his own. But he was unhappily the tool of the worst vices of other men. In this instance he was persuaded, by his selfish and unprincipled court, that the most determined and resolute measures alone were desirable at this crisis; and he accordingly used them. The effect was just what might have been expected. The commons were deeply incensed. The breach was made wider than before; the evil was only aggravated. The nobility and clergy withdrew from the hall after the conclusion of the king's address. The commons remained. Mirabeau made a rude and offensive allusion to the address of the king, whose suggestions were considered by the assembly as tyrannical and impertinent. A subsequent offer by the higher orders to unite with the commons, coming as it did with very bad grace, and produced by the effect of necessity and of apprehension on their part, was not calculated to allay the existing bad feeling. This was the *first* measure of open hostility and contradiction, between the national assembly and the king and court, which had occurred; and it was but a prelude to greater ones.

The next great question which was presented for the consideration of the assembly, was the establishment of a new *constitution* for the French people. The constitution agreed upon by that sage assemblage, after protracted and violent deliberations, comprised among others the following principles: That the nation makes all laws, with the royal sanction; that the national consent is necessary for loans and taxes; that taxes can be granted only for the period from one convocation of the states-general till another; that property and individual liberty shall be sacred; and that the person of the king shall be sacred and inviolable.

While the deliberations of the assembly were progressing, the king, listening to the slanders of the court, dismissed Necker from the ministry. This measure was injudicious, and filled the raving multitude with fury. For the first time in the history of this memorable revolution, the streets of Paris resounded with the cry "to arms!" and the enraged rabble poured like a flood though the thoroughfares of the capital. The citizens of the higher class assembled, to protect themselves against the attacks both of the populace, and of the royal troops. This was the primary origin of the *National Guards.* After various conflicts in the streets between the rioters and the defenders of order, a temporary quiet was obtained. The fury of the rabble, for the present, had spent itself.

The troops which the king had stationed in the *Champs des Mars*, were withdrawn. And yet, the pervading quiet was but a lull in the storm, which was only accumulating, by repose, intenser elements of explosion.

It was now evident to every one who observed the state of feeling in Paris, the great center of excitement and of action thoughout France, that the disaffected multitudes who crowded the purlieus and the dens of the capital, having tasted once the sweets of excitement and license, like the beast of prey which has caught the scent of blood, would not henceforth relapse into their accustomed quiet and apathy. For some days idle and noisy crowds had thronged about the Bastille. This was a memorable edifice, and calculated from its remarkable history and the exciting scenes connected with it, to attract around it the growing vengeance of the new masters of France—the rabble. Gradually the novel shout, "To the Bastille! to the Bastille!" resounded through Paris. The destruction of this ancient fortress of despotism had been alluded to already in some of the deliberations of the national assembly. The populace yielding to the hereditary vengeance with which they regarded that worst adjunct and most offensive appendage of past and present despotism, determined on its immediate destruction.

But arms were entirely wanting to accomplish this desirable end. The Bastille was a fortress of vast strength, whose origin was traced back to the eighth century, and which had been carefully fortified by the fears and the jealousy of many succeeding sovereigns. It was no easy task to scale its stupendous and lofty battlements; to dismantle its strong towers; to demolish its thick and massive walls; within which the cells were built, where the unhappy victims of despotism during so many ages had worn away in solitude, in gloom, and in despair, the cheerless years of their existence. But the populace were determined on its destruction. It was rumored that arms were to be had at the Hotel de Ville. The crowds rushed thither and carried off the cannon, and a great quantity of muskets. An immense concourse of people then crowded around the Bastille. The commandant of the fortress, Delaunay, had determined on a vigorous and desperate defense. But the number of men who manned it were few and feeble. It contained but thirty-two Swiss, and eighty-three Invalides. A fresh mob arrived to the assistance of those already assembled around the building. The garrison summoned the assailants to retire. They refused, and began to press onward to the attack. Two men mounted the roof of the guard-house, and broke with axes the chains which suspended the draw-bridge. It fell down and the crowd rushed upon it. They were met and arrested by a discharge of musketry. The crowd for a moment halted, returned the fire, and then rushed onward. A deputation at this moment arrived from the king, ordering the commandant to admit a *detachment* of the Paris militia within the fortress. This did not satisfy the insurgents. The mob rushed forward to set fire to the building. The garrison discharged one of the cannon which were mounted on the battlements, and this fire was returned by the crowd with the pieces which they had brought with them.

Meanwhile the excitement became intense throughout Paris. The tocsin pealed solemnly and continually. The drums beat the *générale*. The increasing multitude flowed on through every street, screaming, roaring, and raging. The faubourg St. Antoine, with its countless masses of ragged and desperate wretches, seemed marching on the Bastille as one man. The infinite hum of angry voices swelled upon the breeze as they advanced. It was a sublime though terrible spectacle. Never before had such a scene been presented in the history of man.

The attack was beginning at length to make an impression on the small and feeble garrison. But Delaunay was a man of heroic and determined courage. He was resolved that this ancient fortress should never yield to the attack of an irregular and ragged mob. He seized a lighted match, with the intention of setting fire to the magazine and blowing up the fortress. But the rest of the garrison were not quite as heroic as himself, and were not willing to share the desperate fate of the commandant. They prevented his purpose; obliged him to capitulate; and the signal of surrender was made. The crowds rushed in and took tumultuous possession of all the courts; threw open the cells and let in the cheering light of day, upon many a gloomy abode of hopeless sorrow and despair. Then were thrown open and exposed to the unutterable horror of men, the instruments of torture and vengeance which had long been the scourge of France, and the execration of mankind. Within those walls nine feet thick, those torture-chambers, and those dark and damp cells, what terrible cruelties had been perpetrated, during many generations! Let us pause for a moment and consider this matter. There, within those cells, youth and beauty in the prime of their splendor, had often been immolated to jealousy and hatred. There had noble manhood pined away an existence, far worse than death itself, without any hope for the future, or any joy in the present. There had perished the countless victims of the cruelty, lust, and jealousy of Richelieu, of Mazarin, of De Ritz, of Pompadour, of Catherine de Medici, of Louis XIV., and of the many other besotted and infamous tyrants, who at different times had swayed the destinies of France; had expended her treasures in licentious luxury; and had made the ruin of others subservient to their own ends. All this was now to be no more. The victims of absolute power were no longer to pine away beneath its destructive blight. The prisoners who then inhabited those cells came forth—horrid specimens of blasted humanity, frantic with joy, and as terrible in their present exultation, as in their former woe. The mob struck off the head of Delaunay, the commandant, and rushed with it and with the keys of the Bastille, to the Hotel de Ville, where the electors were assembled. The latter sent a deputation to the king at Versailles, informing him of the events which had just taken place. The king immediately resolved to go the next morning to the national assembly, to consult with them on the perilous situation of affairs.

When the king entered the hall, it rang with applause. He came without guards and without attendants. His two brothers alone accompanied him. He made a simple and touching address, which excited the enthusiasm of the assembly. For the first time he called it by the title it had arrogated to itself—the national assembly. The deputies, when the address was ended, escorted him on foot to the palace. The queen beheld the approaching crowd from a balcony, holding her son, the dauphin, in her arms. She was cheered with enthusiasm. It seemed, indeed, as if a reconciliation had at length been made between the alienated powers of the state; between the heir of royalty, and the zealous representatives of the French people. It was but a passing gleam of sunshine, which illumined for a moment a vast hemisphere of lowering storms and destructive tempests.

General La Fayette, but recently returned from his American expedition, was appointed governor of Paris; and the king himself resolved to go thither, and take up his residence in the capital, as a safer and more appropriate asylum amid the existing troubles. He was honorably received on his approach by Bailly, at the head of the municipal authorities, at the gates of Paris; who presented him the keys. He passed on to the Hotel de Ville. He there made another simple and touching address to the multitude. His words were received with applause. The monarch seemed again to have secured a reconciliation with Paris, just as he had already done with the national assembly. He heightened the popular enthusiasm in his favor, at this moment, by announcing his determination to recall Necker to the ministry. An express was immediately sent by the king to Basle, to announce to the exiled minister, at once his recall to power, and the disgrace and banishment of his opponents, the Polignac faction. Necker immediately set out for Paris; and his journey through this land of his adoption was one constant series of triumphs and congratulations.

Meanwhile the national assembly proceeded with its discussions on the provisions of the new constitution. The first great object of their hostility was the feudal privileges, which had, for so many ages, been the curse and bane of France. After long deliberation, the assembly resolved upon the following fundamental principles as the future basis of French government, and French liberty: That the quality of *serf* should be forever abolished; that all seignorial distinctions should be removed; that exclusive rights to keep game, to hunt, to have dovecotes and warrens, and all tithes should be abolished; that all taxes should be equalized; that all citizens should be admitted to civil and military employments; that the sale of offices and pensions without claims should also be abolished. These important and wise decrees were presented to the king, in the new constitution, for his acceptance and ratification. His answer was a simple acceptance, with a promise "to promulgate." He did not in form approve of them. He reserved his final judgment upon the points or decrees already submitted to him, until the whole constitution had been agreed upon by the assembly.

This partial refusal of Louis to acquiesce in whatever the representatives of the people might require of him, filled that excitable assembly with rage. All the good and conciliatory impression produced by the passages of friendship which had just occurred between the sovereign and his subjects were lost, and their influence wholly effaced by the irritating effect of his hesitation to yield an implicit and prompt obedience to their demands.

So far, the objects and the results of the French revolution may be approved of by every rational observer, as commendable. The abolition of old abuses which had been decreed by the assembly, was a good measure. The destruction of the Bastille was a desirable one. And whatever else the revolution had effected, until this crisis, was on the whole, an improvement upon the past, and held forth portents of hope and prosperity for the future. But from this hour the darker side of the revolutionary picture begins to appear. From this hour Louis becomes a persecuted, injured, outraged martyr to the insensate fury of an excited and misled assembly and nation. From this hour nothing but evil can be discerned in the principles asserted, in the measures adopted, and in the crimes committed by the revolution, its leaders, and its agents. We see from this period, a disposition displayed on the part of those who had risen unexpectedly to the guidance of public affairs, to run into the worst excesses; to overturn whatever was an appendage or a product of the past; and to revel in the blood and ruin first of their sovereigns, then of their associates, and lastly of their country itself. The hopes which all wise and good men had entertained, and which many of them had expressed at the beginning of the revolution, now began to be disappointed. They no longer praised and commended this great moving of the popular mind. They saw in it henceforth nothing but injury, and that continually, to all the political, social, and religious interests of the nation.

The representatives of the people were now completely alienated from Louis XVI. and they sought everywhere for grounds to justify the hostility which they had commenced, and were determined to pursue.

Unfortunately, the members of his own family furnished causes of offense to these captious observers. The conduct and character of Maria Antoinette were by no means as unobjectionable as that of her husband. As is generally the case, the few acts of indiscretion, perhaps of vice, which she committed were immensely magnified and perverted; so that she soon lost all hold upon the popular reverence and respect. In the first place, she discarded all the ancient forms of etiquette, observed in the French court, whenever a whim led her so to do. She even violated decorum, and afterward failed to conceal it. She frequently left the palace at all hours of the evening; she would walk alone in the park; she would carefully elude her husband's search after her, by sleeping out of her own chamber, in contempt of the established usages of the court. An ecclesiastic, respectable for his virtues, and his distinction as a physician, being sent for by her, he found her stretched out naked at full length, in her bath. The ecclesiastic modestly drew back; but she summoned him to her side; compelled him there to converse with her; and to admire the beautiful symmetry of her person. It was in this attitude that she had her picture drawn, and exhibited even in a public display of works of art. Madame de Noailles reproved her for these indiscretions; and in return the queen named her *Madam d'Etiquette.*

The French people had learned to regard the queen as an Austrian, not as a French woman. The visit of her brother Joseph II., emperor of Germany, to Paris, increased the popular aversion to the house of Hapsburg.

He penetrated into the manufactories, dock-yards, and ports. He made requests at Havre which were directly promotive of his own maritime interests, to the prejudice of those of France. The merchants and artists thought that he visited France rather as a jealous spy than as an admiring guest. He traveled with his brother, the archduke Maximilian. When on a visit to Buffon, the naturalist, the author as a matter of courtesy offered him an expensive copy of his Natural History. The archduke very properly declined to deprive the author of it; but Joseph II. immediately requested the work for himself in so direct a manner, that courtesy forbade a refusal. On the whole, the visit of the brothers of the queen to her adopted country, produced an unfavorable impression upon a nation, whose suspicions and whose resentment were already aroused.

After their departure, the position of Maria Antoinette became more friendless than before. Slanders more injurious and serious than the preceding ones, were circulated respecting her. She was directly accused, by popular scandal, of admitting her lovers to her embraces. Of this number was Edward Dillon, termed *the handsome*; M. De Cogni, and the Count d'Artois. "We made this discovery at cards," said a lady of the court, at the time it occurred; "for the Count d'Artois trod on the toes, and pinched Madam de B. in a moment of thoughtlessness, thinking it was Maria Antoinette."

So publicly was the queen accused of depraved morals, that Madam de Marsan made serious representations on the subject to the king. She was accused of carrying on a secret connection with Madam Bertin, a famous procuress of the capital, and likewise with M'dlles Guimond, Renaud, and Gentil. It was known, that after the king retired to rest, the queen in company with the Count d' Artois mixed with the suspicious crowd who promenaded at that hour on the terrace. Many persons came there from the palace all disguised—the queen among the rest. The degree of liberty there taken by the maskers, degenerated into licentiousness. Many of the young libertines of the court were present; and on one occasion, a handsome *guard du corps* dared to flatter himself with hopes of the queen. He accosted her, and in a decisive manner said, "Madam forgive my boldness; but either gratify me or die!" The queen immediately replied, "Neither, sir." She however had him followed; and afterward promoted his advancement.

The secret orgies at the small palace of the *Trianon*, excited the apprehension of the king. Within the closed doors of this building the queen and her intimate friends amused themselves with various games. Some of them were not of the most delicate or innocent nature. On one occasion the party, after reading an account in Buffon of the loves of the stags, thought it would be very entertaining to represent those animals, in dresses made of their skins. It is said that after the company had ranged about the recesses of the gardens in the singular costume of those animals, they thought it also entertaining to partake of their pleasures!

The consequence of these indulgences may be easily conjectured. The queen was at length accused even of a love of variety. To the handsome Dillon, to Coigne, and to her other admirers, it was said M. de Fersen succeeded, who was able more successfully than they, to fix and hold her volatile affections. She spared no expense in her pleasures. For her private establishment she yearly spent four millions six hundred thousand livres. Trianon cost the nation seventy-two thousand livres; and the palace of St. Cloud cost four hundred thousand.

There were other disreputable transactions of the court which about this period increased the contempt and dissatisfaction of the French nation, and helped among other causes, to produce the destruction of the government and the triumph of the revolutionary agitators.

The period of which we speak was also the age of empirics and impostors. The names and exploits of Cagliostro, of Mesmer, of St. Germain, and of Bleton, now occur; all celebrated masters in the arts of imposition, of solemn and mysterious *humbug*. We find in the records of that period, materials and events which prove that then it was, that the impostures of modern spiritual rappers and mediums were first practiced, in precisely the same way, and for the same results, as they are in the present day. Unhappily for Louis XVI. some of his own family became the despised victims of the impostures of these wretches. Count Cagliostro enabled Cardinal Rohan to *sup with the deceased D'Alembert*, with the king of Prussia, and with Voltaire, all dead some years before. He convinced his eminence, that the worker of these wonders had himself been present with Christ at the marriage in Cana of Gallilee.

But still higher and nobler game was sought for by those shameless impostors, and the French nation were astonished and disgusted to hear that the duke of Orleans had become the dupe of one of the leading jugglers of the day. One day, on entering his library, he there found a man awaiting him, of austere and remarkable countenance; who told him that he could raise the prince of darkness, and learn from him the mysteries of futurity. The duke accepted the offer of the magician, who required however that he should have courage to trust himself with the latter in a pathless plain, alone, and at the dead hour of midnight. The duke acquiesced in each of these proposals, and went with the impostor to the center of a vast heath unattended, in a dark and stormy night. He overcame the terror which at first arose in his breast, at the sight of the numerous specters which surrounded him. After various admonitions and prophecies he gave the duke a ring. "Keep this carefully," said the infernal spirit; "as long as it remains in your possession, it will be a token of prosperity and happiness; as soon as you lose it, your doom is sealed." The magician refused a purse of five hundred louis which the prince offered him on their safe return. When describing this incident to others the duke would open his breast, and exhibit the ring, carefully attached to his person.

In these incidents we see the origin and the operation of the spiritual communications of the present day. In the triumphs of Cagliostro, of Mesmer, and of St. Germain, which at this period were at their greatest height, we behold another instance of the uprooting of the firm and stable foundations of society in an excessive desire for novelties, and a restless itching after things new, mysterious, and wonderful. The French were in the eager pursuit of such novelties both in philosophy, theoretical and practical; in religion, in moral opinions, in politics, and the organization of their government. While Mesmer declared that, with the point of his finger, he could direct the mysterious magnetic fluid to any part of the body, which was the seat of disease, and thus cure dropsy, the gout, palsy, deafness, blindness, and every other evil incident to the human frame; so in the same way, and with the same degree of truth, did *Voltaire* and *Rosseau* pretend to teach mankind the true principles of religion; and *Murat* and *Robespierre* assume to assert the excellence of their doctrines in support of political equality, and of human freedom.

Other untoward events conspired about this period to increase the unpopularity of the royal family, and to concentrate its misfortunes upon the head of Louis XVI. Among these one of the most important, most mysterious, and most injurious, was the memorable affair of the diamond necklace. It is difficult to obtain a clear and satisfactory account of this mysterious event, which exerted so powerful an influence on the destiny of France. We will however state its origin and its results.

When Cardinal de Rohan, who belonged to one of the oldest and most illustrious families of the French nobility, was sent as minister from Louis XV. to Vienna, he was requested to describe Maria Antoinette to one of his correspondents at Paris. He drew rather an offensive picture of the then youthful arch-duchess. By some accident this unfavorable representation of the cardinal became known to her, and at once filled her mind with implacable hatred toward its author. Upon her arrival in France, Rohan attempted on various occasions, to regain her good will. All his efforts were in vain. Previous to the death of Louis XV. Böhmer the crown jeweler, had prepared a magnificent diamond necklace of immense value, for Madam Du Barry, the king's favorite. That monarch's death diverted the expensive gift from its original destination, and left it upon the hands of the jeweler. Rohan heard of the jewel, and also heard that Böhmer had desired to sell it to the queen, who declined to purchase it on account of its great value and immense price. A prostitute of the Palais Royal, named Lamoth, being in necessitous circumstances, and being acquainted both with the cardinal and with his desire to secure the queen's favor, and even her embraces, conceived a plot whereby to obtain the jewel, and to ruin the priest. She went to Böhmer and told him that the queen had changed her mind, and desired to purchase the necklace, stipulating only that she should pay at intervals, and that the whole transaction should be kept secret from the king. Böhmer agreed to these terms. She added that in support of her assurances, she would present him with a letter from the queen, and that one of the first men of the court would wait upon him, and conclude the bargain.

The cunning courtesan next went to the cardinal. She told him that the queen would not only accord him her friendship, but even her more tender favors, on condition that he would present her with this diamond necklace. The cardinal consented to the bargain. He waited on Böhmer; represented to him that the queen wished the jewel; that she had commissioned him to purchase it for her, stipulating that the first payment should be made in August ensuing. The price was to be fourteen hundred thousand livres—three hundred and fifty thousand dollars. The jewel was then delivered to M'lle Lamoth, to deliver it to Maria Antoinette. In the meantime the cardinal expected his promised interview with the queen. The cunning of the prostitute did not fail her in this part of the intrigue. She informed the cardinal that Maria Antoinette had appointed to meet him in a remote spot of the gardens at Versailles; that she would be dressed in white; and that she would make herself known by presenting him with a white rose. She then selected one of her abandoned associates, whose person and gait somewhat resembled that of the queen, who, at the time and place appointed, appeared in the partial darkness; gave him the rose; allowed him to kiss her hand; and then, an alarm being purposely made, commanded him hastily to retire.

The day for payment at length arrived. The expected money did not come; nor did the queen, the supposed debtor to Böhmer, make any apology or explanation for her neglect. Böhmer sent a message to the queen, desiring to know why the first payment had not been made. She was thunderstruck. It was the first intimation which she had received of the matter. Böhmer was sent for. Among other proofs, he produced a letter from the cardinal, stating that the necklace had been duly delivered to the queen. After arranging all her information respecting the matter, she communicated it to the king. The cardinal, who was then at the palace as grand almoner, was sent for at midnight, into the king's cabinet, where the queen awaited him. The king demanded to know whether he had recently purchased any jewels of Böhmer. The cardinal answered that he had, and he thought that they had been delivered to the queen. The king asked who employed him in that commission? He replied, a lady whom he believed to be connected with the court, named Lamoth. The cardinal then said, that he plainly perceived he had been imposed upon. He was so much overcome with terror, that he was compelled to lean upon the table for support. The king then ordered him to withdraw; and he was arrested on leaving the palace. Md'lle Lamoth was also imprisoned, but she had sent the jewels composing the necklace already to England, and they were then beyond the reach of recovery. She at first denied all knowledge of the affair; and directed the king to inquire of Cagliostro, the famous impostor. The cardinal was afterward tried, and honorably acquitted. Lamoth was executed, after being scourged. Cagliostro was at first arrested; and then banished from the French territory.

Such was the end of this lamentable intrigue. But the impression produced at that time against the queen, and against Louis XVI., by its unfortunate occurrence, was very powerful. The French people thought that the virtue of Maria Antoinette must be very questionable indeed among those who knew her best, if a false appointment, or if even the pretense of a pretended assignation, could be made for her for such a purpose. But whether true or false, whether innocent or guilty, the perverse and excited minds of the nation were determined to put the worst possible construction upon the conduct of the probably innocent and unconscious queen. Nor was this injurious impression afterward removed, or even weakened, by a decree of the national assembly exculpating her from all blame.

It was at this period in the progress of the revolution, that the king said one day to M. Necker, who had been recalled to the ministry, "*For several years I have only enjoyed a few moments of happiness.*" Necker replied, "Yet a little while, sire, and you will feel differently; all will yet end well." Vain and delusive hope! Ever since the refusal of Louis XVI. to approve without reserve all those articles of the new constitution which had been determined upon by the national assembly, and sent to him for his acceptance, his fate seemed to be inevitably and unalterably sealed. The discussions which immediately ensued upon his refusal being reported to the assembly, first called out into prominence three men who afterward became notorious and infamous, on the bloody and tumultuous stage of the revolution—Robespierre, Mirabeau, and Danton. The first of these declared with a violence which, for the first time, attracted to him the attention of the whole assembly, that it was not the province or the prerogative of the king to criticise the decisions of the assembly.

While the assembly was distracted from day to day, by the most violent discussions—the particulars of which are not pertinent to this history—the crowds of Paris were incensed against the court and ministry, in consequence of the scarcity of provisions. A deputation of incensed and frantic women forced their way into the presence of Louis, and laid before him their complaints and their grievances. He received them kindly, as it ever was his custom to do; and by the mildness and moderation of his manner disarmed their fury. Women, if properly addressed, generally listen to reason, and feel the influence of softening emotions. They retired, appeased by the reception which they had received. He ordered the municipal authorities to distribute bread among this crowd, who seemed to be in absolute want of it. For some reason, however, his order was not complied with, and the odium of this neglect rested on the king alone.

The royal family had now taken up their residence in Paris, in the palace of the Tuilleries, which had not been inhabited for a century. A guard of the Parisian militia was placed around it, commanded by Lafayette, who was thus made responsible for the person of the king. By this arrangement the whole appearance of the court was immediately changed. There was in effect no longer any court at all. The aristocracy were excluded from the royal presence by the restraint under which the king was placed. From that hour they considered him in reality a prisoner; and then commenced that process of emigration which deprived France of some of its noblest blood, while it secured many of them from the horrors of the guillotine, which overtook so many of their associates.

From this moment the popular party in France may be regarded as triumphant. It was then under the guidance and control of Mirabeau, Barnave, Lamoth, and the duke of Orleans. While great numbers of the nobles were escaping to Turin, and to Coblentz, the royal family became more and more deserted; the number and fury of its enemies increased; the audacity of the demagogues was elevated; and it seemed an easier task and a richer sport to these unprincipled wretches, to play with the royal prerogatives, and to ruin the welfare and destroy the existence of the unhappy but illustrious family who were then at their mercy.

It was at this period that Mirabeau, who, by his revolutionary eloquence had greatly contributed to sap the foundations of the trembling throne, seeing his ambition of popular supremacy thwarted and intercepted by other demagoges as aspiring, as violent, and as unprincipled as himself, bethought him of the project of standing as a mediator between the throne and the tribune, between the king and the assembly. The court first tampered with him by means of Malouet, an agent of Necker. He stipulated that his debts should be paid, and that he should have a place in the ministry. On these conditions he consented to espouse the cause of the king and the court; to assert that the concessions in favor of liberty which were already gained were sufficient; and that it was now time to arrest the advancing tide of revolution and of change.

CHAPTER IV.

THE TERRIBLE POWER OF ROBESPIERRE AND THE JACOBIN CLUB.

WHEN the period arrived for the dissolution of the national assembly of France, in 1792, it had accomplished far greater results than had ever been expected of it. Not even the most sanguine Jacobins of the day had anticipated that the representatives of the people would, in so short a time, so completely have degraded and debased the throne and all its time-honored institutions, and that it would so thoroughly have established the reign of popular prerogative and supremacy in their stead.

The new assembly which was about to convene as their successors, included among its members men whose names were then wholly unknown to fame, but whose talents soon placed them on an equality in distinction, with any who had already figured in the national assembly. These were the deputies of *La Gironde*, a department of France which produced many celebrated statesmen, of whom Condorcet was the most profound and Vergniaud was the most eloquent.

In addition to this change in the legislative assembly of France, another alteration had taken place in the political machinery of the country. The democratic clubs had now become omnipotent. The most remarkable and dangerous of these, was that of the *Jacobins*, so called from holding their meetings in the old suppressed monastery of the Jacobin monks.

This building, whose form was that of an ampitheater, and was admirably adapted to the purposes of popular eloquence, having been appropriated to their own use by the oldest and largest of the political clubs in all France, the assemblage soon become the most violent, and the most terrible of its associates.

It was at this period, (1792,) that the influence of Robespierre first began to display its baleful supremacy in the French capital. He was excluded from the new legislative assembly, by a decree of the national convention to the passage of which, he had himself contributed; which forbade any of the members of the first representative body to be rechosen as members of the second. But he was now the most distinguished and able member of the Jacobin club; and it was through the proceedings of this club, that he first made his terrible power known and felt throughout France.

After Mirabeau, Robespierre was the most extraordinary man produced by the revolution. It has long been the prevalent fashion to represent him as a person devoid of all talent, and as a mass of moral deformities, without one single redeeming trait. This estimate of the blood-stained Jacobin, bad as he really was, is absurd in the extreme. There never lived in any age, an adventurer who gave more unanswerable proofs of the possession of great abilities. He possessed the very same order of talent for which Demosthenes himself is so justly celebrated:—that impetuous and powerful eloquence which could sway the turbulent passions of men; which could control the feelings and direct the resolutions of vast assemblies; which could arouse, excite, alarm, and convince heterogeneous multitudes; which could govern their stormy impulses, and make them subservient to the orator's purposes. Just as Demosthenes aroused the assembled Athenians against the aggressions of the crafty monarch of Macedon, by the clarion tones of his voice, as it reverberated around the *Bema* at Athens; so did Robespierre excite the Parisians who listened to his impassioned words, against the ancient throne of the Bourbons, and against the inoffensive king who sat upon it; whom, with words as burning and as scathing as any which ever issued from the lips of Demosthenes, he denounced and stigmatized as a tyrant even worse than Philip of Macedon. Both of these orators arose to power from utter obscurity. Both of them aimed their fury against already existing institutions. Both operated only upon the popular will, and used the masses as the obsequious instruments of their purposes. Both passed through great intellectual conflicts. Both employed but one single weapon—the tongue. Both were successful in accomplishing the object of their ambition. And both perished at last by a violent death. Such are the singular coincidences between the lives of these two remarkable men. The only difference between their mental qualities is that, while Robespierre was the more unbending, pertinacious, and penetrating genius of the two; Demosthenes was the more massive, comprehensive, and immense. Robespierre was a suitable representative of the more attenuated intellectual and physical proportions of these latter ages. Demosthenes was a fit model of the larger intellectual and physical dimensions of those primeval times when giants lived; when the race possessed its primitive grandeur and greatness, and before the artificial luxuries and pernicious usages of succeeding generations had reduced the proportions of the race, though they may have conferred more refinement and more cultivation by the process.

Robespierre had been an obscure attorney at Arras, the place of his birth. But many other men have passed their youths in obscurity, from the want of circumstances favorable to the development of greatness. Such was the case with Robespierre. His first efforts at eloquence like those of the great man with whom we have just compared him, were total failures. His delivery was awkward and heavy. But by dint of great perseverance and great resolution, he succeeded in acquiring such a mastery in this difficult and noble art, that he had no equal nor competitor even among the many talented men whom France at that time sent up to her national representation. If the great test of talent, or even of genius, is *success* in whatever men undertake, then was Robespierre gifted indeed. His ability is proved by the fact that, whilst he enjoyed no advantages of birth or influence; while he possessed even no external gifts of nature to recommend him to admiration, or to facilitate his progress toward power, he overcame every obstacle, and every deficiency; and by the pure force of *mind and of thought* alone acquired a supremacy and wielded a scepter as absolute almost as that of Napoleon himself. This was the man, whose obnoxious name and influence were now frequently brought to the notice of Louis, and of the court; and who soon became their most unyielding and implacable enemy.

The first question which engaged the attention of the new assembly, was that of the emigrants. "Monsieur," the king's brother, had already left the kingdom. The assembly demanded of Louis that he would request his return, on penalty of being deprived of the regency, should any event occur which would render the functions of a regent necessary. Louis XVI. addressed his brother a letter, requesting him earnestly to comply with the demands of the legislature. That body also proclaimed certain penalties, and imposed certain disabilities, upon all other French citizens, who had passed beyond the territory of their country, and who then refused to return.

The constituent assembly also required the priesthood to take the civic oath. Those who refused to comply with this demand lost their character as ministers of public worship, paid by the state; though they retained their professional position, and the liberty of exercising their functions in private. The legislative assembly now went a step further. They required the oath to be taken anew, and deprived those priests who refused so to do of all emoluments whatever, and forbade them to exercise their professional functions even in private; just as if an assemblage of debauched secular adventurers, could by any human possibility, deprive men of a spiritual character, derived from a source infinitely higher than any human origin, or dispossess them of a spiritual function which they could neither give nor withdraw! In consequence of the hostile feelings which had long existed between the French nation and Austria, and which had been hourly increasing, the legislative assembly determined to declare war against that country, and compelled Louis to acquiesce in the unwelcome measure. As soon as the compliance of Louis XVI. with this proceeding became known, it revived for a short time, the small remains of regard for the persecuted monarch which existed; and postponed for a time the final and ignominious scenes of his life. The assembly next compelled Louis to another ungrateful task. That was the dismissal of his ministry.

The king's brothers who had emigrated, and to whom he made known the decree of the convention requiring their return, refused to comply with the demand. The convention then decreed them to be under accusation.

The assembly next required Louis XVI. to call upon the princes of the Germanic empire not to allow the assembling of emigrants in their territories. The king having performed this duty, was compelled to inform the assembly that he would declare war, if those princes disregarded his intentions in favoring the revolution. The consequence of this step was, that Austria and Prussia entered into a treaty to quell the disturbances, as they justly called the revolutionary movement, in France.

The assembly continued to attend to its supposed duties, and passed various decrees of more or less general interest. It resolved that the property of emigrants should be appropriated to pay the expenses of the impending war. It decreed the suppression of all religious communities. It resolved on the suppression of all ecclesiastical costumes. To finish this series of outrages, on May 29th, 1792, the national assembly constituted itself in permanent session. It immediately passed a decree ordaining the formation of a camp of twenty thousand troops near Paris, for the purpose of increasing their own absolute control over the capital, and overawing the court and king.

The old ministry having been dismissed, it was necessary to constitute a new one. It was at this crisis that a celebrated man first appeared upon a theater of action, on which he afterward became illustrious. This was *Dumouriez.*

General Dumouriez in the command which he had already held in La Vendee, had displayed extraordinary abilities. Kept down as it were by the times, and the peculiar events then passing, he had spent most of his life in diplomatic intrigues. He was now fifty years of age. He was in truth ready to take any side which offered him the strongest hopes of preferment. His character may be illustrated by this incident: He exclaims in his memoirs, "Honor to the patriots who took the Bastille," yet a few pages after he acknowledges, that being at Caen at the time of that event, he had composed and presented a memorial on the best means of preserving the Bastille, and suppressing the revolution. A sister of the famous emigrant Rivaral was his acknowledged mistress; and probably he was in heart a royalist. Returning to Paris from La Vendee, Dumouriez discovered that the Jacobins were the ruling power in France. He attended the clubs and took part in the proceedings. But he still kept up his intimacy with some of the persons around Louis XVI. By their means it was that Louis was induced to offer him the port-folio of foreign affairs. The other places in the cabinet were filled by Lacoste, Duranthon, Roland, and Clavieres.

This ministry began their functions, by prosecuting

vigorous reforms. The king was charmed at the prospect of accomplishing some good at last through their means. The progress of republican simplicity was noted by cotemporary writers, in the important circumstance that Roland, one of the ministers, appeared in the presence of the monarch without buckles on his shoes; and that another functionary (Chabot) retained his hat!

By this time the royal family had become totally alienated from the nation. The latter displayed feelings of hostility, which indicated that the day for reconciliation was forever past. On one occasion the queen approached the window of her chamber which opened toward the court, to take a little air. A gunner of the guard addressed her with words of vulgar abuse. Said he to her, "I should like to see your head on the point of my bayonet." In the same garden just beneath the eye of the royal captives, a man might often be seen mounted on a chair, uttering to a crowd the most infamous calumnies, within the hearing of the king and his family. One day overhearing these, the queen burst into tears and exclaimed, "What an abode! What a people!" What a sad contrast was presented between her present situation of mortification and danger, and the splendid scenes and the brilliant hopes of her youth! She who had been reared amid the magnificence of the most magnificent of courts; who inherited the chivalrous reverence and admiration of that nation, which had retained beyond all other nations the respectful feelings which characterized the middle ages, in reference to the established rights and the unapproachable superiority of kings; even she was made to tremble at the horrid curses and infamous imprecations which were lavished upon her by a nation whose guest she had become; to whom she had entrusted her dearest hopes, and those of her children; and whom she had never injured nor wronged in the smallest possible degree. Such are the amazing vicissitudes of human life; such the value and the stability of popular applause and popular censure! The queen wishing to feel the public pulse at this time went to the opera. "*There goes Madam Deficit*," said the crowd, as her carriage passed along; alluding to the reported deficiency of the treasury which they absurdly ascribed to *her* extravagance and mismanagement.

On June 20th, 1792, the unhappy king and his family were compelled to witness the most dangerous and formidable outbreak of popular violence which they had yet seen. The Tuilleries on this occasion were attacked by a mob under Santerre, a butcher of the faubourg St. Antoine; and the safety of the king even in his gilded prison, was seriously endangered.

The multitude had assembled first around the hall of the representatives, for the purpose of presenting various petitions. Having accomplished this end through their leaders, and feeling under the influence of an excitement produced by the interest of the occasion, they condescended to extend their journey to the Tuilleries. Santerre, with a drawn sword, marched at their head. Women crowded among the throng. Flags waved with the inscription, "The Constitution or Death." Ragged breeches mounted on poles, were carried along as the colors of this motley and infamous crowd. Cries were heard of *Vivent les Sans-culottes!* On the point of a pike was borne a calf's heart, with the inscription, "Heart of an aristocrat." Such were the scenes of infamy with which the glorious era and triumphs of *Liberty* were about to be introduced into France!

When the crowd arrived at the gates of the Tuilleries, they found them closed, and protected by numerous detachments of the National Guards. The king with his usual sincerity and want of suspicion, ordered the gates to be opened. The rabble not appreciating the feelings and motives of the king, rushed in as if that privilege had been granted them from fear of their numbers and power; and they made the palace resound with shouts of "Down with the *Veto*." "The *Sans-culottes* forever." During this disturbance, the king was accompanied with the aged Marshal Aclogue, some of his household servants, and several officers of the national guard. At that moment the sound of axes was heard, assulting the doors of the private apartments of the king. Louis ordered the doors to be opened. The crowd rushed in. "Here I am," said he, to the enraged rabble. Amid the endless confusion which prevailed, constant shouts were heard of "No Veto;" "No Priests;" "No Aristocrats!" "*Vive la Nation!*" cried they. "Yes," answered Louis XVI., "*Vive la Nation;* I am its best friend." "Well prove it then," said one of the despicable wretches who led on the rabble; at the same time holding before him a red cap on the point of a pike. The king took the infamous emblem and put it on his head. The crowd then "uttered a deal of stinking breath" approbatively, and rent the air with their acclamations. One of the rabble who was drunk, offered the king a dram from a filthy bottle, which he held in his hand. The king drank without hesitation the offered beverage. The queen was then in another of the royal apartments. The intruders penetrated even there. As soon as she was seen, they exclaimed "There is the Austrian." Her daughter was terrified by the furious aspect of the crowd, and wept. Her little son, the dauphin, dismayed at first, recovered his wonted cheerfulness, and smiled in the happy innocence and confidence of his age. A red cap was handed to him; the child immediately put it upon his head. Santerre who still led on the rabble, seeing the boy almost smothered by the folds of the cap, relieved him of the hated incumbrance. It was at this crisis that Louis XVI. did an act which has secured for him the respect and commiseration of a discriminating posterity. Surrounded as he was at that moment by the most despicable and dangerous of all perils—that of an infuriated and brutalized rabble, seeking for carnage and plunder—he took the hand of a grenadier who was standing near him, placed it upon his heart, and said, "Feel whether it beats quicker than usual." At seven in the evening, the rabble retired from the palace, without having accomplished the extremes of violence and outrage which they had expected. Immediately after their departure, the king threw from him with indignation, the red cap which still adorned or disgraced his head. The palace had been defaced and abused by the populace in the most outrageous manner. During their presence there, they had presented a remonstrance to the king setting forth the abuses which they asserted he had tolerated and permitted in his government.

The next day some complaints were made in the Assembly in reference to the manner in which the king and the royal family had been outraged. One member proposed to commence proceedings against those who had created the disturbance. This motion was ridiculed by another member, who answered, "Impossible! what proceedings can be taken against forty thousand men?" Of such an immense number had the crowd consisted!

It was by such gradual approaches that all confidence and respect between the injured king and his people, were totally destroyed. They learned to regard each other with aversion and hatred. Only one or two more similar displays of popular fury were necessary, in order to place things beyond the reach of remedy; to render the existing breach incurable; to deprive the royal family of the trifling share of liberty which they still enjoyed; and to conduct them to their last and final imprisonment—the sad prelude to the melancholy climax of their fate. And these essential and hateful preliminaries were not very long in occurring, under the influence and guidance of Robespierre and his blood-thirsty associates.

CHAPTER V.

LOUIS XVI. AT THE BAR OF THE NATIONAL CONVENTION.

On the 14th of July, 1792, another great popular demonstration was to be made, the king and court were once more to be outraged, and reason insulted. It was the anniversary of the Federation. All the splendor and dignity which characterized the first commemoration of this occasion, which has been described in a previous chapter, had passed away. A mortifying and disgraceful contrast now appeared. Instead of the magnificent altar, the three hundred officiating priests, the sixty thousand National Guards in their uniforms, the members of the assembly, the king, and the court, all proceeding with decorum and dignity as they then had done; the observer now beheld a truncated column on the Champ de Mars, instead of the altar, rising from the center of a vast pile, which bore on its branches the keys of St. Peter, doctor's caps, bags full of law proceedings, cardinal's hats, tiaras, titles of nobility, and coats of arms; all of which were to be burned up. The procession consisted of a confused mob of drunken vagabonds, women, children, and wagons; on one of which was carried a daubed representation of the taking of the Bastille, and on another, a printing press, which halted at intervals, and struck off patriotic songs, to be distributed to the enthusiastic multitude around. After these came the assembly, the court, and the royal family, showing the shame they felt in their downcast countenances. They could not conceal the mortification which they experienced, that France, once the proud land of chivalry, refinement, and elegance, had become so disgraced, so dishonored, as to be the theater of such a scene. The oath of Federation was taken by everybody. When that important ceremony had been concluded, the assembly broke up; and after considerable anxiety and danger, the king and his family succeeded in regaining the palace without further outrage or accident.

It was at this period that the project was once more entertained of saving Louis XVI. by flight; and that project was now conceived by the very man who was so efficacious in defeating the first attempt—by Lafayette. He dictated to M. Tollendal a letter to the king, dated *Paris, July* 9, 1792, in which the details of the proposed plan of escape were minutely set forth.

As might have been expected, Louis XVI. doubted either the sincerity, or the discretion of the man, whose officious interference had prevented his previous success, and he declined accepting the offer made him. The king, moreover, answered the proposal in such terms of severity and reproof, as were richly merited by the vacillating and self-seeking course pursued by the adventurer who proposed it. Said he, "The best advice which can be given to M. de Lafayette, is to continue to serve as a bugbear to the factions, by the performance of his duty as a general."

The project of the king's flight, however, was not yet given up. A retreat to the castle of Gaillon, in Normandy, was resolved upon. The duke of Liancourt, an ardent friend of the king, then commanded that province.

Its capital, Rouen, had declared its opposition to the progress of the revolution. The duke generously offered his army, and even his fortune, to the service of the king. The castle of Gaillon was but a hundred miles from the sea, and would afford an easy flight to Louis through Normandy to England. It was also only twenty leagues from Paris. But this apparently judicious plan of escape was rejected; especially because it would place the king under obligations to Lafayette, to whom the person of the king must be confided during the journey. Doubtless, had Louis entertained any just idea of the greatness and the proximity of the danger which hung over him, he would not have refused this or any other reasonable refuge which might have been proposed. But he never imagined the real extent to which the frenzy and the infatuation of the nation had proceeded.

The 10th of August, 1792, approached; a day of memorable gloom, despair, and woe to the unhappy and persecuted family of the king. The whole history of Louis XVI. almost from the inauspicious hour of his coronation, until that of his death, was one sad procession and tissue of calamities. No other monarch of all the thousands who, in various climes and ages have inherited the dignities and the responsibilities of a throne, excepting perhaps Charles I. of England and Mary Queen of Scots, presents so singular and sad a spectacle. Hundreds of monarchs have fallen on the battle-field; and many by the sudden or secret hand of the assassin. None except the two whom we have named, endured so long, so-unvarying, and so disastrous a series of calamities; tending so inevitably from bad to worse, to terminate in total ruin.

A day had been fixed for the discussing of the *dethronement of the king*. An extraordinary agitation prevailed among the deputies. In the assembly it was doubted whether the dethronement which both people and representatives had determined should take place, ought to be brought about by a deliberation and decree, or by a public and murderous attack. Petion, together with the whole party of the *Girondists*, preferred the former mode. He thought that a decree proclaiming the deposition of the king, would put a stop to all further agitation and violence. Perhaps his judgment was correct. The party of the Jacobins, however, refused to acquiesce in this plan. They declared that the people had resolved to take their liberty and its defense into their own hands. Chabot proposed that the tocsin should be tolled that very evening, and that the last decisive acts of the revolution should now begin.

A general agitation pervaded Paris. The drums sounded in every direction. The battalions of the national guards repaired to their quarters, in ignorance of the real cause of the universal alarm. The sections were filled with the most violent and noisy of the citizens. The insurrectional committees had formed at various points—in the faubourg St. Antoine, in the faubourg St. Marceau, at the hall of the Cordeliers, Danton's clarion voice was heard calling the people to arms. Said he, "The people can now have recourse but to themselves. Lose no time. This very night, satellites concealed in the palace are to rush forth upon the people and to slaughter them! Save yourselves, then! To arms! to arms!"

This cry "To arms!" soon became general, and resounded throughout the streets and palaces of the vast capital. From the center to the circumference of the city, one wide and universal yell swelled up toward heaven, and made night hideous with its terrible confusion. The Marsellais seized some pieces of cannon which had been placed before the Jacobin club; and their procession was joined by an immense crowd. They determined first to send commissioners to the Hotel de Ville, to turn out the municipal officers, and take all authority in their own hands. The tocsin was now ringing incessantly, and its solemn, startling sound reverberated over the whole capital. It was wafted afar on the wings of the midnight winds to the surrounding suburbs. It proclaimed the memorable hour, when the oldest monarchy in Europe was about to fall. That night of agitation, terror, and blood, was to be the last which the heir of so many kings was destined to pass in the palace of his ancestors.

The king, the queen, their two children, and Madam Elizabeth, the king's sister, had not retired to bed; but had gone into the council chamber, where the ministers and many superior officers were deliberating in terror, what steps had best be taken to save the royal family. The Swiss guards were the only troops which yet reremained faithful to Louis. But their artillery had been taken from them; and though they were honorable and intrepid men, their numbers were too small to be able to afford any assistance against the mighty masses of that stupendous popular flood, whose surges were every moment approaching nearer and nearer to the palace. These troops were eight hundred in number. They were commanded by by Generel Mandat. The incessant clang of the tocsin, the booming of artillery, the rattling of ammunition wagons along the streets, the yells of the populace, the march of the approaching column, and the rolling of their drums, were becoming more and more distinct to the terrified ears of the unhappy family, against whose innocent heads the insensate rage of those besotted multitudes was so strangely and so cruelly directed.

General Mandat had made the best dispositions which were possible for the defense of the palace. In addition to these eight hundred Swiss, there were in the edifice a great number of old servants of the royal family, who, arming themselves with swords and pistols, and whatever other weapons they could obtain, resolved to die in defense of the family with whose fortunes they so honorably identified themselves. Well did they acquit themselves of this last sad duty to their benefactors, which devolved upon them.

It is probable that a vigorous defense made at this moment, and especially a determined attack upon the rabble, might still have saved the royal family. But Louis XVI. though a virtuous, was not an able prince. He was devoid of the energy and the resolution necessary for such a fearful crisis; and it was his misfortune, and not his crime, that he did not on this occasion, exercise faculties which nature had not bestowed upon him, and which he therefore did not possess.

It was now five o'clock in the morning. The multitude overcoming every resistance, had reached and surrounded the palace. The dawn of day exhibited to the terrified king and his family, on all sides, a vast sea of angry heads, and every demonstration of popular fury. Their artillery was pointed toward the palace. Their confused shouts and bacchanalian songs were heard within its gilded halls. The commandant, Mandat, had been shot by the insurgents, at the Hotel de Ville, whither he had gone with a message from the king. The monarch immediately sent an order, marked by his usual though mistaken clemency, commanding his Swiss guards not to fire upon the mob, and only to act upon the defensive. His friends now urged him to put himself at the head of his troops, and commence a desperate resistance. It is even said that Maria Antoinette declared to him: "Sire, it is time to show youself," and snatching a pistol from the belt of General d'Affry, she presented it with a lofty and dignified gesture to the king, and reproved him for his pusillanimity. She had just dried the bitter tears which her misfortunes had wrung from her crushed spirit. But Louis XVI. was not a hero; he was *only a martyr;* and was incapable of an act of so much boldness and resolution.

By the advice of his counselors Louis determined to show himself once more to the multitude. He wore a purple suit of clothes, and his hair, which had not been dressed for some hours, was in disorder. On stepping out on the balcony his presence excited some enthusiasm. He now beheld before him many pieces of artillery directed against the palace. The caps of his grenadiers were at once lifted, in respect to the royal presence, and placed upon the points of their bayonets. For the last time, the ancient cry of "*Vive le Roi!*" so long associated with the glories, the splendors, and the calamities of the French monarchy, resounded around the halls of the palace of the Capets. From the balcony the king descended to the courts to review his troops. He was received there with enthusiasm. The attachment of this small body of men to the falling fortunes of the king, commends them to the respect of all ages; for they proved faithful to a man whom they knew to be unfortunate, and not guilty, and had strength of mind enough to resist the delirium which swept away the sanity of so many thousands of mankind. But disaffection had spread among the gunners, who manned the few pieces of artillery which defended the palace; and among some of the battalions of the national guards. As the king passed along these in his route back to the palace, some of the gunners, quitting their posts, ran up to the king, thrust their blackened fists into his face, and insulted him by the most brutal language. Louis was as pale as a corpse; and he was convinced, by the signs of disaffection which were displayed by his own troops—always excepting the heroic and incorruptible Swiss—that all was lost.

It was at the moment of the king's return from this inspection, that he was advised to take a step which proved to be decisive of his future fate. He was induced to take refuge, as he thought, from the impending danger in the bosom of the national assembly. This act sealed his destiny; though at that moment of confusion and terror, it was apparently the best measure which the king could adopt. By it all bloodshed seemed likely to be prevented, and the lives of the royal family would be preserved; for had the palace been taken by storm they would have inevitably been massacred on the spot. But in the end the step proved ruinous to the king's cause. From the assembly he passed to his prison. From his prison he journeyed to the scaffold!

The queen violently opposed this step. Roederer urged her to remember, that by so doing she endangered the lives of her husband and her children. At length the king said with a resigned tone to his friends and family, "*Let us go.*" "Sir," said the queen to Roederer, "you will answer for the lives of the king, and of my children." Roederer replied, "Madam, I promise that I will die by their side; I can do nothing more." They set out for the assembly by the garden, the terrace of the Feuillans, and the courts of the riding school. A detachment of the Swiss accompanied and protected the royal family. A deputation from the assembly met them, and with some small show of courtesy conducted them to the hall. The crowd was immense, and a passage was made for them by the efforts of the grenadiers. The royal family then entered, followed by the two ministers. Said Louis XVI., "Gentlemen, I come to prevent a great crime; I think I can be no where safer than in the midst of you." Vergniaud, the president, replied that he might rely on the firmness of the national assembly, and that they would protect the constituted authorities. Louis seated himself by the president. Chabot suggested that the presence of the king might influence the freedom of public discussion! To avoid this result, the king and his family were removed into the box of the reporters of the assembly—the *loge dé rapporteur;* which box was thus rendered illustrious by the fact, that it was the first and the last instance, in the history of the world, in which the humble seat of a reporter was honored as the refuge of an illustrious king. Even there, Louis was not free from insult. A ragged workman of the suburbs made his way to the iron railing which protected the fugitives, and said aloud to the king, "You are there, are you, Beast of a veto! There is a purse of gold I found in your palace yonder; if you had found mine, you would not have been so honest!"

Roederer proceeded to inform the assembly of the horrid scenes which had occurred. The assembly ordered twenty members to proceed to the crowd, and pacify them. At that moment the report of cannon was heard, mingled with the sound of musketry. It was a bloody conflict which had begun at the palace between the Swiss guards and the multitudinous rabble. The latter were probably ignorant of the departure of the king. They said to the troops, "Give up the palace to us, and we are friends." The duty of the Swiss forbade them to comply with this demand. The firing then commenced. The troops discharged a cannon among the Marseillais rabble, and made great slaughter. Terror seized the defenders of liberty on all sides, and they fled in great confusion. If the Swiss had followed up their advantage at this moment, all might perhaps have been redeemed. But at this juncture the king's order arrived, forbidding the Swiss to fire, and commanding them to follow him to the assembly. A large portion of them obeyed, leaving the palace without its defenders.

The enraged and wounded rabble now rallied. They were led by Westerman and Danton. They poured on in immense numbers, attacking the few troops who remained, slaying the most of them; and at length, after suffering some loss, obtained absolute possession of the ancient home of their kings. From this moment the attack was turned into a promiscuous massacre. The Swiss threw down their arms. They begged for quarter—a privilege granted by the most barbarous of combatants. They were butchered without mercy. The old servants of the king who fled, were pursued into the gardens and there murdered. Some of these climbed up the splendid monuments for refuge, with which the taste and the munificence of many kings had adorned the spot. They were mercilessly picked off by the sharp shooters of the rabble, and fell dead to the earth. The massacre was carried throughout every apartment and recess of the palace. Streams of blood were seen to flow from the roofs to the cellars of that once splendid edifice. Disgraceful and indecent mutilations were perpetrated publicly on the bodies of the dead, such as would only be agreeable to a Parisian revolutionary populace. Most prominent among the perpetrators of this outrage were *women*, who forgetting the natural attributes and decency of their sex, displayed the brutality of infuriated beasts. Seven hundred and fifty Swiss perished on that horrid day. The palace was ransacked. The work of slaughter finished, next followed that of devastation and demolition. The elegant furniture was dashed in pieces, and its fragments scattered far and wide. The rabble penetrated into the private apartments of the queen, which they disgraced with their obscenities. They ransacked every recess; they broke open every lock; they examined every depository of private papers. The cellars were plundered. All the works of art, with which the palace of the most refined monarchs of Europe had for generations been adorned, were destroyed. The butchery and devastation did not cease for some hours. Rapine, drunkenness, and bloodshed increased the revel and the carnage. When the crowds retired they had expended their rage. There was nothing left upon which to wreak it; for they had made a wreck of everything.

Meanwhile the assembly proceeded with its discussions, and awaited the issue of the combat at the palace. The royal family were imprisoned for fifteen hours, in the reporter's box, from which spot they distinctly heard the violent and abusive discussions of the deputies. From that spot Louis XVI. beheld the utter ruin of his hopes, the destruction of his authority, the crumbling of his scepter. The assembly then passed the celebrated decree of dethronement. By its orders Louis XVI. was suspended from the royal authority; a plan of education was appointed for the dauphin; and a national convention was convoked. During the passage of these infamous decrees, the sister and the wife of the ruined monarch were bathed in tears. Their situation, even in their humble refuge, was most unpleasant. The heat was intensely oppressive. The only refreshment of which the king partook, during all this time, was a peach and a glass of water. He sat with his hat off, intently watching the proceedings of the assembly, who assumed the prerogative of deciding his fate. From the hall of the assembly, when that body adjourned, the royal family were conveyed to the building of the Feuillans. There they remained for three days, occupying a suite of apartments, consisting of four very small rooms. In the first were several gentlemen who accompanied the king. In the second was the king himself. The third was occupied by the queen, who had none of her own servants about her. The fourth was appropriated to the royal children, and their aunt, Madame Elizabeth.

The proceedings of the French people and their representatives on this memorable occasion, serve as a powerful illustration of the character of perverted popular rule, in all ages and in every clime. The ignorant multitude, misled as they inevitably will be, in most cases where they possess absolute political power, by designing and unprincipled leaders, will ever become their tools for the perpetration of outrage and despotism. The crimes of kings and princes have indeed been innumerable. But we question very much whether, if the sovereign power had been, during the past history of the world, intrusted to the populace as often as it has been to princes, the crimes and outrages of the former had not been equal in number to those committed by the latter. They all alike partake of the common infirmities and weaknesses of humanity.

After decreeing the dethronement of the king, the assembly proceeded to remove all the high functionaries of the state as being closely connected with the king. Santerre, the butcher, was invested with the command of the national guards. They suppressed the municipal general council, and substituted Petion in their place and authority, under the title of *Procureur Syndic*. The great seal of state was taken possession of by the new minister of justice. This important office was conferred by the assembly on *Danton*, an immortal name in the annals of popular outrage and revolution. *Lebrun*, a prudent, thoughtful, stupid man, was made minister of foreign affairs. *Monge* was equally surprised with the appointment of minister of the marine.

The assembly next resolved, that all those decrees to which Louis XVI. had thought it his duty to affix his *veto*, should now receive the authority of law. By various acts the legislature assumed and exercised all the functions of government. Several months thus passed away, during which the popular attention, and the legislative vigilance, were directed toward the memorable massacres which took place in the prisons of Paris, in the Abbaye, the Conciergerie, la Force, the Bicetre, La Salpetriee, and the Chatelet. In each of these prisons horrid scenes of bloodshed were perpetrated on the captives of the 10th of August. The attention of the nation was also diverted from the royal family for a time, by the vicissitudes and fortunes of the war which was carried on by the nation against their enemies in Belgium and Savoy, under the command of Dumouriez and Kellerman. During the same interval the formal abolition of royalty, and the public proclamation of the republic, took place.

But by a strange infatuation, the thoughts of the nation soon reverted to the condition and the destiny of their royal and noble captives. From the 1st of October, 1791, to the 20th of September, 1792, the legislative assembly had passed two thousand one hundred and fifty decrees, relating to the administration of the kingdom. It does not comport with our purpose to enter into the consideration of any of these. They belong to the history of the revolution. We will confine ourselves strictly now to the events which appertain to Louis XVI. and his unfortunate family.

These unhappy victims of popular frenzy had been transferred to the prison known as THE TEMPLE. They were confined in the small tower, without any interior communication with the rest of the edifice. The body of this building was four stories high. The first story consisted of an ante-chamber, a dining-room, and another room in which was contained a library of fifteen hundred volumes. The second story was divided in nearly the same way. The bed-chamber of the queen and the princes was in the second story. The apartments of the king were in the third story. He slept in the large room and made a study of the turret closet. The fourth story was not used. The king generally rose at six in the morning. He shaved himself, and the faithful Clery dressed his hair. He then went to his reading-room or study. He there read, or wrote, till nine. At nine o'clock the royal family assembled in the king's chamber for breakfast. At ten, the king went with his children to the queen's apartment, and there passed the day. He employed himself in educating his son; giving him lessons in reading, in geography, and in reciting choice passages of the most distinguished French poets. The queen was employed in the instruction of her daughter, during the same interval.

The rest of the time till one was passed in needle-work, and in general conversation. At one o'clock, if the weather was fair, the royal family were allowed to promenade in the garden, under the care of four municipal officers, and a commander of a legion of the national guards. Dinner was served up at two. Santerre usually visited the royal family at this time. The king occasionally spoke to him, the queen never. In the evening, the time was passed in reading from some historical work. At nine the family supped, and shortly after separated for the night. The king kissed his children, and then retired to his lonely turret, where, in solitude and silence he usually remained reading and meditating till midnight. Each apartment was always under the strict watch of an officer.

On the assembling of the national convention the question was soon proposed: what shall be done with the royal captives in the Temple? On the first announcement of this inquiry, a profound silence pervaded the assembly. At length Barbaroux rose and said that this question was premature. It was first necessary to determine whether the convention was a *judicial* body; whether it was a court of justice as well as a legislature; whether it could execute laws as well as make them. He added, that if the trial of Louis XVI. came within the range of the functions of the assembly, it had many more culprits to try besides those already named. The important question was then referred to the committee of legislation, for their determination.

The committee took six weeks for the consideration of this question. This delay was agreeable to some parties, and obnoxious to others. The more moderate and intelligent part of the nation, as well as the nobility and the ecclesiastical orders, hoped that in the interval the popular fury might calm down, and that the delusion might pass away, which condemned Louis as a traitor to his country; as the enemy of liberty; as a man who, on any account, deserved the punishment of death. On the other hand, all the enraged factions loudly demanded the trial of the king. The Jacobin club was pertinaciously active and prominent among the agitators. They accused the Girondists of delaying the trial of the monarch by their quarrels and disorders, with which they distracted the national assembly. It was apparent to every observer, that the memorable day could not be very far distant, when the injured son of St. Louis was to stand, as an accused culprit, at the bar of his country.

The committee to whom was referred the question of the trial of Louis XVI. at length presented its report. That report contained the charges against the monarch, as well as the documentary proofs on which they were based. Two points were to be determined by the assembly. The first: whether the king could be tried at all. The second: if he could, what tribunal was competent to pronounce the judgment? The report of the committee was printed; and being translated into most of the languages of Europe, soon spread throughout the continent.

The doctrine which had universally prevailed throughout Europe for a thousand years previous to this period; which had been founded in the mediæval era of feudal power; and which had been established by the acquiescence of all civilized nations afterward, was that the *person* of a king is sacred and inviolable; that he may be deposed, but being the anointed of God, and the representative of his government on earth, he cannot be imprisoned or slain.

The negative of the question, therefore, of the inviolability of the king's person, found powerful advocates in the national convention. A violent debate ensued, and the ablest men on both sides put forth their best efforts. The Jacobins, as might be expected, contended furiously for the immolation of the king on the bloody altar of their frenzy and ambition. St. Just, who afterward became badly celebrated, made his first great display in the convention on this question. He exhibited considerable power of logic and declamation. He was followed by M. Morisson, the most zealous advocate of the inviolability of the person of the king. The arguments of the latter were answered by Robespierre, who spoke with his usual fierceness and acrimony. He declared that Louis XVI. was fighting against liberty from the recesses of his prison; that he should be condemned to death without any deliberation whatever; that to deliberate was to doubt; that to doubt was to commit treason against the republic, and against freedom; that to call in question the guilt of Louis XVI. was to condemn the servants of liberty, who had brought the revolution on thus far; who had enacted the scenes of the 10th of August, and every other glorious and memorable triumph. Such was the language used by this powerful political maniac. He added, that the foes of liberty everywhere were endeavoring to crush her to the earth, in the person of Louis XVI. by shielding and protecting him.

At length, on the 3d of December, the convention passed the decree, that Louis XVI. should be tried by it. The forms of the trial were then taken into consideration. The assembly then decreed that it possessed all power, legislative, executive, and judicial; that it alone could try the king, and decide upon his fate. It then resolved to dismiss all other business from its consideration, until the destiny of the monarch had been determined, and that the convention should immediately proceed to his trial.

The sad intelligence of this new outrage which was intended for the unhappy monarch, was first communicated to Madam Elizabeth, his sister, by Clery, his faithful servant. He also informed her that during the trial the commune had determined to separate him from his family. He devised a means of communication between the members of the persecuted family, after the separation took place. It could, however, only convey one idea to the king's family. This plan was, to carry a handkerchief from the king to the princes, should he be ill. The king was informed by his sister of the unwelcome truth that his trial was soon to commence.

The executive power was ordered to take all necessary means for the preservation of order during the trial. The declaration containing all the charges against the king was presented to the assembly on the 10th of December; and the appearance of Louis before his accusers and his judges, was fixed for the 11th of that month.

On the morning of that day, a numerous body of troops surrounded the Temple—the prison in which the unhappy monarch was confined. At nine, the royal family repaired as usual to breakfast in the king's apartment. The officers who were present watched the captives closely. At length the family separated. The king desired that his little son, the dauphin, might be left with him a few moments. The request was rudely denied. He desired to know why this request was refused, and that small favor which the most savage of men would have granted, was so cruelly withheld from him. The answer was, that the council of the commune had so ordered it. The king then tenderly embraced his son; and after his departure he walked about the room in much agitation. He then sat down and leaned his head upon his hand. In this position the unhappy monarch remained alone for half an hour, absorbed in the most mournful and crushing reflections. The officer on guard, who stood outside his door, apprehending that something was the matter, went in. The king on being disturbed said, "What do you want with me?" "I was afraid you were not well," was the answer. The king replied in a tone of the deepest anguish, "The way in which they have taken my little son from me, cuts me to the heart." The officer withdrew in silence. The undeserved agony of fallen greatness had melted even his brutal spirit. What an outrage on humanity was perpetrated in the sufferings which were inflicted by fiends incarnate, on this most innocent and amiable of men!

The mayor of Paris at length arrived, and informed the king that the convention summoned him to its bar, as Louis Capet. "*Capet* was the name of one of my ancestors," replied the king; "it is not mine." He then entered the carriage of the mayor, and proceeded to the assembly. Santerre announced to that body the arrival of the king. *Barrere*, the most infamous of all the wretches who disgraced the revolution with his crimes, said, "Citizens, the eyes of Europe are upon you. Posterity will judge you with inflexible severity; therefore preserve the dignity and dispassionate coolness which befit judges." When the king entered, profound silence pervaded the assembly. The dignity and serenity of Louis XVI. under the new and astounding circumstances which surrounded him, struck his accusers and his judges with profound reverence. For a moment even his bitterest enemies were overawed by the moral grandeur of the scene; and by the composure and self-possession displayed by the outraged monarch, which, if he had ever been weak before, now wholly redeemed his fame. Even St. Just, Marat, and Robespierre, lately so fanatical and furious, for a moment appeared to feel the upbraidings of conscious injustice and shame.

"Be seated," said Barrere, "and answer the questions which shall be put to you." Louis sat down and listened attentively to the reading of the *Acte ènonciatif*, which contained all the accusations against him. He was charged, in that document, with a conspiracy to thwart the movement of the 14th of July; with the refusal to sanction the declaration of rights; with a false oath at the Federation on the 14th of July; with conspiring with Talon and Mirabeau to effect a counter revolution; with using his veto on various occasions in oppression of liberty; with the flight to Varrennes; with continuing their pay to emigrated courtiers and soldiers; with refusing to sanction the decree for the emancipation of twenty thousand men near Paris; with the organization of secret anti-revolutionary societies in Paris; and with causing the bloodshed which took place on the 10th of August, in the capital.

To all these charges the king answered with firmness and dignity. He denied some of the alleged facts; he imputed others to his ministers; and he protested that in all cases he had never deviated from the constitution of his country.

The king then demanded the assistance of counsel. A violent tumult arose among the demagogues and fanatics at the announcement of this request. Some of the most infamous of them spoke against granting the demand; pretending that it was only an expedient to protract the final judgment. This was probably the first instance in the history of the world, and among civilized nations, in which a defendant's plea of *not guilty*, and his demand made to the court which tried his case, to have counsel assigned him for his defense, was construed by that court in to a pretext, a mere subterfuge, to avert or protract the verdict. We question whether even the semi-barbarous inhabitants of Morocco or Lapland would have made so absurd, and so outrageous an objection. Yet such an objection was gravely urged, by various members of the legislature of the greatest nation of christendom; so powerful is the force of popular frenzy and delusion on the human mind!

After a violent conflict, the request of Louis XVI. was complied with. He selected Turgot, Malesherbes, and Tronchet. The first of these declined in consequence of his great age; and from the fact, that for many years he had retired from practice. The second had been the bosom friend of Turgot and Maurepas; a man of profound learning and great respectability of character. He was seventy years of age, and had passed with honor through many scenes connected with the glory and splendor of the ancient régime. The third was a younger man, of great ability, who was rapidly rising in his profession, upon whom the principal labor and responsibility of the defense rested.

The convention had decreed that during the preparation for the trial, the king should have his two children with him. But as they refused to allow the whole royal family to be together, the king, knowing that the society of his children was more necessary to the queen than to himself, refused to deprive her of that consolation.

The three advocates of the king found it necessary to add to their number another. This person was *M. Desere.* The counsel had free access to their illustrious and unfortunate client. They had a burdensome task to perform. The mass of materials which they were to digest was immense. They labored night and day. At length the 26th day of December had arrived, the day appointed for the trial. The king rode, as before, to the assembly with the mayor, and was cheerful and courteous in his intercourse with them. There was but little scenic splendor or forensic display at this most important trial of modern times. The forms and proceedings which were somewhat after the fashion of the civil law, did not allow of either. The trial, if such it may be termed, excited the vulgar curiosity of the crowd, and the hall of the assembly contained a singular and miscellaneous multitude, who looked with the same heartless eagerness on the proceedings as they would upon a bull-fight, or a combat of gladiators. But every candid and intelligent observer was convinced that Louis XVI. had long since been condemned by a foregone conclusion; and that all the efforts of his counsel and of his personal and political friends, could not possibly avert the blow which the fanatical vengeance of the revolutionists had prepared for him.

The king's counsel first discussed the principles of law which the case involved, and afterward argued upon the facts. It was urged by them, that Louis looked in the assembly for his judges, whereas he beheld everywhere only his accusers. Their defense of the king was long, learned, and able. The assembly listened to their efforts with dignified attention. After they had concluded, Louis made a few observations which he had written. He ended by saying, "In addressing you, perhaps for the last time, I declare that my conscience reproaches me with nothing; and that my counsel have stated to you the truth. I assert, that the many proofs I have at all times given you of my love for the people, and the manner in which I have always governed my conduct, ought to prove to you that I was not afraid to expose myself to prevent bloodshed; and to clear me forever from such a charge." With these simple words, so true and so impressive, the king took his leave of the convention, with whom it was worse than vain to argue. In leaving, the king saluted an assembly of *Frenchmen* who refused to reciprocate the courtesy! To such a degree may political fanatacism blunt even the amenities of our nature!

CHAPTER VI.

THE DOWNFALL OF THE ANCIENT MONARCHY OF FRANCE.

An immense tumult immediately ensued upon the king's departure from the convention. The next thing in order was the discussion upon the defense which he had made. Some of the deputies, however, raised a great outcry against the endless delays which were thus allowed, as they said, to obstruct the onward path of justice. *They* wanted no discussion. The tempest continued to rage for an hour with great violence. At length order was restored; and the assembly resolved that the final discussion on the king's fate should be resumed on the 27th of that month.

On that day the assembly was addressed by a large number of the ablest orators of all parties. The majority argued in favor of his condemnation, reserving the question of the nature of his punishment, as a subsequent and distinct inquiry. The rest, who were few in number, contended for an appeal to the nation, which was intended to rescue him. Some of the representatives had been deeply affected by the serenity and dignity displayed by this injured prince; and could not refrain from giving utterance to their feelings. Of this number was Vergniaud, the eloquent leader of the Girondists. He spent the whole night after the condemnation of Louis, in tears. There were many others who, upon that memorable occasion, were unable to stifle the innate feelings of humanity and justice, which even the fanaticism and frenzy of the revolution had failed to eradicate. But their influence and their numbers were small, compared with the immense mass of the Jacobins and their coadjutors, whose members constituted the great majority of the assembly.

Robespierre spoke on this occasion with more than his usual fury. This was the greatest opportunity which had yet offered itself to display his talents, and augment his power. Like all hypocrites, he too must pretend to a semblance of humanity and virtue. He had been moved at the sight of the accused, thus humbled before the mighty power of the people. But the greatest sacrifice, he said, that he could make for his country's good, was to stifle those humane emotions, when they endangered the welfare of the state. He then spoke of the constant delays which retarded the cause of justice. He condemned the appeal to the people. He proceeded to quote allusions to instances of ancient republican virtue—Cretias, Socrates, and Cato. He desired the convention to proceed manfully against the worst of tyrants, and not to flinch in the performance of their stern though unpleasant duty. He ended by demanding the immediate condemnation of Louis, and his punishment by death.

The discussions on the fate of the king lasted five days. Vergniaud, Brissot, Gensonné, Petion, Barrere,—each spoke at great length and with much ability. The last of these, especially, by the appearance of calm impartiality which he assumed, exerted a more fatal influence against the king, and displayed deeper turpitude than any of his associates. The 14th of January, 1793, was at length appointed as the period for putting the final vote in reference to Louis XVI. and his destiny.

When that momentous day arrived, an immense multitude surrounded the assembly and filled the tribunes. It was decreed that the votes of the assembly should be taken upon these points: whether the king had been guilty of treason; whether the judgment should be referred to the people; and what should be his punishment. It was also determined that each member should vote from the tribune; that he should write his vote; then sign it; and if he desired, add his reasons for so doing. When the votes were taken, six hundred and eighty-three members declared Louis XVI. *guilty*, without any explanation or reservation. Thirty-seven declared him guilty, but denied the right of the convention to condemn and punish him. Twenty-eight members were absent on various excuses and commissions. Not one single person among that large assemblage of seven hundred and forty-nine intelligent Frenchmen, had either the fortitude or the impartiality to declare Louis XVI. innocent!

The second question to be decided was the appeal to the people. On this point, two hundred and eighty-one deputies voted for an appeal to the people. Four hundred and twenty-three voted against it. The rest of the members were either absent or declined to vote. It was thus decided by a *majority* of the representatives, that the fate of the unhappy king should not be referred to the decision of the nation.

The next day was appointed for the vote upon the third and most important question—the nature of the king's penalty. On that day the crowd was greater and the interest more intense, than they had been at any previous period. The tribune was occupied at an early hour by the most furious of the Jacobins, in order that they might more closely scrutinize the voters, and their sentiments. It was expected that the sitting would be both a protracted and an excited one, and some preliminaries were necessary to maintain the preservation of order and security. These occupied nearly the whole day. It was seven o'clock in the evening when the voting began; and the assembly decreed that the sitting should be permanent, until the voting had been concluded.

A scene and an occasion like the one which was about to ensue, was certainly most memorable in the history of nations. An excited band of adventurers and demagogues were about to decree the destiny of the immediate successor but one of Louis XIV., who was regarded in his day as the most powerful and formidable sovereign in Europe. This band was about to exert an usurped authority over the throne, and over the institutions and prerogatives of ages. What had been the work of many successive generations of men; that which all their toils, their triumphs, and their vicissitudes had established, these irresponsible fanatics were about to blast from the face of the earth and from the sight of men, by one fell sweep of their mushroom power and supremacy. The solemn knell of the mighty Capet dynasty was about to strike forever; its long line of glorious heroes and illustrious kings, was about to be extinguished and descend to the tomb in anguish, ignominy, and disgrace. Those men who were about to dispose of the life—not of a mere citizen, not of a prince, nor even of a statesman, but of a great sovereign—knew not, scarcely, at that very moment, whence the means were to come to pay the humble lodgings which they then occupied! Such are some of the strange vicissitudes which occur in the affairs and the fortunes of men; teaching most impressively the vanity of human greatness, and how despicable may be, and often are, the possessors and the depositaries of human power.

The voting began. The most reasonable and the most honorable of the members of the assembly, voted in favor of the banishment of the king; or for his imprisonment until peace was restored, and for his subsequent banishment. Another class voted for the death of Louis, with the express proviso, that it would be expedient to stay the execution of the sentence for an indefinite time. They did this knowing that the gaining of time would be everything for Louis, and that probably that sentence would be equivalent to an acquittal. The vast majority of the assembly, however, displayed a very different spirit. While each member was ascending the steps of the tribune to deposit his vote, profound silence pervaded the hall, in order that each vote might be distinctly heard, and tokens of censure or approbation were given accordingly. In the intervals, the most violent threats and boisterous shouts pervaded the place; presenting a despicable scene of disorder and confusion, utterly unworthy of the great occasion, and of the important interests which were under consideration.

As the voting progressed, and as the word "Banishment," seemed to be frequently pronounced, the excitement became intense. The fate of the unfortunate king seemed to hang upon an uncertainty. Suddenly an appalling spectacle presented itself. Among the masses which crowded the center of the hall, a singular sight appeared. It was the tottering figure of a man who seemed from his ghastly and death-like appearance, to have left the grave to be present at the sealing of the fate of one who was soon to join him in that sad abode. It was a deputy named *Duchatel*, who had left his bed of sickness, and had been carried to the convention by the still active and hoping friends of the king, that he might cast his vote for "*Banishment.*"

At length all the ballots were deposited. The assembly had been voting all night and all the succeeding day. Seven hundred and forty-nine members had voted. Three hundred and sixty-one had decided for death unconditionally. Two hundred and eighty-six had voted for banishment. The rest had voted either for death and delay of execution, or for imprisonment. After the ballots were counted, Vergniaud, the president, announced with a solemn voice, the following decision: "*The punishment pronounced against Louis Capet is Death!*"

Immediately after the announcement of the horrid decree of the convention, it was asserted that an error had been committed in counting the votes. The assembly resolved to verify the result, and proceeded to examine the votes anew. It was then discovered that the original counting had been correct.

M. Malesherbes, as the oldest friend and confidant of the king, was selected by his counsel to perform the ungrateful task of conveying to him the decree of the convention. When he entered the apartment of the king, he found him resting with his forehead on his hands, absorbed in a profound and mournful reverie. He immediately said to M. Malesherbes, "For two hours I have been reviewing my whole reign, and trying to remember whether I have ever given any cause of complaint to my subjects, and I must say sincerely, that I have been able to remember no instance of the kind. I have always endeavored for their good."

Louis anticipated his fate, and was prepared to meet it. He then said to his friend, "Have you not met the *White Lady* near my prison?" What do you mean? inquired he. The king answered with a smile, "Do you not know, that when a prince of our house is about to perish, a female dressed in white is seen wandering about the palace?" Then assuming a serious and respectful manner, he uttered these sublime words; "*My friend, I am about to depart before you, to the land of the just. There I shall be at rest. My only regret is for my helpless family, whom I leave behind me, uncertain of their fate. But we will be reünited, at last, in Heaven.*" Overcome by his emotions, he added no more.

The convention had yet one more question to decide, in reference to their helpless victim. It was whether there should be any reprieve. It was determined that each deputy should vote in his seat, either *yes* or *no*. Three hundred and ten voted for delay. Three hundred and eighty voted against it. It was thereupon decreed that Louis should die within twenty-four hours!

This memorable session of the convention had occupied seventy-two hours. It might reasonably be supposed that on so solemn an occasion, suitable order and decorum would have characterized the behavior of the assembly. The reverse was actually the case. The most disgraceful scenes occurred. The further extremity of the hall was converted into seats and private boxes. These were filled with notorious prostitutes, dressed in the immodest style which befitted their profession; and there they received the compliments of their acquaintances among the members, and were entertained with ices, oranges, and liquors. Several females particularly attracted the attention of the whole assemblage, by the superior splendor of their dress, and by their majestic and voluptuous beauty. A particular box was appropriated to their use. They were two of the mistresses of the duke of Orleans, (*Egalité.*)

The galleries were also filled with women. Some of these were the insane female Jacobins, who had taken a prominent part in the insurrections of the capital. They were drinking brandy, laughing, and jesting. Bets were lightly made upon the issue of the trial. Impatience and disgust seemed to sit on every countenance. The figures of the deputies, passing silently to and fro, as they deposited their votes, rendered more ghastly and ghost-like by the feeble and uncertain light of the wax tapers as the night advanced, augmented the horrid gloom of the scene. Some of the deputies had fallen asleep, and were only awakened to deposite their ballot of *death* against the king.

As the hours of the night slowly advanced the confusion became more universal. When the duke of Orleans was called on to vote, he proceeded toward the tribune with faltering step, and with a countenance paler than death.

He then read these words: "Influenced exclusively by my duty, and convinced that all those who resist the sovereignty of the people deserve to die, my vote is for *death!*" This unnatural decision given by the first prince of the blood, and evidently extorted by a craven fear of the popular power, called forth from every part of the hall groans and hisses of contempt. Even the fierce Jacobins failed to applaud the base tribute thus rendered to their terrible power, by this unworthy scion of a fallen but immortal race.

The fate of Louis XVI. was now sealed forever. Well might the assembly pause and shudder at the act which it had just perpetrated. Well might all Paris be overwhelmed with gloom and sadness. A deed which filled the civilized world with horror, might readily have caused a few compunctious thoughts to its desperate perpetrators. The dreadful news was officially conveyed to the king, by a committee of the convention headed by Garat. The king received the news with calmness. His last request was for permission to see his family; to have a confessor to assist him in his religious duties; and liberty for his family to retire from France. He then ordered his dinner and ate as usual. He remarked the absence of knives on the table. He smiled and said, "Do not think me so weak as to lay violent hands on myself. I am innocent, and am not afraid to die." M. Edgeworth was the ecclesiastic whose assistance the king desired to have in his last moments.

The most sad and painful duty of all yet remained for the prince to perform; and for this he summoned all his energy. It was to bid a last adieu to his family. History scarcely records among all its harrowing details, a scene more affecting and distressing than the parting interview between this unhappy and persecuted monarch, and his wife and children. The domestic affections of Louis were very strong. His attachment to his children was unusually intense. How great the contrast between the parting interview which was about to take place between the members of that family, and the previous scenes of their history! When Louis first embraced the beautiful and accomplished princess, his wife, whom he was now, for the last time, about to fold to his breast, how widely different had been their circumstances! He was the youthful and happy heir-apparent to a splendid throne, with the prospect of a long and brilliant reign before him. She was the most splendid and magnificent woman in Europe; full of bewitching grace and loveliness; the proud daughter of an illustrious line of emperors; her very presence was fascination; and she was the perfection of a wife, a princess, and a queen. In the possession of her charms, and in the enjoyment of her love, Louis might have been regarded as the most fortunate and happy of men. That once blooming and brilliant form he was now about to press to his breast for the last time—a trembling, crushed, and shattered wreck of the blooming bride she once had been.

The queen was apprised that the hour for the final interview had arrived. She had been informed for some time of the fate which the assembly had decreed to her husband. At half past eight in the evening his door was opened, and his wife and children made their appearance. They all rushed into his arms. A sad silence prevailed for some minutes, broken only by sobs and groans. The king then sat down, his queen on one side, his sister, Madam Elizabeth, on the other, his children between his knees. All were leaning on the king, and pressing him in their arms. The sad interview lasted two hours, during which time the unhappy family exchanged those tokens and expressions of affection, which are always dear to hearts that are bursting with grief, and whose only consolation is their mutual sympathy and their tears. At length the king rose, and moved toward the door. There he pressed each beloved one again for the last time affectionately to his breast. The tears and sobs of the heart-broken family were here renewed. Louis knew that it was for the last time that his eyes rested on those graceful forms he loved so well, though his family yet hoped for one more parting interview. "Farewell! Farewell!" said he, as he tore himself from their embraces, and rushed back into his chamber. The door then closed, and the king was left alone. Here for the first, and for the last time, his manly spirit failed him, as well it might; and the faithful Clery, who waited at his door, overheard the agonizing sighs and moans of his heart-broken master.

In a few minutes Louis recomposed himself, and sent for his confessor. During the night he slept well. The Abbe Edgeworth occupied Clery's bed in the same apartment with the king. In the morning, the priest celebrated mass, at which impressive service the king assisted with proper reverence and devotion. He then confessed, and received the holy communion. The altar was constructed of a chest of drawers, placed in the middle of the apartment. The priest's vestments were borrowed from a church in the neighborhood of the Temple. During the service Louis was seated in an arm-chair, placed by Clery in front of the altar. He knelt upon a cushion which lay before him. It was thus that this last solemn and sacred rite was performed for the dying king.

CHAPTER VII.

THE DEATH OF THE ROYAL MARTYRS, LOUIS XVI. AND XVII.

The enormities of the French revolution would have remained incomplete, had they not been terminated by several additional acts of preëminent and unparalleled infamy. These acts were the execution of Louis XVI., the murder of his wife, the unfortunate and beautiful Maria Antoinette, and the slow but sure destruction of their son, the dauphin.

When Louis was informed that the last hour of his existence had arrived, he gave the signal to the few attendants who yet surrounded him, to advance. He and the Abbe Edgeworth occupied the back seat of the carriage. Several *gen d'armes* sat on the front. During the ride to the scene of this national murder, the king was engaged in devoutly reading in the breviary of the priest, the prayers appropriate to those about to die. It is said that the soldiers had express orders to destroy Louis should the carriage be attacked, and a rescue attempted by his partisans and friends.

The scaffold had been erected in the *Place de la Revolution.* Around this immense area a large number of cannon had been planted, to suppress any movement which might be made in behalf of the victim. A vast multitude lined the whole route from the Temple to the place of execution. At precisely ten o'clock in the forenoon the carriage, the progress of which had been very slow, halted, and Louis XVI. rising with energy, stepped forth into the area. Three executioners, eager for their infamous work, immediately seized his hands, in order to bind them behind him. The king was about to resist this unnecessary insult, when, after a moment's reflection, he yielded, and submitted to this last indignity. He was thus conducted to the scaffold, accompanied by the priest. He ascended the steps with firmness, and having reached the summit of the platform, he looked around him with composure and dignity. There, the descendant of many illustrious kings had at length reached the last stage of his memorable and unfortunate career. From the height of that eminence he looked at the immense multitudes who had once proudly called him their sovereign, and who, but a few short years before, had hailed his accession to the throne with loud and eager acclamations. He then gazed at that immense capital, which had been the brilliant home and seat of his long line of ancestors; which had, for so many generations, been identified with their glory and their power; and which they had so long delighted to adorn and beautify. Then turning from this spectacle, so pregnant with affecting reminiscences of the past, and directing his eyes to the crowds immediately around the scaffold, he uttered in a voice loud, clear, and unwavering, these words: "*Frenchmen, I die innocent of the crimes imputed to me. I forgive the authors of my death. I pray that my blood may not fall upon France.*" He would have said more, but the commandant, fearing perhaps that the words of the king might excite a diversion in his favor, ordered the drums to beat. The loud and deafening clatter immediately drowned the voice of the king, and he desisted. The executioners then took hold of him. They rudely dragged him beneath the ax of the guillotine, and laid his head down upon the block. In a moment, the glittering blade fell heavily, and the head of Louis bounded with violence into the basket placed beneath the scaffold to receive it. In an instant, the earth and all its scenes faded from the consciousness of the murdered king; and as the ancient blood of the Bourbons crimsoned the soil over which they had so long swayed the scepter; and as the freed spirit of Louis passed away forever from the earth; the Abbe Edgeworth, overcome by the mournful grandeur of the scene, raised his hands, and exclaimed with impressive sublimity, "Son of St. Louis, ascend to heaven!" The execution occurred on the 21st of January, A. D. 1793. After a short time, the immense assembly gradually dispersed. The body of the king was immediately conveyed, not to the royal sepulchre of St. Denis, where the long line of French monarchs lay buried; but his remains were hurried to the cemetery of the Madeleine, where the last sad burial rites were performed in silence and solitude, without the least circumstance of parade, by a few faithful and attached adherents of the royal family. The corpse was covered with quick-lime, which was intended to produce rapid decomposition, so that if the popular fury might, at any subsequent period, make an attempt to violate the sanctuary of the tomb, and commit any additional outrage upon these remains, the purpose might be prevented. The decomposition was so rapid and complete, that after the downfall of Napoleon in 1815, when an effort was made by the restored family to recover the remains, not the least traces of them could be found.

Louis was executed on the same spot, upon which afterward Maria Antoinette, his sister, the princess Elizabeth, and many of the noblest spirits in France terminated their existence in blood. It was also the very spot on which Danton and Robespierre subsequently expiated their innumerable crimes. It was the same spot on which the heroic Charlotte Corday met her fate, with a dignity worthy of immortal honor, as one of the most resolute and devoted friends of true liberty.

Years of mighty change and vicissitude to France rolled by; and this same spot was again made memorable by the fact, that on it the assembled sovereigns and princes of Europe took their position, when the armies of the allied powers entered Paris in 1815, and once more restored the exiled Bourbons to their rightful throne. What affecting associations must cluster around the spot, which has been the scene of such amazing and such contradictory events!

The will of Louis XVI. which he prepared some time before his death, in anticipation of his fate, gives utterance to such sentiments as might be expected from so good a man, and so amiable a prince. What sublime resignation and heroic courage are contained in the following words, which occur in it: "Abandoned by the whole universe, I now have none but God to whom I can address myself. Shut up with my family in the tower of the Temple at Paris, by those who were once my subjects, and implicated in a process of which it is impossible for me to foresee the issue, I thus declare my last wishes and sentiments:

"I die in the bosom of our Holy Catholic, Apostolic, Roman church. I pray God to receive my deep repentance for having affixed my name, though it was done against my will, to any acts which were contrary to the discipline of the Catholic faith, to which I have ever remained sincerely attached. I request those whom I may have inadvertently offended—for I do not remember to have given offense to any intentionally—and those whom I may have unjustly charged with faults, to pardon the injury they may suppose me to have done them.

"I forgive with all sincerity, those who may have been my enemies, without having received from me any injury; and I pray God to pardon them as well as all others who may have done me harm.

"I commend to Almighty God my wife, my children, my aunts, my brothers, and all others who are connected with me by ties of blood. I pray God to look upon my family who suffer so much with me, with an eye of mercy, and to support them with his grace when I am dead. I commend my children to my wife. I have never doubted her maternal tenderness for them. I exhort her particularly to make them good christians and honest members of society; to teach them to look upon the grandeurs of this world, if they should be so unfortunate as to possess them, as dangerous and perishable treasures, and to direct their attention to the only solid and durable glory of eternity. I entreat my sister to continue her tenderness to my children, and to supply the place of a mother, should they ever have the misfortune to lose their own.

"I beseech my wife to pardon all the miseries which she endures on my account, and all the vexations I may have occasioned her, during the period of our union. And she may rest assured, that should she think that she has anything to reprove herself with respecting me, that I have no such feeling or remembrance.

"I recommend to my son, should he ever become unfortunate enough to become a king, to reflect that he must devote himself to the happiness of his fellow-citizens; that he ought to forget all hatred and resentment, especially what may relate to the sufferings I have endured; that he may promote the happiness of his people by reigning according to the laws; but at the same time, that a king cannot cause the laws to be respected, unless he possess a necessary degree of authority, and that otherwise confined in his operations and unable to inspire respect, he becomes more injurious than useful.

"I recommend to my son, the dauphin, to take care of every person attached to me, as far as the circumstances in which he may find himself placed, may permit. There were some of those who were about me, that have not conducted themselves toward me as they ought to have done, and have been ungrateful. I forgive them, and I entreat my son only to think of their distresses.

"I request the gentlemen of the commune to deliver to Clery my effects, my books, my watch, my purse, and the other little articles which were deposited at the council of the commune. I forgive the ill-treatment of those who have been my keepers during my captivity, and the harsh restrictions they thought themselves bound to practice toward me. I have found *some* compassionate souls.

May they enjoy that tranquillity in their hearts, which their reflections can bestow upon them.

"I request M. M. Malesherbes, Tronchet and Desere, to accept my sincere thanks, and the warmest expressions of my sensibility, for the care and trouble they have given themselves on my account.

"I conclude by declaring before God and the world, and as ready to appear in His presence, that I have not to reproach myself with any of the crimes which have been laid to my charge.

"Written at the Temple, December 25th, A. D. 1792."

But a few months after the judicial murder of Louis XVI., in October, 1793, his unfortunate wife and queen was compelled to undergo the same ignominious fate.*

* The act of accusation against her consisted of several charges, the substance of which was that she had contributed to the derangement of national finances, by remitting from time to time considerable sums to her brother, the Emperor Joseph; that since the revolution she had continued to hold a criminal correspondence with foreign powers; that in every instance she had directed her views to a counter revolution, particularly in exciting the body guards and others of the military at Versailles, on the first of October, 1789; that in concert with Louis Capet she had distributed counter revolutionary papers and writings; and even, to favor their purposes, some in which she was personally defamed; that in the beginning of October, 1789, by the agency of certain monopolists, she had created an artificial famine; that she was a principal agent and promoter of the flight of the royal family in June, 1791; that she instituted private councils in the palace, at which the massacres, as they were termed, in the Champ de Mars, and at Nancy, were planned; that in consequence of these councils, she had persuaded her husband to interpose his veto against the decrees concerning the emigrants and the refractory priests; and that she influenced him to form a guard composed of disaffected persons, and refractory priests.

We know of no instance, in all the wide range of human vicissitude and misfortune, which furnishes so impressive and so affecting an illustration of the uncertainty and mutability of human greatness, as the case of this unhappy woman. We will not even except the sufferings of Mary, Queen of Scots; because her long imprisonment of eighteen years had gradually weaned her mind from earth, and had blunted her sensibility to pain. But the once fair daughter of Maria Theresa, born in the most brilliant court in Europe; the daughter, the sister, the wife, and the mother of kings; descended from a long line of illustrious sovereigns, and allied by blood and marriage to every distinguished monarch in Europe; she was not only executed as a common felon, but her body, in which coursed the proudest blood among a hundred royal dynasties, was buried with beggars in a common ditch. The bill of the undertaker, who prepared the deal coffin for the fallen princess, was worded thus: "*For the coffin of the widow Capet, seven francs!*" She, whose imperial ancestors had for many generations been entombed with stately and imposing ceremonies, with solemn and seraphic melodies, in marble and gilded mausoleums, beneath the towering spire and Gothic dome of St. Stephen's ancient cathedral at Vienna; upon whose exquisitely beautiful sarcophagi the most accomplished talents of the sculptor had been expended; even she was consigned to the grave at last by brutal hands, amid savage and indecent jests, in a rude box, whose utmost cost to the state was seven francs! And when twenty years afterward, the restored dynasty of the Bourbons endeavored to find, amid the mouldering and undistinguished dust of that common *fosse*, the remains of her who had once occupied so high a place, and had possessed such imperial state, only one poor mark or remnant of all her former glory could be found, rescued from the oblivion of the past. The crumbling dust of the murdered queen, after a protracted search, was recognized by the *garter* bearing upon it the royal arms of France, which still clasped the ghastly remains of those knees, before which chivalrous and gallant men of many nations had once been proud to bow in courtly admiration. By that garter alone, Maria Antoinette was then distinguished from the common herd of prostitutes, assassins, and vagabonds, which had so long surrounded her, and had commingled with her dust!

The great concern expressed by Louis XVI. in the destiny of his son and representative, the dauphin of France, and the intrinsic interest of the subject itself, render it proper that the history of the one should be made complete by some details respecting the life and fate of the other. Nor would we be able to form a correct idea of France and her people during the first revolution, were we to omit all statements respecting a theme so closely indentified with the subject of the preceding pages.

Charles Louis, the dauphin of France, was the second son of Louis XVI. and Maria Antoinette; and was born at Versailles, March 27th, 1785. The cardinal De Rohan administered to him the sacrament of baptism, immediately after his birth. At the period of his father's death he was in the eighth year of his age; and was remarkable for several things: for the fairness of his complexion, the beauty of his person, and the vivacity, intelligence, and amiability of his disposition. In 1789 his elder brother died, and thus it was that Charles Louis became, in regular succession, the dauphin of France, and heir-apparent to the throne of St. Louis.

The earliest years of the child were passed in the amusements and exercises usual with persons of his rank and age; and as he became older, the charms of his disposition rendered him more and more an object of interest and attention. On the 28th of January, 1793, immediately after the murder of his father, his uncle, the Count de Provence, who was then residing at one of the minor German courts, proclaimed him the successor of Louis XVI. under the title of Louis XVII. He thus became a legitimate sovereign, and a suitable subject for the scrutiny of history.

On the first day of July, 1793, it was decreed by the "committee of public safety" that the dauphin should be separated from his mother in the Temple, and confined in another apartment. At ten o'clock at night, after the dauphin had retired to rest, his mother was informed of the sad intelligence which was to separate her from her son. She was distracted at the thought, and besought the officers by every moving and affecting appeal, which a mother's love could suggest, not to distress her with so heavy an affliction. Her efforts to move their pity were all in vain, and the little dauphin, overcome with astonishment and distress at this strange and sudden change, was torn from her embraces, and taken to that apartment in the tower of the Temple which had been occupied by his unfortunate father.

By this transition the young prince was placed under the control of the famous Simon, an *artist* in shoe-leather.

This individual was a creature of Marat, who had proposed him for this trust, and had been approved and appointed by Robespierre. He was a rude, ignorant, passionate, and vulgar wretch; just such an one as we might suppose would be a favorite and congenial associate of Marat, "the friend of the people."

It is matter of undisputed truth that the treatment bestowed by his jailor upon the young dauphin, was most brutal and cruel. Whenever news arrived of some partial triumphs gained by the royalist forces in La Vendee, Simon was sure to punish the prince for their successes by severe blows, and by the most unfeeling persecution. "It is your friends," said he, "you young villain, who are cutting our throats, and ruining the cause of liberty." The dauphin, scarcely knowing the meaning of the cobbler's allusions, smothered his sobs, while the unbidden tears rolled down his cheeks.

The day after he had been separated from his mother, she sent him his books, his writing materials, and his toys. Simon appropriated the former to the intellectual purpose of lighting his pipe, while the latter he would amuse himself with breaking up, and defacing in the presence of the weeping prince, who in vain implored to have them spared. On the 2d of August, 1793, the national assembly added another to the long list of its outrages, by decreeing that Maria Antoinette should be entirely removed from the Temple and confined in the prison of the *Conciegerie.* From that hour the heart-broken queen never again beheld her unhappy son!

After this period the cruelty of Simon became more excessive and severe. On one occasion when the child refused to sing a revolutionary song, in which his mother was honored with the epithet of *Austrian she-wolf.* Simon threw an andiron at his head, which would inevitably have destroyed him, had he not, by a sudden movement, evaded it.

The only regret of Maria Antoinette in leaving a world in which her destiny had been so sad and so singular, was solicitude for the fate of her two children. After her execution their situation became sufficiently friendless. The dauphin's sister was confined in the Temple, though her condition was somewhat more tolerable than that of her brother. The treatment of Simon was intended both to destroy the health of the child, and to demoralize his mind. The wretch succeeded in accomplishing both purposes previous to his removal from the Temple. The health of the latter amiable individual began to fail from the constant state of brutal intoxication in which he lived, together with the confinement of his situation; and he obtained permission to retire. He took leave of his unhappy little victim with these words: "Oh, the young villain! he is not yet quite crushed, but he never will escape now, even if all the priests in the world should come to his aid."* After Simon's departure, the dauphin was removed to another larger apartment, which was then bolted and fastened up, as if it was intended that the prince should never come forth again alive. His food was put in to him between the iron bars of the door. He had

* It is a comfortable reflection, of which we would not, on any account, deprive the reader, that this despicable wretch Simon was afterward guillotined with his friend and patron Robespierre. Avenging justice, though slow, was sure, in this as it is in all other cases to measure out deserved punishment to the guilty.

neither light nor fire. No human soul was ever allowed to enter the room. It remained unswept and uncleansed for some months, and amid its damp and heavy shades the lonely and friendless child was left to while away the tedious hours of his existence, in solitary communion with his own thoughts. The little victim never even beheld the hand that gave him his bread and water. No friendly voice ever cheered him by its sympathy. The cold and massive walls of that ancient dungeon chilled his tender frame through and through; and if a curious stranger ever was permitted to look through the grated door, he beheld the bent and shivering form of the unconscious and lonely child, *somewhere* amid the heavy glooms of his prison house, silent, cheerless, and almost unconscious of his sad being. He was thus cut off entirely from all intercourse with his relations, and with the external world. He was allowed no amusement, no occupation. On the 10th of May, 1794, his aunt, the princess Elizabeth was guillotined and added another to the royal victims of the revolution; and the little prince and his captive sister, were left alone in the world. One more murder of helpless innocence and youth was yet wanted, to fill up the measure of the damnable infamy of the "Friends of Freedom."

The treatment of the dauphin had now been such for some months, that it must inevitably end in idiotcy or in death. He became more and more reduced. He could at length hardly leave his bed, and crawl to the stone jug which contained his water. He lost all appetite, and his tasteless food was left scattered about the floor of his prison, which became infested with rats, mice and the most offensive vermin. No cleansing had taken place for months, and the atmosphere became putrid and poisonous. As a necessary consequence, the health of the little sufferer became ruined, his frame became emaciated, his arms and knees were attacked with scrofulous swellings, his back became crooked; and death, more merciful than the "Friends of Liberty," would soon have ended the woes of his existence.

At this period, by some accident, it became noised abroad through Paris that the condition of the son of Louis XVI. was most pitiful and miserable. The rumor at length reached the convention; and curiosity induced that body to send Laurent, a member of the revolutionary committee, to examine into the state of the dauphin, and to assume the post of guardian over him. This person appears to have possessed an ordinary share of humanity, and to have been capable of feeling for the misfortunes of others. As soon as he was installed in his new post, he visited the cell of the dauphin and called him by name. He received no answer, and immediately ordered workmen to remove the iron bars of the door. He entered, and a horrid sight indeed presented itself to view. On the filthy bed there appeared to be laying something in the shape of a child, half covered with rags; offensive from the dirt with which it was covered; unable to move from the position in which it then was; and looking with mingled terror and astonishment at the visitor who thus disturbed his accustomed solitude. His head and neck were covered with sores; his wrists and knees were swelled enormously; the nails of his hands and feet had grown to long claws, and his whole appearance bore the impress of mingled idiotcy and death. His mind seemed to be gone. To the various questions put to him he made no answer; he only gazed with a vacant stare upon the intruders, and seemed striving to discern in the gloom and darkness of his horrid abode, their features and their forms. At length, being asked whether he wanted anything, he answered in feeble and almost inaudible accents; "*I want to die!*"

No time was to be lost if their unfortunate little sufferer was to be rescued from immediate death. His prison was cleaned. The barred windows were opened, so that the light and air might enter. A comfortable bed was prepared for him. His sores were dressed. His person was washed and clean linen provided for him. His hair was cut and combed; and other necessary changes were made in his situation. The child could not suppress his surprise at these marks of unaccustomed kindness; and expressed his gratitude to his benefactor in the most touching and affecting manner.

Notwithstanding this favorable change in the condition of the dauphin, his health seems to have gradually declined. The fatal work had already been accomplished; the seeds of death had been planted within him. In March, 1795, Laurent obtained permission to leave his post in the Temple, and bade farewell to his young friend, who was filled with gloom at his departure. The successor of Laurent was named *Lasne.* This man had been a soldier, and had frequently been on guard at the Tuileries, where he had seen the dauphin, and had become familiar with his features and person. He immediately recognized the young prince, and contrasted his present appearance and condition with the brighter and happier period of his existence. Though he treated his ward with the greatest kindness, three weeks elapsed before he could get a single word from him; so completely had terror and abuse subdued the spirit of the child, and filled him with continual apprehension. At length Lasne recalled to the recollection of the dauphin the little regiment of boys of which he had been the commander, at the Tuileries, and the maneuvers which Lasne had himself witnessed when on duty at that palace. It was the first pleasing reminiscence of the past which had cheered his youthful spirit for many months. After that incident the child became affectionately free and confidant to his keeper.

But his health continued to decline. In May, 1795, the convention was informed that the dauphin was dangerously ill. Dessault, a distinguished physician of Paris, was appointed to visit him. He expressed the opinion, that the child was gradually wasting away from the combined effect of scrofulous disease, and of confinement and ill-usage. He recommended that the invalid should be sent to the country, and declared that nothing but the air of the country could revive and restore him. But this only remedy which could accomplish so desirable a result, was positively refused. M. Dessault paid but two visits to the prince, and died on the first of June. There were those living at the time, who said that he had poisoned the dauphin, and had then himself been taken off to prevent any disclosures. Others asserted that he had detected that the invalid in the Temple was not the true dauphin but a substituted child, and that to prevent *this* disclosure, he was poisoned by the authorities. The answer to all these conjectures is that M. Dessault, who had been the physician formerly to the royal children, and knew their persons well, never expressed to any one any doubt as to the identity of the dauphin; nor did he leave any proof on record or in existence that he entertained such doubts.

After the death of Dessault, M. Pelletan was appointed by the committee of public safety to continue the medical treatment of the prince. He arrived after an interval of six days, and found his patient in a hopeless condition. All that he could do was to order his removal to another apartment, which was better aired, and had a more cheerful appearance. For a day or two the child seemed to revive. But the improvement was only temporary. On the 8th of July he again became much worse. Lasne, who was the first to see and converse with him, immediately discovered the traces of the advancing disease. At length he remarked to him, "How unhappy I am to see you suffering so much." The answer which he received was one of singular interest and mystery. "Oh yes," he answered, "I am suffering; but the music is so sweet!" Lasne was surprised, as well he might be, at this remarkable fantasy. He knew that there was no music anywhere in the Temple, or in the neighborhood of it. He therefore asked the prince, "Where do you hear the music?" "Above," said he. "How long since?" "Since you have been praying. Don't you hear it? Listen!" Lasne had knelt by the side of the bed, and had devoutly repeated several prayers. After a pause of surprise and pleasure, the dying child added with increased ecstacy, "In the midst of all the voices, I hear my mother's." After a further interval the child inquired, "Do you think my sister has heard the music?—how happy it would have made her." Lasne, overcome with emotion, could make no reply. The child turned his large eyes toward the opened window, and gazed intently upon the blue sky beyond it. His soul seemed wrought up to a high degree of tension, in listening to the unnatural melody which was soothing his dying moments. While he appeared thus engaged his eye began to grow dim, his countenance to lose its vitality, his body gradually sank into the arms of Lasne, and in a few moments, without a struggle, he ceased to breathe. The persecuted prince was free; his spirit had taken its everlasting flight. It was the eighth of July, 1795, a little more than two years after the execution of Louis XVI.

It might be an interesting inquiry to the philosopher and the psychologist, to account for the singular phenomenon just narrated, respecting the death of the dauphin; whether the hearing of the music in question is a proof that the spirits of the departed are permitted to cheer, with heavenly melody, the last moments of the dying; or whether it is to be regarded as a mere delusion of the departing and exhausted spirit; or whether its faculties can and do become so much strengthened, as its union with its clay tenement loosens, that it has power to hear in the spirit-land what is unheard by ordinary mortals. It is not our purpose to enter into a philosophical or theological inquiry on this subject; but it is worthy of remark that the historical truth of the incident in question is undoubted, and rests upon the most satisfactory authority. Such cases are not without parallels in the history of minds; though we know of no *satisfactory* solution which has yet been given of them.

CHAPTER VIII.

THE FALL OF ROBESPIERRE AND THE MOUNTAIN.

Until the year 1794 the power of Robespierre continued to increase with amazing rapidity, and to an unparalleled magnitude. In the preceding year he had boldly accused the most distinguished and able leaders of the Girondists,—Brissot, Vergniaud, Gaudet, and Gensonné,—as being secretly attached to Dumourier, and to the Royalist cause; and he had followed up that daring blow with attacks of such intense fury and resolution, that he had at length dragged those eminent men to the guillotine, along with an immense number of their more obscure associates. In the next place, he had directed his power against the anointed and crowned head of Maria Antoinette—and that head, once so brilliant and beautiful, rolled beneath the ax of the executioner. Passing on to other members of the royal family, his insatiable ferocity found new victims in the Duke of Orleans and Madam Elizabeth, the amiable sister of Louis XVI.

Then, not satisfied with the destruction of the highest of earthly powers and dignities, and of those who bore them, Robespierre even dared to confront the majesty of heaven, and impiously decreed the abolition of the Christian religion; he denied the future immortality of the soul; and elevating a half-naked prostitute of Paris on the high altar of the cathedral of Notre Dame, proclaimed in her person the universal reign of the Goddess of Reason.

And when other demagogues, as desperate and as unprincipled, but not as able as himself, advanced to the possession of a degree of power which endangered his own supremacy, he boldly struck at their heads, and sacrificed them, after a prodigious conflict, to his insatiable ambition. The powerful Danton, Hebert, and Camille Desmoulins, once his associates in nameless crimes, but afterward his rivals in the exercise of an infamous power, all fell victims to his superior and jealous nature; and expiated their career of blood and ambition on the scaffold.

Then followed the cruel and bloody war in La Vendee, all the excesses of which seemed to be instigated and protected by the power of Robespierre. And indeed after the death of Danton and Hebert, the authority which Robespierre had obtained was absolute and uncontrolled; and he exercised that power to the utter desolation of his native land, and to the destruction of everything which promotes the happiness and well-being of society. Whole cities, such as Lyons and Nantes, were razed to the ground; and thousands of their inhabitants were massacred in cold blood. The committee of public safety composed of Robespierre, St. Just, and Couthon were the possessors of absolute authority throughout France, and of that memorable committee, Robespierre was the heart and soul, and is personally responsible for all its atrocious deeds. He held under his control the National Guards, commanded by the brutal Henriot. He ruled the mountain in the convention; he was the divinity of the Jacobin club; and through these he governed the municipality and the departments of France. In June, 1794, Robespierre was more absolute in France, and far more terrible, than

Louis XIV. had ever been before him, or than Napoleon ever was after him.

A proof of this assertion may be seen in the fact, that at this time, by means of his emissaries and associates, he had thrown seven thousand persons into the various prisons of Paris; and the number of those in confinement throughout France was two hundred thousand. Their condition was wretched beyond description; and the amount of misery endured may be inferred from the fact, that the most of these prisoners were persons of respectability, who had been accustomed to the comforts of life, and were now deprived of everything adapted to make life endurable. The state of despair to which the community was reduced, the suspicion, the fear, the pervading terror, which spread a pall of sadness and gloom throughout the land, it would be impossible to describe. Every man regarded his neighbor as his hidden foe; and awaited with breathless apprehension the moment when his accusation would come from some unexpected, but inevitable source. The ties of relationship, the power of affection, the suggestions of honor, the impulses of gratitude, seem all to have wasted away beneath the withering effect of selfishness, suspicion, and hatred. The counting house of the merchant and the chateau of the nobleman were continually invaded by the insensate rabble under the pretext of searching for aristocrats; and no age or rank or sex were secure from the fangs of these human harpies.

The usual number of executions per day, during the height of Robespierre's supremacy was eighty. The carts which conveyed the victims to the place of execution were frequently filled with the most accomplished and beautiful women; and with the most distinguished and cultivated men. The princess of Monaco, in the prime of her blooming loveliness, was conveyed to the scaffold in the same wagon side by side with some of the most distinguished members of the Academy of Sciences; with Lavoisier, the illustrious chemist; with Florian, the eloquent novelist; with the son of Buffon the naturalist; and with the daughter of Vernet the painter. And these, with thousands more of the victims of the insensate ferocity of the revolutionary leaders, were condemned to death, without any form of trial or impartial examination whatever; and for no possible crime, but that they were not as infamous and blood-stained as their persecutors, but loved order, decency, and humanity. In the city of Arras, Le Bon, by Robespierre's orders, executed two thousand persons. Twenty thousand victims more fell beneath the relentless fury of Carrier at Nantes. In that city hundreds of children of both sexes, under the age of fourteen years, were shot. The shortness of their stature occasioned the bullets in many instances to pass over their heads. The terrified innocents rushed forward and clung around the knees of their executioners, praying for mercy. But no mercy was shown them. They were murdered at the point of the bayonet. From the 10th of June, 1794, to the 17th of July alone, the revolutionary tribunal at Paris condemned to death and executed twelve hundred and eighty-five persons. It will not be difficult to believe the truth of this enormous estimate, when we remember the process by which convictions were brought about. "Do you know of the conspiracy in the prison?" "No." "I expected you would say so, but that will not save you. You are condemned." To another the question was put, "Are you not a noble?" "Yes." "Go—you are guilty." To a third, "Are you not a priest?" "Yes." "Then follow him." Sometimes jests and jokes were used to diversify the horrors of the tribunal of death. An aged man who had by paralysis lost the use of his tongue, was placed at the bar. Being unable to make any answer when accused, the judge said jestingly, "Very well, we don't want his tongue, but his head!"

With such feeble hopes of justice before them when arraigned, and with such a dread atmosphere of suspicion and terror around them, it may readily be believed that the whole nation began to endure a living death, and to look around them for the means and the period of their deliverance from such unspeakable thraldom. Happily, the day of release was not far distant. Robespierre, as is always the case with tyrants, invited his own ruin by carrying his atrocities to an extreme which no human power could endure. The enemies of his person and his power were first found among those who had been his associates in revolutionary violence, but whom he now determined to remove from his path and to destroy.

It was to a woman, to Charlotte Corday, that the immortal honor belongs of having delivered France from the detested presence and diabolical influence of Marat. It was also to a woman far more beautiful but less virtuous than she, that the credit is due of having nerved the arm of Tallien to strike the deadly blow, at the very thought of which so many stout hearts trembled, but which was necessary to deliver France from the fatal despotism of Robespierre.

It was when on a political mission to Bordeaux, that Tallien first beheld the majestic beauty of the woman who afterward exercised so potent an influence over his destiny. She was in feeling a royalist. She detected in the eloquence of Tallien a powerful instrument by which she might recall her countrymen back to reason and humanity. She first obtained complete control over the mind and soul of Tallien, till at length the latter idolized her with an intensity of devotion never surpassed. Then it was that she stirred his spirit with a mighty spell, and invoking the nobler elements of his nature, led him to the determination to attempt the delivering of his country from the fell power of a bloody tyrant, or to perish nobly in the attempt.

On the 26th of July, (8th Thermidor,) Robespierre delivered a speech in the national convention, in which he made charges against the committee of general safety, and various members of the convention, as being hostile to liberty and to the complete triumph of the revolution. He urged the abolition of the committee of general safety, and the concentration of all power into the hands of one person. He urged the convention to punish with death all its unworthy members. Here was a demand for greater power, and for more blood of the representatives of the people. Robespierre had drawn up a list of the representatives whom he proposed to immolate on his bloody altar. This list was headed by the name of Tallien, and contained the names of Thurist, Guffroi, Bourdon de l'Oise, Legendre, Vadier, members of the committee of general safety, and many more. By some accident Tallien became aware of the purpose of Robespierre, and of his own unenviable prominence on the fatal catalogue. He saw that it was now time to strike the decisive blow; and he communicated to the others proscribed, the purposes of Robespierre concerning themselves. The period had now arrived for the occurrence of one of the most furious and deadly conflicts ever displayed in a deliberative assembly. The 27th of July at length dawned, a memorable day in French history. During the preceding night the conspirators with Tallien at their head, had held a long and secret meeting, in which they had matured their plans, and determined on the course to be pursued, to overturn the power of the tyrant. When the Assembly met the next day, an air of decision and desperate determination marked the demeanor of the representatives, indicating their purpose to succeed or perish in the impending struggle.

At one o'clock, St. Just ascended the tribune, and began to speak upon the proposition contained in the address of Robespierre on the preceding day. "I belong," said he, "to no party. I will oppose them all. This tribune may become a Tarpeian rock to me, when I tell you that the members of the convention have wandered from the path of wisdom." Here Tallien, determined no longer to delay, arose and interrupted St. Just. "Shall you," said he, "arrogate to yourself the right to denounce, accuse, and proscribe the members of this assembly? You are but the satellite of a tyrant, who yesterday began to raise the vail before our eyes, of the horrors he still proposes to perpetrate. I will tear that vail asunder, and will exhibit the danger in its full extent, and the tyrant in his true colors."

Robespierre had taken his seat opposite the tribune, determined to overawe the hostile speakers by the fierceness of his countenance. But when the clarion tones of Tallien's eloquence resounded throughout the hall, he began to tremble, and his face became deadly pale. He would have risen to interrupt Tallien, but the energy and resolution of the latter were indomitable. He then proceeded to describe the plans of blood on which Robespierre had determined. "The massacre," said he, "was to have begun with the committees of public safety and general security, and other members of the convention. Let us take instant measures to prevent the purposes of the assassins, for they are more than one. I will name them. First, there is Dumas, the president of the infamous revolutionary tribunal. There is Henriot, the drunken commander of the National Guards. And there is Robespierre, the center of this blood-thirsty conspiracy, and his associates in the committee of public safety, St. Just and Couthon. Is there a voice among you, who will not declare that Robespierre is a tyrant? Tremble! wretch, tremble!" said he, pointing to the form of Robespierre which then shook with agitation and fury before him. "We enjoy your agony; and I declare, that if the convention refuses to pass the decree of accusation against you, I will plunge this dagger into your heart;" and he drew forth the glittering blade, and brandished it before his foe, while the hall resounded with the acclamations of the deputies.

Robespierre attempted in vain, during the loud tumult

which followed this outburst, to obtain a hearing from the convention. The president of that body was his personal foe; and whenever the distracted deputy endeavored to speak, he rang his bell so loudly as to drown his shrieking voice. In vain Robespierre turned from one side of the hall to the other, imploring to be heard. "Pure and virtuous citizens," exclaimed he, "will you not permit me to speak?" Finding that the tumult of the assembly would not be calmed by the use of persuasive tones, and seeing their determined purpose to drown his utterance, he at length screamed at the top of his voice: "President of assassins! for the last time I demand to speak!" The tumult only increased; and Robespierre at length sank down upon his seat exhausted, panting, and foaming at the mouth. His voice was gone, and he in vain attempted to recover his self-possession and his utterance. After a few moments, the eyes of the exulting assembly being still fixed upon the exasperated but enfeebled wretch, a voice exclaimed, "It is the blood of Danton which chokes him!" And then the overthrown but unconquered despot uttered one of his sudden repartees, which, under the circumstances, is one of the finest and sublimest things recorded in history: "Is it Danton whom you would avenge? Wretches, why then did you not dare to defend him!"

Immediately the act of accusation was proposed and carried. Robespierre, his younger brother, Le Bas, St. Just, Couthon, Dumas, and Henriot, were put under arrest, and sent to prison; and the assembly adjourned at five o'clock.

The moral dignity and grandeur of this celebrated scene were certainly of a high character. In the convention Robespierre had yet many ardent adherents. The terror of his name was still overpowering; he possessed the prestige of his past immense success; and before that day, to have seriously opposed any measure which emanated from him, was the certain death-warrant of the bold adventurer. But on this occasion for the first time, the will of the blood-stained dictator was directly resisted; and Tallien, with a degree of heroism deserving of immortal honor, dared not only to oppose but to stigmatize, to accuse, to condemn him. And then, the means employed to crush the will, and drown the eloquence of Robespierre, were peculiar. It was only a matter of strength of lungs between one feeble, agitated, screaming wretch, and five hundred vociferating deputies; who, when the perilous pathway had once been opened by their heroic leader, all joined with hearty good-will in defeating and baffling the attempts of the fallen tyrant to regain the power which he had so suddenly lost. Robespierre, it must be confessed, possessed but a small chance of success with five hundred deputies doing their best to cough, scream and roar him under!

No sooner however had the magistrates heard that Robespierre had been arrested, than they sent a force to Conciergerie prison to release him. He was immediately conducted to the Hotel de Ville, where he found his brother, and St. Just. They were received by the magistrates with acclamation.

The assembly met again at eight o'clock the same evening, and were informed of the release of the prisoners. Terror and irresolution for a few moments pervaded the stoutest hearts. In this emergency, Tallien again displayed his indomitable heroism. Said he, "Everything conspires to secure the liberty of France. Robespierre, by resisting the decree of the assembly which declared him under arrest, has placed himself *hors la loi*." The assembly instantly decreed that Robespierre and his associates were opposing the government. The sections were convoked, and Barras placed in command of them. The *générale* beat. The sections were ordered to the defense of the convention. The municipality were summoned to their bar. A message was sent to the cannoniers in the Place de Carousal to attack the Hotel de Ville where Robespierre still remained.

The rapid adoption of these measures saved the lives, and decided the fate of Tallien and his party. While their execution progressed, all Paris was in a state of the most fearful and anxious excitement. On every side the bewildered multitude hurried to and fro, uncertain what to do or what to believe. The solemn tones of the loud tocsin resounded through the heavy air of night, carrying terror over the whole capital, and far beyond the barriers, through the adjoining country. The hundreds of proscribed persons who had been long concealed in the hidden recesses of Paris, hearing the rumor which men whispered with pale lips, that Robespierre had been arrested, cautiously crept forth from their secret dens, to be assured of the glorious tidings. Even into the prisons the deep sounds of agitation penetrated. The prisoners knew that some great crisis was transpiring beyond their gloomy walls. Their relatives and friends approached their grated windows, and whispered the welcome news that their great butcher was at length shorn of his power, and that they might yet escape his deadly fangs.

Robespierre and his party still remained at the Hotel de Ville, hoping that the arrival of the National Guards would soon put an end to the doubtful conflict; for at their head he had determined to march to the hostile convention, disperse them, and then resume the reins of power which had fallen from his grasp. But the National Guards had been won over by the active agents of the convention, and did not advance to the protection and support of Robespierre. Henriot, descending the stairs of the hotel, and finding the square in front deserted, returned in despair to his associates. He informed them of the hopeless posture of their affairs. Here was the turning point of the revolution. At this moment had Robespierre possessed resolution sufficient to enable him to arouse the hesitating attachment of the National Guards, the cannoniers, and of the municipality, he might yet have succeeded in crushing the power of the convention, led on by Tallien, and still divided in its purpose.

But this eloquent and pertinacious orator, Robespierre, was devoid of the energy and moral courage necessary to this great crisis. As soon as Henriot informed him that the National Guard had failed to march to the Hotel de Ville, he gave himself up to despair. At this moment, determined not to fall into the hands of his enemies, he discharged his pistol at his head. He escaped immediate death, but inflicted a frightful wound on his lower jaw. Le Bas blew out his own brains. Couthon attempted to stab himself, but had not courage to accomplish the deed.

Coffinhal and the younger Robespierre endeavored to escape by the window.

The bleeding body of Robespierre was soon dragged by the mob to the assembly. They refused to admit him; he was then conveyed, together with Couthon, to the hall of the committee of general safety, where they lay for nine hours, their wounds still bleeding, stretched upon a table on which they had signed the death warrants of thousands of their victims. From this spot, on the next morning, they were conveyed to the revolutionary tribunal, where, with a rapidity of process which they had themselves so often used, they were immediately condemned to death.

Early in the morning of the 29th of July, all Paris was in eager motion, to witness the righteous retribution about to be inflicted on the fallen tyrant. He was placed in a wagon between Henriot and Couthon, and commenced that dismal journey on which he had sent so many of his fellow creatures, in the prime of life and hope. Along the route the immense multitude gave utterance to their joy in loud shouts of exultation. He was conducted to the Place de la Revolution, the spot on which his illustrious victims, Louis XVI. and his unfortunate queen, had expired. When the bandage which confined his broken jaw broke, the blood overflowed his dress. Ere he reached the spot, frantic men and women, approaching the wagon, hurled the bitterest curses against him. Said one, "Murderer of all my kindred, descend to hell, burdened with the execrations of every mother in France!" When the executioner tore off the bandage which supported his jaw, it fell to the ground; and he uttered a yell, which filled the gazing multitude with horror. As the ax descended which severed from its body the head which had been the greatest curse which ever afflicted France, the shouts and exultation of the vast multitude shook the earth, and resounded far and wide over the desolated city.

The amount of misery which this great, bad man inflicted on his unhappy country, during the several years of his fatal supremacy, can scarcely be computed. Some idea however may be formed from the actual number of executions which took place during this period of the revolution. It has been accurately computed by Prudhomme, that there were slain one thousand two hundred and seventy-eight noblemen, seven hundred and fifty noble women; of wives of laborers and artisans one thousand four hundred and sixty-seven; of nuns, three hundred and fifty; of priests, one thousand one hundred and thirty-five; of common people, thirteen thousand six hundred and twenty-three. Of those guillotined by the revolutionary tribunals, there were eighteen thousand six hundred. Of men slain in La Vendee, there were nine hundred thousand. Of the victims of Carrier at Nantes, there were thirty-two thousand. Of women killed in La Vendee, there were fifteen thousand; making a sum total, including a few other items, of one million and twenty-two thousand persons, of all ranks and ages, immolated on the bloody altar of revolutionary fury and violence. Such were the terrific consequences of the perverted talents of these revolutionary heroes.

And yet it is related, that until a few years since two maiden sisters of Robespierre survived at Paris, living in genteel retirement, and that they always expressed astonishment at the censure and execrations which were heaped upon the head of their brother throughout the civilized world! They only remembered him as an affectionate relative, who had provided for their wants with fraternal solicitude, and they could not comprehend how such a man as they knew their brother to have been, could ever display qualities so savage and ferocious as those which were universally ascribed to him. It was indeed an impressive commentary on the undying strength of a sister's attachment, that the only lips which ever uttered words of esteem or regard for the fallen and murderous Jacobin throughout all the world, were those of the two persons to whom we have just referred!

When the head of Robespierre and his associates fell beneath the avenging ax of the guillotine, they left France in a state of prostration, poverty, and ruin, of which the mind can scarcely form any conception. The monthly expenses of the revolutionary government had been three hundred millions of francs. The receipts of the treasury never exceeded one third of this sum. The only possible mode of supplying this deficiency, was by the issue of assignats, or paper-money; which were intended to pass at par, but which soon fell to one-twentieth of its nominal value. The losses of those who held this worthless scrip may readily be imagined. The whole nation became afflicted with a grinding poverty. The nobles had all been despoiled of their wealth; and the middle classes were oppressed by the issue and depreciation of the paper currency. Excitement, idleness, and debauchery had rendered the lower orders more impoverished than ever.

Hence the degree of wretchedness which existed will scarcely be credited. Even the highest servants of the government subsisted on the most trifling pittances. *Pichegru*, at the head of an army of fifty thousand men, received only forty dollars per month. The gifted *Hoche*, commander of the army of La Vendee, composed of one hundred thousand men, wrote to the convention asking them to procure him a horse, as he was utterly without means to obtain one. And if such was the state of destitution which afflicted men of the highest eminence in rank and power, how much more desperate must have been the condition of the multitudes who occupied inferior stations, both in the public service and in private life.

Then in addition to these pecuniary distresses, imagine a whole nation clad in the deepest mourning, for the murder of a million of its noblest and best citizens! The country was covered far and near with chateaux sacked and burned; with villages desolated; with crops destroyed; with all the implements of husbandry, and all the materials for manufactures, lost and ruined. It must surely be admitted that if ever, in the blood-stained history of this earth, any nation presented a close resemblance to all the horrors of Pandemonium, France, once the land of gay revelry, of refinement, and of distinction in art, letters, and every form of elegance and magnificence, presented that resemblance, when she lay agonizing beneath the deadly fangs of the demons of revolution, debauchery and infidelity.

After the death of Robespierre and his most infamous accomplices, the convention received an infusion of the friends of order and constitutional government. After a severe struggle a new constitution was prepared; and on the 4th of October, 1795, the government took the form of two representative bodies called the councils, together with an executive branch consisting of five persons denominated the directory. The officers selected were Moulin, Gohier, Sieyes, Barras, and Roger-Ducos. While these men feebly guided the destinies of France, the meteor-star of Napoleon's glory suddenly arose on the rugged isle of Corsica; and began from the ensanguined plains of Italy to cast abroad its bright effulgence over the continent of Europe.

CHAPTER IX.

NAPOLEON'S EXPEDITION TO EGYPT.

From his earliest youth, the glowing imagination of Napoleon had been haunted by the brilliant idea of establishing a new empire in the east. There was to him a nameless grandeur and romance in the project, of leaving behind him the effete and worn out climes of Europe, and invading with a mighty and irresistible armament, those same countries which had witnessed, two thousand years before, the triumphant march of Alexander's legions; and of establishing there an empire as magnificent but more durable than his. There was a novelty and glory in the idea of a bold and gifted adventurer from the west, such as himself, of advancing as a conqueror without an invitation or a warning through the remote and unique climes of the east; and his mind glowed with a new rapture at the thought of erecting on the ruins of crumbling oriental dynasties, a throne of stupendous majesty and power, which would not only surpass those of all other eastern potentates, but also one which would extort the admiration of the monarchs of Europe itself.

Of all the countries of the east, Egypt was on many accounts the most important and suitable, as an incipient conquest. It was an immense country, possessed of vast resources. It was still a dependency on the feeble crumbling scepter of the sultan. It was the highway of England, Holland, and other great commercial communities of Europe, to their rich possessions in the east. It was a central country from which, having made a triumphant beginning to his vast career of conquest, he could extend his power to Abyssinia, to Arabia, to Persia, and other neighboring countries. His majestic and powerful fleets could ride securely on the Nile; whose broad bosom would be covered, by his means, with the rich commerce of the world. The waters of the Mediterranean would waft to his dominions the luxuries and polished products of the west. The Red Sea would form a convenient channel through which he could secure the rich and rare commodities of the farther east—of China and the Indies. The Grand Cairo would form a capital whose magnificence and extent, whose gorgeous palaces and luxuriant gardens would be worthy of so great and powerful an empire; while Alexandria, renovated by him from the crumbling decrepitude of ages, would regain her pristine splendor, and become a fit sea-port for an empire to which the commerce, the arts, refinement, and luxury of the world had, by so sudden, yet so potent a charm, been irresistibly attracted.

Such were some of the brilliant phantasies which glowed in the ardent mind of Napoleon. After his successful career in Italy he returned to Paris, and was received by the directory in the Luxembourg palace, with great state and splendor. The colors taken from the Austrians in Italy were presented by him to the directory, together with a copy of the treaty of Campo Formio, in which the most humiliating concessions had been made by Austria to France. After his return, however, Napoleon's mind was not unoccupied, though he was not engaged in any public trust. His brilliant victories in Italy had already won him an European reputation, and he was balancing in his restless and sagacious mind the course which it behooved him next to pursue.

To remain long idle in Paris was not in the nature of Bonaparte. Besides, he had now become so powerful, that he was already an object of jealousy to the directory. If he aspired to a place with them in the government, they knew that he would soon become absolute ruler, and they absolute cyphers. If he did not obtain a seat in the directory, they feared, and with justice, that he would become the center of all the discontented intriguers and adventurers in the capital, and might soon ascend to the possession of power over their ruins. In either case, to permit Napoleon to remain long unoccupied at Paris was the presage of ruin to the directory. Hence it was that in January, 1798, at the suggestion of Barras he was appointed to the command of the army of England. But after carefully examining the coasts of the British channel on both sides, he came to the sagacious conclusion, that the time for the invasion of England had not yet arrived. Accordingly, he declined the appointment which had been tendered him. His mind again reverted to his schemes of oriental conquest; and after a short interval he persuaded the directory to appropriate the armament intended for the descent upon England to the expedition to the east. The principal motive which induced Barras and the directory to acquiesce in a project which to their short-sighted vision appeared chimerical in the extreme, was the same prudent wish to get rid of the insatiable ambition and the dangerous popularity of the conqueror of Italy. They indulged the secret hope that both of these would find an early and a nameless grave beneath the treacherous and shifting sands of Lybia.

The preparations made by Napoleon for this memorable expedition, were on a large and magnificent scale. He obtained from the directory the appropriation of forty thousand of the best troops of the army of Italy. The fleet of Admiral Bruyes, composed of thirteen ships of the line and fourteen frigates, was placed under his orders. Three millions of francs which had been seized by the directory at Berne—the ancient and long accumulated treasure of that republic, the product of Swiss industry and economy for two hundred years—was granted for the purpose of defraying the expenses of the expedition. To the possession of this cherished store of the Bernese republicans, the directory had no other claim, whatever, than the claim of the stronger over the weaker, of the triumphant over the defenseless.

It was on the 19th of May, 1798, that the French fleet set sail from the port of Toulon. This magnificent armament had been considerably augmented by the indefatigable exertions of Napoleon. It now consisted of thirteen ships of the line, sixteen frigates, seventy-two brigs, and four hundred transports. It carried thirty-six thousand soldiers of every description, and ten thousand sailors. Napoleon sailed first to Ajaccio, and Civita Castellana, and there united with his fleet the squadrons then cruising in those ports. With his force thus increased, he set sail for Malta; and on the 10th of June he hove in sight of the imposing and magnificent works of that celebrated fortress which extended for several miles along the horizon, presenting a front of vast extent and magnitude.

It was Napoleon's purpose to storm the fortifications; but the necessity for hostile measures was obviated by the successful intrigues which he had for some time past been carrying on with the grand master and the leading knights of the order of St. John. Baron Hompesch, the grand master, after considerable secret negotiation with Napoleon, had stipulated that he would surrender the fortress, on condition that he should receive six hundred thousand francs, a principality in Germany, or a pension for life of three hundred thousand francs; and that the French cavaliers should receive a pension of seven hundred francs a year each, for life. On these ignoble terms this ancient fortress, so renowned in the history of christian warfare and chivalry, was surrendered; with the possession of all its vast bulwarks, splendid churches, magnificent palaces, and the treasures of plate and munitions of war, which the noble knights of previous ages had secured and erected as the fruit of many memorable achievements of heroism and fortitude.

Napoleon gazed with rapture on the innumerable fortifications which he had so easily won. The luxury and splendor of the palaces which the successive grand masters had erected, filled him and his officers with admiration and astonishment. So deep was the harbor, that the L'Orient, a vessel so immensely large that it had grounded on leaving the port of Toulon, sailed up without obstruction to the very quay; and its extent was so great, that six hundred ships of the line could securely and conveniently ride within it. Napoleon strongly manned all the batteries with detachments of his own troops; and on the 19th of June set sail for the coast of Egypt.

On the 1st of July the French fleet came in sight of the low coast of that country. Napoleon narrowly escaped the English fleet under Lord Nelson, which had been scouring the seas for some weeks, in eager search of him. The English fleet had only deserted the roads two days before the arrival of the French armament; and it is certain, that if the hero of Trafalgar had then fallen in with the object of his pursuit, a furious battle would have ensued, which would materially have altered the fortunes of the world. The English commander would undoubtedly have achieved a signal victory, because his force was superior to that of the French, and the latter were encumbered with the vast number of land troops which the fleet was conveying to Egypt. The sea would have been strewed with wrecks of the French fleet; thousands would have found a watery grave; and this bold and wonderful expedition would have had a premature and an inglorious termination.

But a more brilliant fate was reserved for the adventurous Corsican. Exulting in the narrow escape which he had just made, he ordered his troops instantly to disembark. Early the next day he advanced at the head of five thousand men and attacked the ramparts of the city of Alexandria, which were defended by an insufficient number of Mamelukes. After a short conflict the latter were driven from their posts; the gates were opened, and the French troops entered on their first conquest in Egypt. They found the city, which the mighty Alexander had founded, a confused mass of magnificence and ruin. Yet as a presage of future triumph, its subjugation was an event of great importance. The invaders were quartered in the city, which they found already impoverished and reduced by misfortunes and grinding exactions, to a most lamentable degree. The harbor which was situated in one of the mouths of the Nile, was nearly choked up with sand. No ships could now approach the spot where once all the navies of the world could easily and securely ride at anchor. The city was ruled by the Mamelukes, a body of Turkish soldiers, who had been sent by the sultan to exercise civil and military authority over the abject and feeble Egyptians. The Mamelukes themselves were under the authority of their Beys, officers conferred directly by the sultan.

Having garrisoned the works of Alexandria with as many of his own troops as were necessary for its defense, Napoleon determined immediately to advance into the interior of the country. The grand Cairo, the ancient capital of Egypt, was the next object of the invader's ambition; and he resolved instantly to commence the perilous march across the desert to reach it.

From Alexandria to Cairo the pathway lay across the treacherous sands of a sterile waste, some three hundred miles in extent. This boundless plain of sand was cheered and relieved neither by shade nor water; for no tree or bush could draw subsistence from the barren soil, and the few wells which existed had been filled up by the Bedowins, the untamed children of the desert. A tropical sun poured down its burning rays on the troops, and scorched and seared every living thing. The fine, light sands came floating along in clouds over the plain, and filled the eyes and mouths of the parched and thirsty travelers. The hostile Arabs hovered around the advancing columns, and harassed them with unceasing attacks. Every now and then, the exhausted troops were cheered by a delicious vision in the far distance, of a calm and refreshing lake, reposing on the bosom of the wilderness. They shouted for joy, and rapidly advanced to plunge into its cooling and invigorating waters. They approached the spot, and found that they had been deceived by the *mirage* of the desert; and disappointment and deep despair began to overwhelm the spirits of the most daring and intrepid.

It would require at least a week for the French army to pass through the desert; and already on the third day, the most horrible disasters had befallen them. Their sufferings from thirst had already become unendurable. Hundreds of men, horses, and camels had perished by the way, from want of water. Even the intrepid Lannes and Murat threw themselves on the ground, and rolled upon it in paroxysms of despair. The drifting sands destroyed the eyesight of hundreds of the soldiers. Their eyeballs rotted and fell out. Desaix, who commanded the vanguard, sent a courier to Napoleon in the rear, declaring that if the army did not hasten forward with the utmost rapidity, it would perish. "The whole desert," said he, "does not contain water enough for a thousand men, and we are thirty thousand. For heaven's sake do not leave us in this situation, but give the order either to retire rapidly or to advance. I am in despair, at being compelled to write to you in the language of despondency;

but when we have escaped our present horrible position, I hope my usual firmness will return."

At length, after a march of a week marked by the most horrible sufferings, and by considerable losses, the parched and wearied army arrived in sight of the wished-for Nile, and beheld its bright, silver stream rolling sluggishly along before them, glittering on the bosom of the desert. The ranks were immediately broken, and the tumultuous crowd rushed with rapture to the banks of the river, to quench their burning thirst. Many even threw themselves into the cool and flowing flood, and all forgot, in the gratification of the present moment, the mortal agonies of the past.

After resting for several days on the welcome banks of the river, the French army resumed its march along the stream toward Cairo. For seven days the journey continued. The troops passed through a deserted country, from which all the inhabitants had fled in terror. At length, on the 21st of July, Napoleon, riding at the head of his columns, first beheld with rapture the distant summits of the mighty pyramids, and not far off, the glittering minarets of the capital of Egypt.

To resist the approach of the invaders, Mourad Bey, at that time governor of Egypt under the Porte, had collected together all his best troops, consisting of eight thousand Mameluke cavalry—the most splendid and effective in the world—together with ten thousand Arabs, Copts, and Fellaks. His camp on the bank of the Nile was defended by forty pieces of artillery. It was also protected by rude field-works; and the force thus opposed to the French army was altogether the most formidable which had been mustered in Egypt for many years. His army was already drawn out on the plain in battle array, to oppose the further advance of the French.

Napoleon immediately made his dispositions for the battle. He formed his columns into hollow squares, and advanced to the attack. It was an anxious moment. In a far distant clime, a few adventurers were now about, for the first time, to meet a formidable foe. Defeat would be synonymous with destruction. Napoleon in a few words eloquently harangued his troops. Pointing toward the pyramids, whose vast summits loomed far up solemnly and sublimely into the clear, azure heavens before them, he said, "Remember, that from the top of those pyramids forty centuries contemplate your conduct in this battle!"

Mourad Bey, perceiving that the French had formed in order of battle, and were slowly advancing, detached his eight thousand Mameluke cavalry from the rest, and approached the hostile squares at the height of their speed. These troops presented an imposing and magnificent appearance. They were splendidly accoutred, and the harness of their powerful horses glittered with silver mountings. The beys were all around with cimeters and pistols; and as their long line rapidly advanced over the plain, the earth shook beneath their heavy tread; and the shock which ensued, when they clashed with the advancing columns of the French, was prodigious. At the first collision several of the squares of the latter were broken. But they were soon reformed again, and the rolling fire of their musketry did tremendous execution among the serried ranks of the Egyptian cavalry. The latter, in their desperation, exerted themselves to break the solid squares of the French; but in vain. Slowly they rode around them, and whenever they could perceive the slightest chasm, they attempted to dash in and penetrate. These few, more successful than the rest, soon were dispatched, and the squares again closed over and around their prostrate bodies. Again and again they dashed their horses against those ramparts of steel, but could not break them; and they gradually wasted away beneath the flaming walls of unremitting fire, upon whose deadly and immovable front they could make no impression.

After an hour's hard fighting, the Mamelukes began to discover the hopelessness of their endeavors to produce any effect whatever upon the squares of the French, and panic began to spread through their ranks. Several thousand were already slain, and at length the rest took to flight. They retreated toward the pyramids. The French, adroitly extending their squares like a fan, pursued them. They attacked the entrenched camp, and soon the works, together with all the ammunition and baggage of the Mamelukes, fell into the hands of the French. Seeing the total rout of his army, Mourad Bey fled with the remains of his once formidable cavalry across the desert into Upper Egypt, and the proud conqueror of the "Battle of the Pyramids," entered Cairo, and quartered his troops in its sumptuous palaces without the least resistance.

Plunged into the great vortex of oriental luxury in the capital of Egypt, the French army for a short time seemed to have realized their most romantic dreams; while Bonaparte, in swaying the scepter of the ancient Ptolemies, for a moment may have imagined that his ambitious projects in the east were about to be accomplished. He endeavored to obtain the confidence of the inhabitants of Cairo, by joining with them in their religious ceremonies. He permitted the *imans* still to administer justice as before. He disturbed none of the municipal arrangements of the city. He only held with a firm hand the reins of political authority. The consequence was that the Egyptians, for the first time in their lives, enjoyed the advantages of a regular and impartial government; and soon the evident benefits which resulted from the presence and supremacy of the invaders, made the vanquished hug and cherish the chains which bound them.

But after a short time spent in the full enjoyment of the novel luxuries and pleasures of the Egyptian capital, the French troops began to weary of them. The monotony of eastern life soon commenced to pall upon their senses, and they felt an irresistible inclination to return to their home in the west. Even the project of further conquest in the east had lost all its charms for them. They had secured and enjoyed the richest conquest which that whole hemisphere contained; and of it they had already become satiated and disgusted. At length the disaffection become so great, that Napoleon threatened to shoot any one, officer or private, who would dare to speak to him in reference to the project of abandoning the expedition.

On the first of August, 1798, was fought the celebrated battle of the Nile, between the fleets of France and England—a battle so disastrous to the power and supremacy of France in the east. The number of vessels in each fleet was about equal. Nelson commanded on board his vessels ten thousand men and ten hundred and twelve guns. The French admiral, Bruyes, had eleven thousand men and eleven hundred and ninety-six guns. The British ships were all seventy-fours, while several of those of the French were much heavier, some carrying eighty guns, some one hundred and one—the celebrated flag-ship, the L'Orient, one hundred and twenty guns. The French fleet lay at anchor in the bay of Aboukir, admirably disposed in line of battle, in front of the harbor of Alexandria, which they had been unable to enter in consequence of the shoals of sand which obstructed its mouth. Nelson, having reconnoitred the position of his foe, determined to force his way through his line, and thus double his whole fleet around a part of the line of the French ships. The advantage gained by this novel and sagacious device was evinced by the issue of the battle.

This memorable conflict began at three o'clock in the afternoon. The shores of the bay were covered with thousands of Arabs and Egyptians, who beheld with awe and wonder the horrible havoc, and the prodigious skill and fortitude displayed by the two foremost nations of the world, in a great conflict which all felt would be decisive and memorable in the history of their own country, and in that of the powerful and bold invaders who had so suddenly appeared in their midst. The combatants themselves were fully conscious of the vast importance of the occasion. Nelson had been scouring the seas in pursuit of the French fleet ever since the surrender of Malta. For days he had neither eaten nor slept. At length, when he saw the object of his search advantageously anchored in line of battle, his exultation was extreme, and he instantly gave the signal for action. The French on their side were equally ready and eager for the conflict. They had waited long, in a state of inactivity, for the decisive moment to arrive; and the vast size of their vessels, and their advantageous position, led them to indulge in the hope of certain victory. Their admiral, Bruyes, was the most experienced and distinguished seaman of whom their country could boast, and every circumstance conspired to give them confidence.

As the English ships, the Leander, the Culloden, the Alexander, and the Swiftsure, passed within the line of the French vessels, they suffered severely from the tremendous raking fire of the French; but no sooner had they taken up their positions—one vessel on the outer bow, and another on the outer quarter of the French ships—than the tide of conquest began to turn. The conflict was tremendous. The combatants fought with desperate courage; and seemed determined to end the conflict only with victory or death. The scene was fearfully sublime. When the darkness of evening settled down over the contending fleets, the horizon was illuminated for many miles by the incessant discharge of two thousand pieces of artillery, and the earth and ocean shook with the prodigious concussion. The vast sea of blazing fire appeared like some fierce volcano, whose mouth belched forth an ocean of flame in the midst of the watery waste.

At length, by nine o'clock, the English had obtained a complete and unparalleled victory. About that time the L'Orient, a vast ship of one hundred and twenty guns, which carried the French admiral, was found to be on fire, and soon the flames extended beyond the possibility of their being subdued. As the fire approached the magazine, many of the sailors and officers fled from the ship; but her commander determined to die the death of the heroic and unconquerable; and remained on board. At length, at ten o'clock the explosion took place. The concussion was terrific—without a parallel in ancient or modern warfare. The earth and sea shook for miles around, and soon after, the burning fragments of the unfortunate vessel fell from the prodigious height to which they had been carried, far and wide over the fleets. The sea was now covered with the floating, burning, and shattered wrecks of the French ships; and when daylight dawned upon the horrid scene, a spectable was presented which has no parallel in naval history. Not a single ship except two remained in the possession of the French, of all that vast and imposing armament, which on the day before had defied the world, and rode triumphantly upon the wave. The Guillaume Tell and the Generaux alone escaped, to carry back to France the dreadful story of this unequaled and memorable disaster. All the other ships of the French fleet fell into the possession of the English; except the L'Orient and La Serieuse, which had sunk. Eight thousand of the French troops had been wounded or slain. Admiral Bruyes perished with his vessel. For twelve miles the shore was covered with fragments of the wrecks, and the surface of the sea was filled with the floating bodies of the dead. The commanders of all the French vessels had been either killed or wounded. The English had lost but nine hundred men in killed and wounded, in that dreadful conflict.

This battle was the death-blow to French conquest in

the east. Napoleon heard the disastrous news at Cairo, and for a moment, even his daring and desperate courage was appalled and overpowered by the magnitude of the disaster. Despair completely prostrated the minds of the French soldiers, and with the impulsive ardor of their nation, many blew out their brains, and others threw themselves into the Nile. The troops now saw that their only means of transport to their native land had been taken away from them; and they felt as if doomed to die in a strange land, eternal exiles from the homes which they now loved the more intensely, as the prospect of returning to them became the more remote and uncertain.

Disasters accumulated around the unfortunate invaders. Immediately on receiving intelligence of the battle of the Nile, the sultan formally declared war against France. At the same time, an insurrection against the French occurred in the streets of Cairo. The Turks took refuge in the mosques against the forces ordered out by Napoleon to suppress the riot; and some of these sacred edifices were assaulted and battered to the ground. After five thousand of the inhabitants had been slain, order and peace was again restored.

It was not difficult for a man of Napoleon's sagacity to discover, that the only means of counteracting the effect of all these disasters, of saving himself from disgrace, and his army from ruin, was to commence active operations on the offensive, and by some new and bold conquest again to overawe the vacillating inhabitants of the east. Accordingly, he ordered Desaix to march with a strong detachment of troops into Upper Egypt, and there pursue and attack the broken remains of Mourad Bey's troops.

On the 7th of October Desaix with twenty-five hundred men attacked the Turks at Sidiman, numbering four thousand Mamelukes and six thousand Fellahs, and again the hollow squares into which the French were formed, defied the fiercest assaults of the heavy cavalry, and at the same time mowed down, with their continuous rolling fire, the serried ranks of their assailants. The Egyptians and Turks were again defeated with great slaughter; and the battle was decisive of the future fate of Upper Egypt. The French advanced through the rich country, until at last they rested in triumph beneath the shade of the stupendous ruins of Luxor, and of the mighty sphinxes and sepulchral monuments of Thebes.

In pursuance of his plan of continued conquest Napoleon meanwhile determined to anticipate the attacks which he expected from the sultan's power, by an hostile invasion into Syria; where the sultan was then assembling a formidable force. On the 11th of February, 1799, he commenced his march, over the desert which marks the confines of the two continents, Africa and Asia. In six days he reached El Arish, where he defeated the Mamelukes, assaulted their camp, and stormed the fortress. Having continued his march toward Palestine, he at length entered that celebrated country on the 4th of March. The first town and fortress that lay in his way was Jaffa, the Joppa of sacred antiquity. The garrison resisted valiantly; but after a fierce and continued conflict of several days, the works were carried, and the town was given over to all the horrors of war. Four thousand troops of the garrison became prisoners; and in the horrible fate which soon awaited them, is found the blackest stigma of infamy, perfidy, and atrocious inhumanity which disgraces the whole career of Napoleon—a career not otherwise devoid of scenes of sanguinary ferocity. These prisoners were disarmed; but it was a question of much more difficulty to determine what was afterward to be done with four thousand prisoners, under the peculiar circumstances in which the triumphant invaders were then placed.

During two days this difficult question was debated in a council of war. It was urged if these prisoners were released, though unarmed, they would at once unite with the hostile ranks of the Turks at Acre, or with the Arabs of the desert who continually harassed the rear and flanks of the army. If they were retained and guarded in captivity by the French troops, it would be impossible to find subsistence for them. The difficulty of procuring rations for the French soldiers was already very great. At the same time, the difficulty of guarding so large a body of prisoners was immense; and would require the services of half the army. Napoleon resolved at last that they should be shot, as the only expedient which it was safe to adopt under the circumstances! In pursuance of this bloody and inhuman purpose, these four thousand defenseless human beings were marched handcuffed down to the sandy shore of the sea-coast, were formed into small squares and there were deliberately shot down in cold blood by continued discharges of musketry! Several hours were occupied in the execution of this terrible and diabolical decree; and the horrors of the scene are said to have surpassed all that has ever occurred, amid the heat and fury of conflicts on the battle field.

After defiling his name and character with the eternal stigma of this massacre, Napoleon again resumed his march. After various conflicts with the Turkish forces, he was rapidly approaching the celebrated fortress of *Acre.* On the 16th of March the French army arrived under its walls. The pacha of Syria had taken refuge within them, with all his artillery, his treasures, and his armes; and had determined to defend them to the very last extremity. During the progress of this memorable siege the utmost heroism and desperate valor were displayed on both sides. The Turks were incited to their greatest exertions by the horror produced by the massacre which had just taken place at Jaffa; and they justly feared a similar fate, if they fell into the hands of the victorious and implacable French. The latter on their side saw before them the vast fortifications of a city, the possession of which was of the most vital importance to them. Should they fail before Acre their march of conquest was forever ended in the east. They could not advance a step farther, and leave so important a place behind them, in the hands of a powerful and desperate foe. As Napoleon remarked with his usual sagacity, pointing to the great tower of the fortress, "The fate of the east lies in yonder fort; the fall of Acre alone will lead to the possession of Damascus, and to the submission of Aleppo!"

Both sides were fully conscious of the vast importance of the fortress, to their respective interests; and this consciousness gave a degree of desperation to the conflicts which took place around and within its walls, which is not exceeded in the annals of warfare. We will not attempt to describe the prodigious exertions of the besiegers, led on by the vast genius of Napoleon himself; nor will we endeavor to depict the heroism and desperate resolution displayed by the besieged during the many assaults made upon the works.

The siege continued until the 20th of May. During its progress the French had several times forced an entrance within the walls, and had been as often repulsed with great losses by the Turks. The utmost efforts of valor and skill could not triumph over the immense strength of the fortress when defended by such heroism as then actuated the enraged, desperate and implacable Ottomans.

At length, the white sails of the English fleet, under Sir Philip Sydney, appeared in the distant horizon, bringing succor to the besieged fortress; and Napoleon perceiving the hopelessness of further exertions, gave the order to commence the retreat. The fire of the Turks was kept up from the walls, until the retiring army passed forever out of the sight and beyond the vision of the sorely besieged, but invincible garrison. Napoleon had lost three thousand of his best troops beneath the walls of Acre. In his retreat he left all his artillery behind. His dream of oriental glory had passed away, and he awoke, at length, to a reality of horrors.

We will not follow the baffled invader of the east through all the incidents of his remaining stay in Egypt. From Acre he retreated through the desert to Cairo. From Cairo, he advanced to Aboukir Bay, to attack the large force of Turks which the sultan had sent to Egypt, to assist in crushing the power of the French. On the 25th of July the great battle of Aboukir Bay was fought; and after a long and desperate struggle, victory once more was won back to the standard of Napoleon. Seven thousand slain Turks attested the fury of the conflict, and the magnitude of the triumph on that memorable field.

Immediately after the occurrence of this battle, Napoleon received information of the disasters which had befallen the directory in Italy and Switzerland; and he immediately formed the resolution of secretly leaving his army behind him, and of returning to Europe. Accordingly, on the 22d of August he set sail from Alexandria, having entrusted the command of the troops in Egypt to Kleber. He was accompanied only by Murat, Lannes, Berthier, Marmont, Bourrienne, and several more of his personal staff. After a voyage of several months, during which the frigate which bore the then obscure party narrowly escaped capture by the English cruisers in the Mediterranean, he reached Ajaccio. He sailed thence, after a sojourn of eight days in his native place, for the coast of France. He arrived attended only by his suite, in the Bay of Frejus, on the 8th of October; and immediately commenced a rapid journey to Paris.

Thus terminated, without any decisive results, the most romantic and remarkable expedition of modern times. It resembled, in the brilliant prospects which attended its commencement, and in the disasters and disappointment which beclouded its termination, the more stupendous venture of the great Corsican against the empire of Russia, which afterward occurred during his career.

CHAPTER X.

THE EMPRESS MARIA LOUISA, AND THE COURT OF ST. CLOUD.

The splendor of Napoleon's military reputation after his return from Egypt, rendered him the most considerable personage in France; and while the directory was rapidly crumbling on its throne, Napoleon was as rapidly rising upon its ruins. On the 9th of November, 1799, Napoleon dispersed the council of five hundred, while assembled in their hall, at the point of the bayonet. The directorial government was abolished, and the consulate was established, consisting of Napoleon, Sieyes, and Roger-Ducos. The two latter were subsequently succeeded by Cambacéres and Le Brun; but the strong arm and irresistible will of Napoleon already governed the destinies of France. Then came the consulate for life. At length, in 1804, Napoleon ascended the imperial throne. Meanwhile, his splendid triumphs on the field of battle, his profound wisdom in the council chamber, his energy and capacity as a ruler, had filled the world with his glory. Mankind seemed after the lapse of many ages, to behold the revival of the immortal epoch of the conquerors of old; and looked with mingled admiration and terror at the rising star and amazing conquests of the modern Alexander.

But one additional title to glory Napoleon still wanted, and that title he determined to possess. The humble

Corsican desired to unite his low-born race to one of the ancient reigning dynasties of Europe. This union would identify himself and his cause with the powerful legitimacy and conservatism of the past. The princess destined to realize for him this wish, was the grand-duchess Maria Louisa of Austria, the youthful heir of the most ancient, the most powerful, and the most illustrious race of kings, who had inherited the title of the Cæsars.

Let us narrate briefly some of the events which preceded the union of this princess with Napoleon; the state of the respective kingdoms which they represented; and the strange events which blended their families and destinies into one.

During the year 1809 occurred that celebrated campaign, which may be said to have laid the Germanic empire in the dust. On the 9th of April, Prince Charles, commanding the forces of Austria, took the field, and the Emperor Francis Joseph declared war against France. Napoleon immediately put himself at the head of his armies, then concentrated at Donauwerth. On the 23d of April he made himself master of Ratisbon. Immediately followed the decisive battle of Eckmühl, and in one month from that period, Napoleon entered Vienna in triumph. That capital had been defended by the Arch-Duke Maximilian, and during the siege which preceded its fall, the well known incident occurred which for the first time connected the name of the future empress of France with that of the conqueror. The city was fiercely bombarded, and Napoleon was informed that the safety of the arch-duchess was endangered by his artillery, which was then throwing its iron hail-storm on the imperial palace to which she was confined by a serious indisposition. Napoleon instantly ordered the direction of his pieces to be changed. Vienna at length capitulated, and the victor took up his residence at the palace of Schönbrunn.

During this short campaign of a few weeks, Napoleon had performed some of his most memorable achievements. The Austrian emperor had entered the field with an army of nearly five hundred thousand men. Napoleon's forces under Massena and Davoust, were far inferior in number to their opponents. The battle of Landschut was the first of that remarkable series of victories which now crowned Napoleon's arms. In that battle the Austrians lost nine thousand men. At the victory of Eckmühl the Austrians lost twenty thousand prisoners. Next follow the memorable conflicts of Asperne and Essling, and so immense were the struggles, and the losses on each side during these conflicts, that each of the combatants claimed the victory. Immediately afterward was fought the decisive battle of Wagram. The struggle was indeed long and bloody. The Arch-Duke Charles, generalissimo of the Austrian forces, had extended his line over too wide a space; and Napoleon took advantage of this error to concentrate his strength upon the most exposed point of his enemy. The defeat of the Austrians was complete. Twenty thousand prisoners, beside all the artillery and baggage of the archduke, fell into the hands of the conqueror. An armistice was the result of this decisive victory. Napoleon returned again to Schönbrunn where the terms of the treaty were matured and completed.

It was by this treaty of Schönbrunn, that Napoleon

most effectually humbled and weakened the Austrian power. By it Francis II. was compelled to descend from the high and ancient dignity of emperor of Germany, to that of emperor of Austria. He had been compelled by the treaty to make other heavy sacrifices. The immense territories known under the name of the Illgréan provinces were ceded to France. Napoleon thus added to his title of emperor of France, that of king of Italy. In October he left Vienna and passing through Würtemberg, arrived in haste at Paris. The thunder, the carnage, and the horrors of Wagram, had effectually prepared the way by which the Austrian princess was conducted to the nuptial couch of the conqueror, who had so nearly laid the dominion of her revered father forever prostrate in the dust. She may be easily justified for the ideas which she is at this period represented as entertaining of Napoleon; that he was a monster in human shape; that he was half-man, half-devil; that he was the evil genius of her family; that he was the scourge and curse of Europe; and that he was the embodiment of everything hateful and detestable. She changed her sentiments on this point, in a remarkable degree, upon a more tender and intimate acquaintance with their subject. She became convinced that he was a man without any infernal compound; and one indeed whom an affectionate and sentimental woman might most devotedly love. It was during Napoleon's temporary sojourn at the palace of Schönbrunn, that he first conceived and expressed the singular purpose of demanding the youthful arch-duchess as his spouse.

Immediately after his return from Vienna, Napoleon

began seriously to contemplate the project of his divorce. Impelled by the irresistible power of his ambition, he determined that it should take place; though by so doing he did violence to his affections, and to all the nobler sentiments of his soul. A stupendous struggle took place within him, beneath the mighty violence of which, even his master mind for a time staggered. But at length the splendor of his contemplated alliance, whereby his upstart fortunes would be allied to the most ancient and august dynasty in Europe, was too strong an allurement to be resisted. He determined that, cost what it would, of burning tears, of sad regrets, of breaking hearts, and of ruined and blasted hopes—Josephine, the beloved wife of his youth—his best, his most devoted friend, should descend from the high place to which he had elevated her, and that another should occupy it in her stead.

It was on the 15th of December, 1809, that this divorce took place. Several affecting scenes previously occurred between Napoleon and his wife, respecting their separation. Josephine, from the first, bore this reverse of fortune with magnanimity. When Napoleon resolved to mention to her the necessity for a divorce that he might obtain an heir to his empire, he approached her; he gazed affectionately upon her for a few moments; and then with emotion pronounced these remarkable words: "Josephine, my excellent Josephine, thou knowest if I have loved thee! To thee, and to thee alone, do I owe the only moments of happiness I have enjoyed in this world. But my destiny overmasters my will. My dearest affections must be silent before the interests of France."—"Say no more," she replied, "I was prepared for this;

but the blow is not the less terrible!" She at length fainted, and was carried to her chamber. When the time arrived for publicly proclaiming the divorce, the grand saloon of the Tuileries was crowded. The whole Bonaparte family were present. All the courtiers were in full costume. Napoleon wore a splendid suit of ceremony, with magnificent drooping plumes. He stood motionless as a statue, with his arms crossed upon his breast. At length the door opened by which Josephine was to enter. She appeared; her countenance was pale, but calm and self-possessed. She leaned upon the arm of her daughter Hortense, whose tears fell fast, and who could scarcely control her feelings. Josephine approached the center of the apartment, where an arm chair had been placed for her, before which was a small table, with writing apparatus of gold. She wore a dress of white muslin, without a single ornament. She moved with her usual grace to the seat prepared for her, and there listened to the reading of the act of separation. Her children, Eugene and Hortense, stood behind her chair, and in vain attempted to suppress their sobs and tears. Josephine heard with calmness the words which there placed an eternal barrier between herself and the tenderly cherished object of her pride and her affections. The reading over, she arose; pressed for a moment her handkerchief to her swimming eyes; pronounced with a clear voice the oath of acceptance; and taking the pen from the hand of Count St. Jean d'Angely, signed her name in full and bold characters to the instrument before her. Then, leaning on the arms of Eugene and Hortense, she retired from the saloon as she had entered it.

But the interest of this sad day had not yet terminated. Josephine remained shut up in her own apartment until her usual hour of retiring to rest. Napoleon then repaired to a separate chamber from the one which he had long shared with his now dethroned empress. He came not that night to his usual resting-place. He sought not then the communion of that tender and faithful breast in which for many long and troubled years he had deposited his cares as into a holy sanctuary, and had ever found sympathy and affection. The contrast was too painful to Josephine's feelings, and her agony at length became insupportable. She arose from her couch. Napoleon had just placed himself in bed, when suddenly and silently the door of his apartment opened. Josephine appeared, her dress and hair in disorder, and her face swollen with weeping. She advanced slowly toward the bed, and with clasped hands gazed upon the covered form of him, who had so long been the god of her idolatry. Forgetting everything else, in the fullness of her grief, she threw herself upon the bed, clasped the neck of her husband, and gave full vent to her grief. Napoleon wept. He dismissed the attendant who waited at the door of the apartment; and after an interview of an hour, the emperor parted forever from the woman who had been the benignant angel of his checkered and turbulent destiny. The next morning she bade adieu to the Tuileries, which she never entered again. Such was the woman, and such her spirit, whose successor Maria Louisa was to become, upon the throne of France.

It was indeed a singular fate which was about to unite the destinies of these two beings. Napoleon had fought and gained twenty pitched battles over the armies of Austria. He had spread terror during ten years throughout her dominions. He had twice entered her trembling capital as a conqueror. He had frequently brought his future father-in-law to the brink of destruction. And yet, he was now to be united in the tenderest and most endearing ties with the princess whose family and whose dominion he had so nearly ruined. There were men then living also, who remembered well the day when this haughty and all-conquering aspirant to the fairest and noblest hand in christendom, had left his watch, his only possession, as security for a small sum of borrowed money. There were women then living who had disclaimed him as a suitor, and even as an associate, when he first appeared in Paris, a poor, meager, unknown, and undistinguished youth. Now, indeed, he might command the approving smiles, and the yielding heart of the most beautiful and most high-born of the daughters of the earth. Human destiny is indeed a wonderful enigma! Truth is strange; often far stranger than the most erratic flights of the distempered imagination.

The marriage having been duly determined upon by the plenipotentiaries of both monarchs, its announcement was received both at Paris and Vienna with every demonstration of delight. Splendid fêtes were given in honor of the imperial nuptials. Berthier, Prince de Neufchatel, was sent to Vienna to conduct the empress to Paris. She was married by proxy to her uncle Prince Charles, with all the forms and ceremonies which are so scrupulously observed by the court of Vienna, on the

1st of April, 1810; and the day of her departure from the palace, and from the city of her forefathers, was fixed.

It is recorded that the young arch-duchess often shed tears of regret at her contemplated separation from her family, and her connection with a man who had been so long the object of her terror and her aversion. Her family have always been remarkable for the unusual affection and attachment which has ever existed between its members. She shed bitter tears at the prospects of the future, which, while they seemed fraught with splendor and distinction, might nevertheless be pregnant with danger, with mortification, and with indignity to herself and her family.

When the day of departure arrived, Maria Louisa bade adieu to all the members of her family. Etiquette required that she should then retire to her apartment, to wait till Berthier came to conduct her to her carriage. When the prince entered her apartment he was surprised to find her bathed in tears. She apologized gracefully for her weakness; "but," said she, "see how I am surrounded here by so many objects which are dear to me, and which I must leave forever. These drawings were made by my sister; that tapestry was wrought by my mother; those paintings are by my uncle Charles." In fact, almost every ornament of her apartment was the cherished work of some beloved hand. She expressed her regret also at losing her singing birds, her parrot; and above all, a separation which more than all the rest seemed to wring her heart with sorrow, was the loss of *Fortuné*, her lapdog. To lose all these, was a misfortune which at least excused the tears shed by the tender and affectionate princess. So mutual was the attachment between her and her little favorite, that they parted with an affecting adieu of regret and complaint.

A thought at this moment entered the mind of Berthier, which certainly did him great credit. "I have merely come," said he, "to acquaint your majesty, that you need not yet depart for two hours. I will therefore withdraw during that time." He immediately went to the emperor and acquainted him with his plan. Francis II. the most affectionate of fathers, gladly assented to his proposition. The requisite orders were given, and in two hours all was ready for their departure and the execution of his mysterious scheme.

The young empress rapidly passed through the dominions of her father, and reached the confines of the French territories. She was surrounded everywhere with festivities and rejoicings; and her affection for her parrot and her dog, had almost faded from her memory. It was at Compiegne that she first beheld her future husband. The incidents connected with their first interview are well known; how Napoleon had sent an escort to meet the cortege of his young empress, while he determined to await her arrival; how his impetuosity overcame his prudence and his decorum; how he rode forth at a furious rate to meet her carriage; how he himself opened the door and rushed into her arms; how she was at first overcome with sudden terror, but being reässured by his tender embraces was about to kneel, when Napoleon prevented her, and overwhelmed her again with his impetuous caresses.

The imperial couple spent the first night of their union

at Compeigne. The next day they proceeded directly to St. Cloud, and thence to Paris. The empress at this period was eighteen years of age. Her personal appearance was interesting. Her hair was of a light color, her eyes were blue and expressive, her carriage was graceful, and her figure was elegant and beautifully proportioned. Her hands and feet were perfect, and might have served as models to the sculptor. She enjoyed good health; possessed a florid complexion; had an expressive and amiable countenance; and might indeed have been regarded as handsome, though by no means as intellectual.

Upon her arrival at the palace of the Tuilleries, Napoleon took the first opportunity to give her the agreeable surprise, which the stratagem of Berthier had prepared for her. He led her into one of the narrow corridors of the palace, lighted only by a single lamp. "Where are we going?" said she. "Come, Louisa, are you afraid to follow me?" replied the emperor, who pressed his young bride to his bosom with affectionate tenderness. Suddenly they stopped at a door, within which they heard the impatient barking of a dog which seemed dissatisfied with its prison. Napoleon opened the door, and desired Louisa to enter. Imagine her surprise and delight to find herself in a splendid apartment, greeted by her little favorite from Vienna; while in glancing around her, she saw the room furnished with the same chairs, carpets, paintings, birds, drawings, and all the other cherished mementoes of her former happy home, placed in the same order and arrangement which they had formerly occupied. Maria Louisa, overcome by her delightful emotions, threw herself into her husband's arms, who embraced her with delight, very much in defiance of all the established rules of court etiquette.

To complete the interesting scene, Berthier now entered, when Napoleon said: "Louisa, it is to him that you owe this unexpected pleasure. I desire you to embrace him as a just reward." Berthier took the hand of the empress; but the emperor added: "No, no, you must kiss my old and faithful friend." His agreeable order was obeyed; and the marshal saluted with mingled confusion and pleasure the blooming and blushing bride of his master.

Thus, at length, after so many storms and struggles, after the convulsions which had shaken a continent, and the mighty upheavings which had overturned thrones and dynasties, the loud clarion of battle had ceased to resound; the drum no longer beat to arms; and the imperial eagle having soared in the highest heaven of glory, had folded its wings and paused on its ambitious way. Universal peace prevailed. The harsh words of command had given place to the gentle and endearing accents of love. Mars was neglected and Hymen honored. The gates of the temple of Janus were closed; while Concord and Cupid with their benignant scepters reigned over the rejoicing nations.

> "Grim visaged war had smoothed his wrinkled front,
> And now, instead of mounting barbed steeds
> To fright the souls of fearful adversaries,
> He capers nimbly in a lady's chamber
> To the lascivious pleasing of a lute!"

The Court of St. Cloud, to the magnificent portals of which the youthful empress was conducted by her illustrious spouse, and the empire which she was invited to share with him, exceeded in splendor, in renown, and in every element of human grandeur, all other courts which ever existed. The brilliancy of the alliance which now took place, excited the admiration of all the world. Mankind had never before witnessed a union by which so many glories, such imposing historical associations, such renown and such splendor had been combined together. The union of Arragon and Castile by the marriage of Ferdinand and Isabella, had led to the establishment of the Spanish monarchy, which became the greatest in chivalrous power and heroism in its day, which vanquished the Moorish empire in one continent, and the Peruvian in another. The union of Hungary and Bohemia with the hereditary states of Austria, by the marriage of Maria Theresa with Francis I. had produced a great monarchy. The consolidation of Scotland and England under James I. had greatly increased the magnitude and promoted the aggrandizement of the British realms. But these were insignificant combinations compared with the one which now had taken place. There on the one hand was the vast and ancient inheritance of the house of Hapsburg, of Charles V. and of Maria Theresa, combined with that of Charlemagne, of the long line of the Capets, and of the Bourbons. The former sovereignty had been the result of the steady and careful accumulation of ages, of long struggles and of numerous vicissitudes. The latter empire had been won by an untitled adventurer from a remote island of the sea; by the victorious hero of an hundred battles; by a man whose ambition had convulsed Europe, and whose god-like genius was the wonder and the terror of his race. Napoleon had mounted a throne upon which fifty-five anointed sovereigns had sat in succession, from the day that Childeric I. ascended it in the fifth century, down till that period. He was their successor, their heir, their representative.

The court over which Maria Louisa was invited now to preside, was brilliant in proportion to the magnitude of the empire over which it ruled. Paris was then the metropolis of the civilized world. Thither tended as to a mighty and all-devouring vortex, the luxurious expenditures of Europe's princes and nobility. Thither clustered, as around the great center of social refinement and splendor, the most beautiful, the most accomplished, the most fascinating women, as well as the bravest, the noblest, and the most illustrious men.

There, as the acknowledged head and supreme sovereign was the modern Achilles; a hero as brave, as gifted, and as ambitious as Cæsar or Alexander, and more powerful and fortunate than either. His first wife Josephine, like the evening star, had retired in sweetness and in beauty from the scenes of her former grandeur which she had so well adorned and dignified, to the shades of private life at Malmaison; where she remained unseen by a world who remembered her only to admire her virtues and to regret her absence; but where she was still adored by the few who were allowed to behold her subdued splendor. That court was now graced with the presence of Pauline Bonaparte, the most lovely and the most seductive of women; the modern Venus, as beautiful and as frail as the goddess whom she so aptly represented. There was Queen Hortense, the wife of Louis Bonaparte, who had inherited her mother's amiability and intelligence. There was Caroline Bonaparte, the queen of Naples, and the princess Eliza; both of them worthy to be the sisters of an emperor; whose accomplishments were the praise, but whose intrigues were the scandal of all Europe. There was Talleyrand, the most sagacious and far-seeing of statesmen; Fouché, the most cunning and intriguing of ministers; and Cambaceres, the most dignified of courtiers. There were clusters of renowned warriors who had vanquished the embattling foes of France on many a blood-stained field; the heroic Ney, the impetuous Lannes, the dauntless Massena, the resolute Macdonald, and the prudent Soult. There the ambassadors of mighty kings and the representatives of distant and renowned republics were assembled; and added a brighter luster to scenes already sufficiently resplendent. There, too, was the charm produced by the presence of dramatic genius—of Mlle. Mars, the most brilliant of actresses, of Talma, the most consummate of tragedians. The ancient nobility of France were represented by the Princess DeRohan, and by others of its most illustrious scions. Peerless beauty also illumined the gilded halls of St. Cloud by its fascinating presence; for there was Madam Tallien, who still retained the undiminished splendor of her majestic beauty; whose heroic love had inspired her husband in other days to strike the first death-blow to the terrible power of Robespierre. There too were Mesdames Janot, Grandt and Recamier, her equals in personal charms, though not in genius and in fame. Around the court and within the capital of the great Napoleon, were assembled the most eminent men of that day, in every art and science known to human genius; Isabey the painter, Paër the composer, Champollion the antiquary, Corvisart the physician, the doctors of the Sorbonne, the savans of the institute, peers of ancient houses, and statesmen and soldiers of immortal name. All these governed from that spot, under the guidance of their great chief, the interests of many climes. Around the court of St. Cloud, the anxious curiosity and interest of mankind from Moscow to Madrid, and from the bleak hills of Scotland to the balmy shores of the Bosphorus were there concentrated, as toward the great center of affairs; as the spot whence all absolute decrees proceeded, which controlled alike the world of fashion, the republic of letters, the fortunes of war, and the destinies of nations.

Such was the court over which the young and timid empress was suddenly called to preside. Shortly after the marriage, Maria Louisa accompanied Napoleon into Belgium. This journey was taken by him in consequence of various disputes which had taken place between the emperor and his brother Louis, the king of that country, which had terminated in a complete rupture. At Antwerp, and indeed throughout the whole tour, the empress received the homage of the Dutch, and the imperial pair were everywhere greeted with public rejoicings, fetes, and manifestations of popular joy. Louis had been forced to abdicate; and Belgium and Holland had, by an imperial decree, been annexed to the French empire. This journey was intended to afford an opportunity to inspect the actual wants of the countries, whose government he was thus constrained personally to assume. He returned by way of Ostend, Lille, and Normandy, to St. Cloud, where he arrived with his empress in June, 1810.

The festivities which took place at Paris in honor of the imperial nuptials had not ceased before a most lamentable event took place, whose sad details will long be remembered. This was the dreadful accident which occured at Prince Schwartzenberg's ball, in July of the same year. The prince occupied the Hotel Montesson, but its capacious proportions were not sufficient to accommodate the large and brilliant company which honored the ball with their presence. A temporary saloon had been constructed in the garden, which resembled a fairy palace, filled with flowers, perfumes, delicious music, and the dazzling splendor of diamonds and jewels. The walls were covered with gold and silver brocade, while hundreds of crystal chandeliers shed their glittering luster over the gorgeous scene.

Maria Louisa and Napoleon were present. The dancing had just commenced when the fire was discovered. The empress was then engaged in conversation with some ladies near the throne which adorned one end of the apartment. With great self-possession and courage she immediately ascended the steps of the throne, seated herself there, and waited till Napoleon came to conduct her from the scene of peril and disaster. This he immediately did; he placed her in her carriage and accompanied her as far as the Place Louis XV. But there were other and much more deplorable scenes connected with this catastrophe. The beautiful and accomplished Princess Schwartzenberg fell a victim to the flames. In escaping from the ball room, a ponderous luster fell upon her head and fractured her skull. She fell into an opening caused by the burning of the floor; and being unable to rise or to escape, was soon overpowered by the flames. Her body was found burnt to a cinder, except her bosom, and a part of one arm. She was recognized by the brilliant jewels which she wore around her neck, which were still attached to her mutilated remains. A Swedish officer also discovered among the ruins, the almost lifeless remains of another female. Her countenance was so blackened, as to be utterly undistinguishable. The silver mounting of her diamond tiara had melted, and penetrated into the head. A faint groan issued from what seemed to be but a mass of cinders—which was the only proof that life was not yet extinct. It proved to be the Princess de la Leyen, who expired the following day in the most indescribable agony.

Such was the sad and horrid omen which immediately followed the splendid nuptials of the ambitious Corsican; and which filled the minds of thousands with superstitious terror. Every one was reminded of the similar catastrophe which had occurred at the marriage of Louis XVI. and Maria Antoinette; and which might forbode, and actually did precede the extermination of that new dynasty, whose inauguration had been so triumphant and so propitious.

The birth of the king of Rome, Napoleon II., occurred on the 20th of March, 1811. This event may be termed the last benignant smile of fortune which beamed upon the turbulent career of Napoleon. Maria Louisa suffered a long and a difficult *accouchement*. For some time her danger was imminent. Baron Dubois ran to acquaint

Napoleon of her peril. He found him taking a bath to cool the feverish excitement under which he was laboring. On hearing of the danger of the empress, he threw on a *robe-de-chambre* and hastened to her chamber. "Save the mother," said he to Corvisart, the attendant physician, "treat her as if she were a girl of the Fauxbourg St. Antoine." As soon as the child was born, the emperor entered the apartment, and first embraced the mother without bestowing a look upon the son. The latter, indeed, seemed to be beyond the reach of human sympathy. Nearly ten minutes elapsed before he exhibited any signs of life. Every expedient was resorted to, to produce animation; he was rubbed with the hand; drops of brandy were blown into his mouth; warm napkins were wrapped around him. All seemed unavailing. Meanwhile the loud thunder of the artillery which announced to the expectant Parisians, the happy event of the birth of a son to their renowned emperor, reverberated over Paris, and shook the ponderous walls of the palace. At length the royal infant uttered a feeble cry. It is confidantly asserted that the concussion produced by the discharge of the cannon alone resuscitated the expiring infant, gave to Napoleon an heir, and to France the cause of boundless joy and congratulation.

Strange to say, some doubt has been expressed as to whether the king of Rome was really Napoleon's son. All such doubt is absurd. The actual eye-witnesses of the event of his birth were twenty-two in number. Nor was there anything singular in the fact, that Maria Louisa, at nineteen years of age, healthy, blooming, and vigorous, should become the mother of a son to Napoleon, after eleven months of marriage.

The king of Rome was baptized on the day of his birth, in the chapel of the Tuileries. The whole imperial family were in attendance, and Napoleon witnessed the ceremony with the deepest emotion. The emperor himself bore his son to the baptismal font, and knelt upon a stool covered with white velvet during the progress of the ceremony. When the first gun announced that Maria Louisa had become a mother, all Paris was convulsed with joy. All business was suspended; the people flocked to the Tuileries; an immense crowd surrounded the palace; hats were thrown up into the air; people kissed each other in their frenzied enthusiasm; and tears of joy were seen to flow. At eleven o'clock, Madame Blanchard rose in a balloon from the square of the military school, and scattered bulletins over Paris announcing the particulars of the joyful event. A chamberlain was placed at the door of the palace who communicated from time to time the condition of the empress and her son, to the immense crowds who still besieged its portals. In contemplating the birth of the king of Rome, even at this distant day, when all the splendid hopes and august associations connected with it have passed away forever, we cannot fail to be struck with the singularity of destiny. What stupendous hopes surrounded that infant head! And yet, how sadly were they all blasted by the disastrous progress of events; how dark and cheerless was the early setting of that youthful sun, whose rising splendor was so gorgeous and magnificent!

Napoleon, who had so long desired a son, now that his

wish was gratified, exhibited as that son grew older the strongest paternal feeling. He frequently took the king of Rome into his arms and tossed him up into the air. The child would then laugh till the tears stood in his eyes. Sometimes the emperor took him before a looking glass, and put his face into all sorts of grimaces, till the child would cry out with terror. At other times at table, the stern conqueror would besmear the boy's face with gravy, which always highly amused the young innocent. These displays of youthful happiness and of childish affection, remind us strongly of those memorable lines of the poet Gray, whose truthfulness to nature has made them household words to all generations:

> Alas! regardless of their doom,
> The little victims play!
> No sense have they of ills to come,
> No care beyond to-day.
> Yet see how all around them wait,
> The ministers of human fate,
> And black misfortune's baleful train;
> Ah! show them where in ambush stand
> To seize their prey, the murderous band;
> Ah tell them they are *men!*

As the king of Rome grew in years, his character became more interesting and remarkable. His intelligence and spirit were unusual, and indicated a nature of more than ordinary talent and power. He possessed, however, a very violent temper. His governess, Madame de Montesquieu, once corrected him for the excessive fury of his passion. On another similar occasion, she ordered all the shutters of the windows to be closed, though it was broad day light. The child, astonished to find the light of day excluded, and the candles lighted, inquired the reason of the novel proceedure. "In order that no one may hear you, sire," she replied. "The French would never have you for their king, if they knew you were so violent." "Have I cried very loud?" said he, "and did they hear me?" "I fear they have," was the answer. He then fell to weeping, and throwing his arms around his governess' neck, said—"I will never do so again, Mamma Quiou; pray forgive me!"

On another occasion, later in his history, the emperor took his son to a review in the Champ de Mars. "Was he frightened at the shouts of the veteran Guards?" inquired the empress. "Frightened? no, surely," replied Napoleon; "he knew that he was among his father's friends." After the review Napoleon conversed for some time with the architect, Fontaine, respecting the palace to be built for the king of Rome on the elevated ground facing the military school. The word *Rome* brought to the mind of the emperor the fact that he had never visited the eternal city, and was a personal stranger to its memorable scenes. "But," said he "I shall go there some day, for it is the city of my little king." Alas! the little king, for whom so rich an inheritance had been prepared, never entered upon its possession. His was a much smaller domain at the age of twenty-one—that of the grave.

We will not dwell upon the succeeding events of Napoleon's career, during which time Maria Louisa remained his nominal wife. The short reign of the great hero in his diminutive empire at Elba; his return to France in 1815, the bold and desperate daring of which, took the whole world by surprise; his wonderful struggles during the hundred days, by which the mastery of his genius over the combined diplomatists and soldiers of a continent, was most signally apparent; and the accidental though ruinous reverse to his aspiring fortunes at Waterloo; these events are too familiar to all men, to require a repetition here. But it will be sufficient to remark, that had Maria Louisa possessed the least spark of romance in her soul, or the least superiority of intellect, or the least affection for her immortal spouse, her efforts to spend with him the decline of life, and her endeavors to alleviate his sufferings, would have added to the history of both a charm and an attraction, far superior to any which is now associated with their names!

As soon as the influence of Napoleon's mind was removed from her's, and his elevated sentiments no longer inspired her conduct, Maria Louisa displayed the true meanness of her nature; and that was done apparently in utter and innocent unconsciousness of her degradation and her debasement in the estimation of the world. By the treaty of Vienna in 1815, she became the sovereign of Parma and Modena. Through the intrigues of her own family, an Austrian colonel was placed in connection with her, as prime minister, with the covert design of her seduction and disgrace as the wife of Napoleon. Count Niepberg soon accomplished this disgraceful purpose, and became her acknowledged paramour. She had two children by him; and while the great Napoleon still lived and languished on the bleak height of Helena, his recreant wife reveled with the unprincipled seducer in shameless excesses, amid the sumptuous palaces and retreats of

Parma. After a few years Niepberg died, and Maria Louisa became almost frantic at his loss. Yet after a short time her mind, incapable of stability and of exalted sentiment of any kind, solaced itself with other and successive attachments. Her son, the Duke of Reichstadt, died in Vienna, the victim of the state craft of his unnatural grandfather; who surrounded him with various temptations to debauchery, which, through the adroitness of Prince Metternich, were so skillfully applied, that he soon became their unconscious victim, and died a premature death. His mother, disgraced and despised by all the world, soon followed him to the tomb, having furnished in her life a memorable evidence of the fact, that ignoble minds, however much they may have been elevated for a time above their kindred degradation, by connection with more exalted natures, when that better influence is removed will relapse again to that condition, which possesses greater consonance with their own inborn and ineradicable baseness. And among the existing instances in which greatness has been thrust upon its possessors, and persons of the most ordinary qualities have become the object of the curiosity, wonder and congratulation of the civilized world, the case of Maria Louisa is probably the most remarkable; for without the aid of her exalted birth, and her still more exalted alliance in marriage, she would inevitably have passed down to the shades of the common oblivion, without having scarcely excited a remark, or generated an emotion!

CHAPTER XI.

EXPEDITION OF NAPOLEON IN RUSSIA.

NAPOLEON, having determined upon the invasion of Russia, immediately prepared to achieve that gigantic enterprise. Well might even *his* stupendous genius hesitate and reconsider its purpose, when contemplating an expedition more astounding and audacious than any ever before conceived by the human mind. Russia was at that time the most formidable opponent whom he could confront in Europe. The three hundred Spartans stemming the mighty tide of Persian invasion at the strait of Thermopylæ; or Cæsar crossing the Rubicon with his legions, thus bidding defiance to the hostile power of Rome; or Cortez with five hundred Spaniards, invading the vast empire of Mexico; these and other renowned instances of desperate and intrepid adventure, were trifles in comparison with the vastness, grandeur, and heroism of Napoleon's invasion of Russia; a country containing at that time fifty millions of inhabitants, an army of five hundred thousand men, with the howling tempests, the furious snow storms, and the intense cold of a Russian winter, superadded to the infernal horrors of the scene.

Yet all these obstacles did not for a moment daunt the fearless "child of destiny." The solemn and mysterious voice of fate, still seemed to say to him in audible tones: "Onward! to the city of the czars! All Europe will then be beneath your feet," and that voice he had sworn to obey, whether it whispered to him beneath the fair skies of Italy, amid the sandy waste of Egypt, on the fruitful plains of Spain, or amid the cheerless snows of Russia.

Napoleon set off on this memorable expedition, from Paris, in the month of May, 1812, accompanied by Maria Louisa; who had expressed a desire to see her father. Austria was at that time in alliance with France. Toward the Vistula, as to a common center, were then moving by the emperor's command, countless multitudes of troops, cavalry, artillery, carriages, provisions and baggage of every description; and the grand army composed of nearly six hundred thousand troops, well equipped, and experienced in war, commanded by Napoleon himself, assisted by his most celebrated marshals, was an armament unequaled for effectiveness in the whole history of warfare. The millions of imbecile Persians who once deluged Greece, under the command of Xerxes; the hostile hosts which combatted at Cannæ and Pharsalia; the Ottoman force which beseiged Vienna, and which was scattered to the winds by John Sobieski; all these were inferior to the stupendous and well appointed armament which now marshaled under the orders of the modern Achilles, and boldly menaced the capital and the throne of the czars. Yet that immense host, and its renowned commander, were marching under the fatal spell of an evil genius; and were allured by splendid chimeras, onward to the vortex of inevitable ruin.

During the short residence of Napoleon at Dresden, a scene of magnificence and splendor was presented, to which no parallel can be found in modern history. The once humble Corsican was surrounded with a degree of glory and grandeur which had fallen to the lot of no human being before or since, whether he was born the heir of kings, or of beggars. Napoleon occupied the palace of the ancient monarchs of Saxony, surrounded by his marshals, generals, and all the brilliant male and female members of his court. Day after day, and night after night, the most splendid *fêtes* were given him, while adulation and homage more profound than had ever before been offered to a sovereign were lavished upon him. An innumerable crowd of courtiers, generals, ministers, princes, dukes, and even kings, swarmed assiduously around him, upon whom he, in return, not only bestowed benignant smiles, but lavished rich gifts, worthy of the munificence of so great a conqueror. It is related that on several occasions as many as four sovereigns of great states, were waiting patiently at the same time in his ante-chamber. Many queens were proud of the dignity of being maids of honor to Maria Louisa. The streets were thronged with splendid equipages, passing to and fro, from audiences asked and happily obtained from this king of kings; while the rapid departure and arrival of messengers and couriers to every part of Europe, indicated the vast supervision exercised by him over the greater portion of the European kingdoms. Then indeed had the power of this wondrous adventurer reached a pinnacle, unequaled by that of any other mortal; for his imperious will alone seemed to determine the conduct and the fate of five hundred millions of the human race, who received with mingled curiosity and apprehension whatever he might decree respecting their interests and their fate.

On the 24th of June, 1812, the grand army passed the Niemen by three bridges, which had been erected by the orders of Napoleon; and thus they set their foot for the first time upon the forbidden territory of their great foe. Two entire days were occupied with the passage of the troops. Two hundred and fifty thousand men at that single point marched under the order of Napoleon; and never before had a more magnificent display of all the glorious yet delusive pomp and circumstance of war been made. The French army passed this fatal boundary line in high, exulting hope, anticipating a brilliant and triumphant campaign, and the speedy subjugation of the power of Russia. In six months alas! how sad and frightful a wreck of this once splendid armament, tottered back again to the banks of this same river, a few exhausted and straggling thousands whom the sword of the avenging foe, and the more relentless and deadly embrace of a Russian winter, had spared to tell the tale of the unexpected ruin of this great and brave armament.

It is said that the emperor Alexander of Russia was at a ball in the neighborhood of Wilna, when he first heard that the French army had at length crossed the Niemen, and invaded his territory. He immediately issued a proclamation, calling upon his faithful subjects to defend their country and their religion; and concluded it by declaring that he himself would not sheathe his sword as long as an enemy remained within the Russian dominions. The policy which he had determined to adopt on this memorable occasion, was one which proves the sagacity and prfound wisdom of Alexander, to which his own triumph and the ultimate defeat of his foe are alone attributable.

Had Alexander determined to resist the invader upon the field, he would have been vanquished; for Napoleon's ability as a commander was unequaled; his military force was in perfect discipline and effectiveness; and defeat after defeat would have been the inevitable result of a rash purpose to confront directly so great a general with so powerful an army. Alexander wisely resolved differently. His purpose was to retire slowly with his armies as the invader advanced; never to risk the hazard of a general engagement; thus to preserve his troops unimpaired, until the period for the summer campaign being ended, the terrible fury of a Russian winter would descend upon the presumptuous foe, and inflict that penalty which no mortal hand seemed to possess the ability to accomplish.

The wisdom of this policy began immediately to display itself. After passing the Niemen, the first city of importance on the route of the French army was Wilna. Napoleon entered it on the 28th of June; and at the same moment Barclay de Tolly, the Russian general, deserted it by the opposite gate. But ere Napoleon reached Wilna, he was compelled to pass through a territory which his foe had already desolated; his horses perished by thousands from the want of wholesome provender; and twenty-five thousand sick and dying men already filled the hospitals of Wilna. It was not yet too late for him who was so boldly defiant of God and man to recede from the brink of ruin; but the lesson was in vain.

After an imprudent delay of seventeen days at Wilna, Napoleon resumed his march toward Moscow. On the 26th of July he reached Vitepsk, and endeavored to draw the Russian commander, Barclay, into a general engagement. On the evening of the 27th, the latter seemed to be preparing to meet the invader in the large plain which surrounds the city. During the night the watch fires in the Russian camp continued to burn with their wonted brilliancy. On the morning of the 28th, however, no trace of the Russian army could be found in the camp. To the astonishment of Napoleon, during the night, Barclay had effected a retreat in such excellent order, that not the slightest sound had been heard, even by the watchful Murat who had bivouacked with the advanced post of the French army. The great conqueror had again been eluded by his intended victim, who had thus adroitly slipped once more from his deadly grasp.

While Napoleon halted at Vitepsk, he received information which by no means served to increase his enthusiasm. He there learned that the Russian emperor had concluded a treaty of peace with the Turks; which at once rendered a large army of some fifty thousand men, then employed on the Danube, available against his French foe. The latter also learned, that the czar had concluded a treaty with Sweden, by which means Bernadotte, the sovereign of that country, was detached from the interests of Napoleon, and rendered at least neutral in the present conflict.

These were events of great importance to the French emperor; and these, together with the immense losses of men and horses which he had already suffered, and the advanced stage of the season, induced some of Napoleon's more prudent and experienced marshals to advise him to advance no further into the Russian territory; but to defer his invasion until the succeeding spring, and to agree to a temporary armistice with Alexander.

The great mind of Napoleon was, on this occasion, strangely and painfully agitated by conflicting purposes. Many grave considerations proclaimed the propriety and justice of these more prudent counsels. He had already lost many thousands of men, by the inevitable vicissitudes of the campaign. He had discovered in the Russian commanders and troops, a degree of desperate heroism which he had not anticipated. He already found it exceedingly difficult to obtain the necessary provisions for his immense host. He was surrounded by a hostile and treacherous population; and above all, the indescribable horrors of a Russian winter would soon overwhelm his exhausted troops.

On the other hand, it was then but the middle of summer. Ought the hero of Austerlitz to take up his winter quarters, in the month of July? Besides, by pressing forward he would soon arrive beneath the walls of Moscow; and there, in a great and decisive battle, he would meet and vanquish his foe; he would dethrone the hostile and humbled Czar; he would enter Moscow in triumph; he would then himself wield the scepter of the Russian empire, and would date his decrees to the four quarters of Europe from the Kremlin, the ancient palace and citadel of the Muscovite kings. Then, after a winter spent amid the frozen splendors of that northern capital, he would return with triumphant eagles to the sumptuous halls of St. Cloud.

It is said, that while Napoleon balanced in his mind the relative weight of the arguments on both sides of this great and momentous question, he was agitated as he never before had been. For several days his mind was in a terrific state of excitement. He slept neither by night nor by day. He could not rest for a moment. He could bear no clothing upon his bed; but during the hours of darkness, rolled and tossed in ceaseless agitation, weighing in his mind the doubtful probabilities of the great venture before him. At length, after several days of painful uncertainty, he arrived at the determination to advance. "We must be in Moscow in a month," said he, "or we will never be there. Peace awaits us only under its walls." The die was then cast; and his destiny must needs be fulfilled.

Giving the general order to advance, his troops arrived under their respective leaders, on the 16th of August, before the ancient walls of Smolensko. The two most able generals of the czar, Barclay de Tolly and Prince Bagrathion, had succeeded, after some severe skirmishes with the enemy, in reaching this venerable fortress, and in throwing their troops within its walls. This city is situated on the banks of the Dnieper. Its fortifications were old, but were still able to resist the shock of artillery. The Russian generals appear at first to have resolved to defend the city to the last extremity. An ancient wall thirty-five feet high, and eighteen feet thick, surrounded the whole city, which presented an appearance in the highest degree picturesque. The most prominent buildings, among the many which still remained as monuments of former Sarmatian splendor, were the citadel and the cathedral. The former was chiefly conspicuous for its size. The latter was a venerable and majestic edifice surmounted by vast gilded domes, and adorned with lofty spires which glittered afar in the beams of the sun. From the spire of this cathedral the Russian generals beheld the hosts of the French hero as they successively arrived in immense masses, resplendent with steed and gold, and all the glittering trappings of war. As far as the eye could reach even with the aid of the telescope, the plain around Smolensko was covered with the martial hosts. From their high perch the Russian generals anxiously surveyed the scene; and endeavored to compute the magnitude and power of the armament thus brought to bear against the beleaguered city. In silence and with the utmost precision, division after division wheeled into its appropriate place; and two hundred thousand men were ready to advance to the attack of Smolensko, defended by a hundred thousand troops under the command of the Russian generals.

The latter after a long and anxious survey of the French forces from the gilded spires of the cathedral, determined not to stand the hazard of a siege, but to withdraw from Smolensko, and continue the retreat toward Moscow. The Russian troops accordingly defiled out of the city on the only side which was uninvested by the French, the one which led to Moscow. Bagrathion commanded the retreat; Barclay de Tolly defended the walls.

When Napoleon discovered the intention of the Russians still to retreat, he was exasperated beyond measure; and he determined at once to order a general assault. At two o'clock Marshal Ney attacked the great citadel. At the same time Davoust led his division against the ramparts. Poniatowsky brought sixty pieces of artillery to bear upon the bridges which connected both sides of the city over the Dneiper. The Russians were prepared to receive their assailants. In vain their batteries thundered against the ancient walls eighteen feet in thickness. In vain did Ney "the bravest of the brave," attack the citadel. The utmost exertions of the assailants availed nothing against the combined power of the fortress and the heroism of its defenders. At length night came, and Napoleon had not yet won victory to his standards. At seven in the evening he called off his troops from the hopeless attack. The Russians had successfully resisted the seventy thousand men whom Napoleon had led forward to the assault, during which he had lost fifteen thousand men.

At nine o'clock in the evening, total silence pervaded both camps; but soon an appalling spectacle was presented to the view of the besiegers. Their red-hot balls had set fire to some wooden buildings within the ramparts, and soon the lurid flames of a vast conflagration illumined the darkness of the whole horizon. The fire rapidly extended toward a more central part of the city. High above the tumultuous ocean of flame and smoke, towered the glittering domes of the cathedral, which they seemed in vain to assail. As the conflagration increased, its extending flames threw a clearer light over the assembled hosts who peopled the plains around, and who gazed in silent awe and wonder upon a scene of such terror and sublimity. But even this scene was but an humble precursor of one of far greater magnitude and terror, which they were destined afterward to behold.

The Russians retreated from Smolensko during the whole of this memorable night, along the Moscow road. When morning dawned Davoust penetrated without any resistance within the walls, and found a deserted city. The French troops however saw nothing but desolation and ruin on every side. The Russians had even destroyed the magazines, and left nothing to the possession of the invaders, but naked walls and mouldering masses of ruin.

On the 22d of August Napoleon left Smolensko, and advanced with his army on the road to Moscow. Already that capital began to tremble with terror, as the dread conqueror approached nearer and nearer to her walls. No city, not even Rome with Hannibal thundering at her gates, was ever agitated with so intense a dread, as was the ancient capital of Russia, when the news arrived that Napoleon with three hundred thousand troops had left Smolensko, and resumed his march for Moscow. At this crisis an aged and experienced general of Russian birth returned to that city from his conquests on the confines of Turkey; and to him, the universal voice of the nation requested the emperor Alexander to confide the supreme command. This veteran was *Kutusoff*. It was thought that his great talents, and his greater experience would afford a surer presage of victory, under the unparalleled circumstance of peril and disaster which seemed to threaten the Russian throne and empire at that moment. Since the days of the dauntless Suwarrow, no Russian general had won so many great triumphs over the Turks, or had given so many proofs of unconquerable heroism, as he had done during a long life of vicissitude and warlike adventure.

Since the entrance of Napoleon into Russia the emperor Alexander had ordered his generals not to venture upon a general engagement. But as the French approached Moscow—now only fifty leagues distant, the increasing panic of its inhabitants imperatively demanded that the invader should be met in the field; and the appointment of Kutusoff to the supreme command was a proof that a great battle was at length determined upon by the Russian monarch. The memorable field of *Borodino* lay in the pathway of Napoleon, ere he could place his eager hand on the crown of Russia, deposited in the treasure-chamber of the Kremlin; and to that spot the forces of the czar were now concentrated, for the purpose of confronting the foe.

On the 5th of September the head of Napoleon's columns came in sight of the humble village, whose name has since become immortal on one of the bloodiest pages of history. When evening came, the watchfires of both armies shed a gloomy light over an immense plain, forming two vast opposing semi-circles, which closed in the whole horizon on both sides. The hostile armies passed a sleepless night. They were on the eve of one of the great decisive battles of the world, which was to control the future fate of millions. Napoleon passed the night in his tent, alternately racked by anxious thoughts and fearful forebodings of the future; and with emotions of tenderness as he gazed with rapture on the portrait of his fair child, the king of Rome, which Isabey had completed since his departure from Paris, and which had but a day or two before arrived in his camp.

At length the long and tedious night passed away, and the morning sun shone brightly on the hostile hosts. It was the sun of Borodino, forever memorable in the annals of blood and all the horrors of war! Early in the morning Napoleon rode along the far-reaching lines of his grim warriors, and encouraged them with words of confidence which he did not himself feel; for already the unexpected disasters of the campaign had much diminished his first assurance in its ultimate issue. He reminded them that they were the unconquered heroes of Austerlitz and Friedland; that this was the last great battle to be fought by them, before Moscow opened her gorgeous gates to receive them; and that a triumph now would insure the speedy end of their toils, and their quick return to their native France. His words were received with shouts of rapture and exultation by the whole army.

In the Russian camp a somewhat similar scene was enacted on the morning of this great day. A large concourse of Russian priests, headed by a prelate of high rank, who carried in his arms an image reputed to possess miraculous power, passed along the ranks, which knelt as they approached. The prelate blessed the prostrate warriors as they lay; and as the procession returned along the lines, the swelling sound of sacred melody chaunted by the strong voices of the priests, ascended upon the morning air, and floated sweetly over the plain so soon to be deeply deluged with human blood. Kutusoff himself rode along the lines, and by his dauntless yet solemn air, infused new courage and devotion into the hearts of his warriors. The impressive sounds of prayer and praise as uttered by the Russian priests and soldiers, were even wafted by the breeze to the French camp, and did not fail to call forth the ridicule and satire of the gay and irreverent children of the Seine.

Thus fortified according to their respective tastes for the terrific scenes before them, the two armies prepared for battle. Their strength was nearly equal. The Russian force consisted of one hundred and thirty thousand men, together with six hundred and fifty pieces of artillery. The French army was about equal to these in number, with a similar quantity of artillery; though thirty thousand of the French troops were cavalry, which gave them some advantage over their opponents.

The Russians had fortified themselves in a strong position in and around the village of Borodino. In the center they had erected a great redoubt which mounted a hundred guns. Around this work the most bloody and desperate conflicts of the day were destined to take place. By Napoleon's orders, the fierce Davoust commenced the battle by advancing against the Russian lines on the right. Slowly and steadily his columns approached the terrific line of flame which already marked the position of the Russian batteries. Before reaching them, Davoust had his horse shot under him, and Generals Rapp and Desaix were wounded. Confusion began to prevail among the advancing host, but they were rëassured by the loud clarion voice of their dauntless leader, and were again led forward to the attack. After a fierce struggle the redoubts on the Russian left were taken, and Davoust established himself in the position wrested from the foe.

The center of the French army was led on by Marshal Ney. He ordered three divisions to advance, supported by ten thousand cavalry under Murat; and protected by seventy pieces of artillery. They were opposed by the flower of the Russian troops under Prince Bagrathion. Soon the French columns came within range of the terrible deluge of shot and shell which was belched forth from the Russian batteries. On the heights of Borodino, undaunted by the fearful havoc made in their lines, which crumbled like frost-work beneath the Russian fire, they still advanced. Whole files and companies were swept down by the murderous flood; but the cavities were instantly filled up, and still the tide of dauntless warriors rolled onward. On the heights of Borodino the most terrific conflict took place perhaps recorded in the history of warfare. After four hours of desperate fighting the Russians still maintained their position; and Marshal Ney anxiously demanded from Napoleon rëinforcements to enable him to maintain his position. Napoleon ordered the Young Guard, all the cavalry yet in reserve, and four hundred pieces of cannon to advance, and to assail the great redoubt in the Russian center. Prince Eugene had already narrowly escaped being captured at the head of his column, which had saved themselves only by forming into squares, and thus presenting an impenetrable barrier to the attacks of the Russian cuirassiers.

The immense rëinforcement ordered by Napoleon against the Russian center, after prodigious conflicts and immense losses from the artillery of the foe, succeeded in driving back the Russian line. At this crisis Prince Bagrathion perceiving the advantage gained by the French, ordered the whole left wing to advance to the attack. Then occurred one of those tremendous shocks of battle beneath which the very earth itself trembles. Eighty thousand men and seven hundred pieces of artillery contended on the plain during the space of an hour for deadly mastery; and prodigious feats of heroism, of desperate valor, of undying resolution, on both sides, to triumph or to perish, were exhibited. Blood flowed over the surface of the battle-field in torrents. Thousands of the dying and the dead lay heaped in piles, before, around, and beneath the surviving combatants; and it seemed that nothing could terminate the furious and deadly conflict, except the entire destruction of the contending hosts.

At length Prince Bagrathion being severely wounded, the Russian ranks began to give way. They withdrew with all their artillery from their first position, and established themselves in its rear, in the ravine of Semenowsky. Still the great redoubt in the center remained untaken. Napoleon with his eagle eye, readily discovered the importance of that point, and about the middle of the day, he ordered Eugene, with two hundred cannon, to advance together with Monbran's division of cuirassiers to penetrate the Russian line, and wheeling round, to enter the entrenchment through its gorge. It was defended by the regiment of Osterman; and soon the redoubt was enveloped in a vast cloud of flame and smoke, through which the glittering steel trappings of the cuirassiers were seen at intervals, gradually ascending its slopes, and approaching its summit. After a prodigious conflict the redoubt was won; but not until the regiment which defended it were entirely massacred by the savage onslaught of the French. They refused to give or to receive any quarter; and the whole of the corps of Osterman were slain within the works, which they had so heroically defended.

Driven to madness by the loss of their main fortress, the Russian lines which had taken up their position in its rear now again advanced, determined if possible, by unheard-of efforts, to retrieve the fortunes of the day, Kutusoff himself led on the attack. In admirable order they advanced toward the works which they had lost, which were now manned by the victorious French, whence eighty pieces of cannon thundered against their approaching ranks. They succeeded in taking some of the smaller redoubts; but their heroism was in vain. Thousands fell upon the field, displaying a degree of resolution unequaled in war, but without effect. Distressed at the fruitless and hopeless butchery resulting from his advance, Kutusoff at length gave the order to retire, and resumed his former position on the heights, in the rear of the works won by the French. Seeing no decisive advantage gained either on the Russian right or left, toward the close of the day, he ordered a general retrograde movement of the whole line to the works in the rear of those which had been occupied by the Russians at the beginning of the conflict; and thus, when the shades of evening settled down over the ensanguined plain, the whole line of the first Russian positions had fallen into the hands of the French.

Once during the progress of this memorable day, victory seemed about to perch upon the standards of the Russians, and to desert the proud invader. Kutusoff seeing the weakness of Napoleon's left, ordered Ouvaroff, with eight regiments of Cossacks, to cross the Kolotza, a stream in front of the Russian lines, and attack the left of the French. The impetuous and savage fury of the Cossacks was irresistible, and the French lines, then unsupported by the artillery which had been dispatched against the grand redoubts, wavered, broke, and retreated before their desperate assault. The whole French line began to give way. Napoleon, from the eminence on which he stood, saw by the aid of his spy-glass the greatness of the disaster; and his imperial cheek was paled with terror. The trembling phantoms of royalty and victory appeared about to desert his standards; and the wan finger of destiny seemed for a moment to point toward destruction as his doom. Then it was that he himself rapidly rode to his wavering lines, accompanied by the cavalry and artillery of his guards; and by prodigious efforts redeemed the fortunes of the day, and drove the Russians back again to their first position.

Night came and the battle ended. The victory remained with Napoleon, but such a victory and at such a sacrifice! The triumph itself brought no benefit with it; for the Russians merely withdrew the next day toward Moscow, leaving thousands of dead and wounded as obstacles in the pathway of the invaders. The sacrifices which this triumph cost Napoleon were indeed dreadful. Another such victory, and like Pyrrhus of old he might exclaim that he was utterly ruined. For the space of six miles the plain was thickly covered with the dying and the dead. Prince Bagrathion and thirty generals, fifteen thousand killed and thirty thousand wounded, were the losses of the Russians; while Napoleon mourned the death of Generals Monbrun and Canlaincourt, and the loss of twelve thousand killed, and thirty-eight thousand wounded. Nearly ninety thousand human beings, either killed or wounded then lay weltering in their blood upon that memorable field; while as far as the eye could reach there was visible nothing but a tumultuous heap of human bodies, horses, broken guns, casques, cuirasses, helmets, and other faded and bloody trophies of the glory and magnificence of war. Wounded horses maddened with the pain, struggled among the piles of slain. The wounded soldiers filled the air with their shrieks of agony calling in vain for help and succor; for the resources of the French surgeons were totally insufficient to meet a thousandth part of the demands made upon them. Napoleon from the eminence on which he had watched the progress of the battle, gloomily surveyed the appalling spectacle after the conflict was ended. His triumph instead of filling his mind with exultation, savored more of the sadness of defeat. His losses had been terrible. His only advantage was that he remained possessor of the battle field, and this was no equivalent for the immense losses which he had endured. In the resolution and fortitude displayed by the Russians, he saw an ominous presage of future resistance and disaster which he had not anticipated. He rightly judged that the worst was yet to come.

The condition of the French army after the battle of Borodino, was in the highest degree unfortunate and discouraging. For miles on both sides along the road to Moscow, the retreating Russians had devastated the country, had burned the houses, destroyed the provisions, and rendered it almost impossible for the invaders to procure means of subsistence. Thousands of horses perished from hunger. Nor was the want of food the only disaster which befel them. The French army had nearly exhausted their amunition, and had barely enough remaining to suffice for one more battle. At Borodino they had expended ninety-one thousand cannon shot; and not an equal quantity remained in the possession of the invaders. The soldiers were compelled to the necessity of subsisting almost entirely on the flesh of horses. So reduced indeed had they become after the battle of Borodino, and during the subsequent march toward Moscow, that had the Russians been acquainted with the real condition of their foe, they would not have sacrificed that ancient capital, but would have hazarded another great battle, in which it is very probable they would have gained a decisive victory.

But ignorant as they were of these facts, the Russian generals in a council of war, adopted the wisest, and at the same time, the most extraordinary resolution not to venture another great conflict, nor yet to attempt the defense of Moscow; but to abandon the capital to the French, set fire to its myriad houses, and thus, between the lurid flames of the immense conflagration, and the intensity of the approaching winter's cold, to vanquish a foe who seemed invincible by any ordinary resistance or resources.

Count Rostopchin, who was then governor of Moscow, acquiesced in the stern purpose, and was the first to proclaim and commend it to the astonished inhabitants. With a degree of self-sacrificing patriotism which has no parallel in the history of nations, the inhabitants of Moscow immediately obeyed the mandate; and three hundred thousand people at once began to travel forth by the eastern gates leaving behind them their splendid palaces, their valuable merchandize, and the accumulated wealth and rare treasures of ages, to become the prey of the devouring element. In three days the city was entirely deserted except by a few hundreds of the lowest and most abandoned of the inhabitants.

It was at eleven o'clock on the 14th of September, 1812, when the advanced guard of the French army, under Murat, reached the heights on the Smolensko road, from which the first view of Moscow could be obtained. There, reposing with stately magnificence in the plain below them, appeared the celebrated city, whose gilded spires and temples of mingled Asiatic and European architecture, proudly pierced the heavens, and seemed to herald the entrance of the invaders within the precincts of another continent, and proclaim their sudden advent into the gorgeous portals of the east. As far as the eye could reach the plain was covered with a heterogeneous variety of palaces, churches, gardens, rivers, public and private edifices, and the innumerable dwellings of the various classes, all basking in silent and stately loveliness, in the mellowed rays of an autumnal sun.

As the different divisions of the French army reached the eminence from which this view first greeted their gaze, their enthusiasm burst forth in shouts of frenzied triumph; and the words "Moscow! Moscow!" reverberated over the waste, as the sound was taken up and repeated by the enthusiastic French, from rank to rank. The excitement even reached Napoleon himself. He hastened forward to obtain a view of that gorgeous prize for which he had already risked and endured so much. He gazed for some moments in silence at the city, and then exclaimed: "Behold! at last there is Moscow," and after a pause he added with a sigh—"It was high time!"

Napoleon delayed a day in the expectation that a deputation of the magistrates would wait upon him, and deliver the keys of the city into his hands. He waited in vain. Disgusted at their apparent ignorance or indifference, he gave the order to advance, and his legions approached and entered the gates of Moscow. As he rode along the streets the sight of the antique towers, and the Tartaric style of architecture which characterized the palaces and temples, charmed and delighted him; and his admiration was raised to the highest pitch when he approached the Kremlin. This was a vast assemblage of palaces, a city within itself, partaking also somewhat of the character of a fortress; for it was defended by walls and towers, containing loop-holes and embrasures for the use of cannon. This stupendous and irregular pile of palaces and churches had for ages been the home and the burying place of Muscovite kings; and Napoleon's imagination was powerfully impressed with the thought that he had at length added this vast trophy of barbaric pomp and oriental splendor, to the long list of his other conquests. He had dreamed in his youth of an expedition to the farther east, by which he would dethrone some Persian or Arabian monarch and assume his scepter. That dream had never been realized. His expedition to Egypt had been but a partial and feeble substitute for it. But now, as the peerless Moscow lay unresisting at his feet, he seemed once more to approach nearer to the literal fulfillment of his youthful hope.

Napoleon had reached the Kremlin before he became aware of the appalling fact that he had entered a deserted city. No living creature appeared except his own soldiers, either to welcome or to oppose his entrance. At length he became fully aware of the real fact in the case, and he gave utterance to his astonishment and indignation in unmeasured terms of execration. No deputation of magistrates or nobles waited on him, humbly tendering him the keys of the city. No joyous population greeted him as their deliverer from antiquated tyranny. No smiling princesses hailed him as the modern Alexander, carrying his conquests toward the confines of the east; or lavished such compliments on him as beauty alone can bestow on the heroic and the illustrious. He was surrounded by an unbroken silence, the suspicious silence and solitude of a city of the dead. At length Napoleon entered the Kremlin, and established his head quarters in its gilded halls.

During one night, the night of the 14th of September, Napoleon slept in peace in his newly found home. His officers and soldiers freely pillaged the unoccupied palaces which had been deserted by their owners. Tumultuous riot and revelry, such as only attend in the pathway of conquest, prevailed throughout the vast city, thus suddenly deprived of its legitimate owners. In entering many of the palaces, the French soldiers found the richly furnished apartments with all their valuable contents of art, and furniture, and plate, precisely as their proprietors usually disposed of them. No attempt had been made at concealment or protection. Napoleon slept that night at least in peace. The extraordinary exertions which he had recently undergone, at length overpowered his physical frame, and nature gave way beneath them. He dreamed, as he reposed under the gorgeous hangings of the royal couch of Alexander, the absent czar; and his thoughts wandered far away over a thousand hills and vales, to the spot which contained his beloved wife, and idolized child, the king of Rome. His faithful attendants during the night saw a smile playing upon his lips, and heard the name of his fair son uttered in tones of deepest tenderness. It was a pleasing dream, a sweet illusion; from the gentle spell of which the stern conqueror was soon to wake to behold scenes of horror and dismay, unparalleled even in his memorable career of peril, vicissitude, and suffering.

On the 15th of September a fire first appeared in the Bazaar, which rapidly extended until a considerable portion of the surrounding city was in flames. A large part of the French army was at that moment so intoxicated by the wines and liquors which they found in the cellars of the deserted palaces, that they could afford no effectual resistance to the progress of the flames. The conflagration continued to rage with terrific fury, and unseen hands carried the torch of destruction in a hundred secret places, thus adding to its extent, and to the difficulty of subjecting it to control. During the night of the 15th, and during the whole of the 16th, 17th, and 18th of September, the fury of the flames increased, until at length the whole city seemed enveloped in one vast conflagration, which filled the entire horizon, and gradually approached nearer and nearer to the Kremlin.

At night the spectacle was terrific and sublime, far beyond the power of language to depict. A brighter light than that of the noonday sun banished darkness from the earth for many miles around. Immense palaces, temples, tapering and lofty spires, enveloped in flames, fell with a tremendous crash which shook the ground. Loud explosions of combustible materials continually occurred, which seemed like the report of an unseen battle. Floating fragments of burning material were wafted by the fitful winds through the midnight heavens, carrying destruction where the hands of the secret incendiary could not reach. At length on the 19th, the Kremlin itself took fire, and the mighty but humbled conqueror of a hundred battles, was compelled to evacuate a conquest in which he took so great a pride, and for the attainment of which he had made such immense sacrifices. So general had the conflagration by this time become, that it was with great difficulty, and amid imminent peril, that Napoleon and his suite could pass through the burning streets on their way to the gates. He arrived however, at length, at Petrowsky, a palace situated several miles from Moscow, and from this retreat the baffled invader had leisure to contemplate the unparalleled circumstances of disappointment, disaster, and danger, which at that moment surrounded him. As he gazed from the hot windows of this palace at the tumultuous ocean of fire and flame which extended for miles along the horizon before him, Napoleon is said to have exclaimed: "This sad event is the presage of a long train of disasters!" Nor did his usual sagacity desert him in making this prediction, as the sequel abundantly proved.

By the 20th of September the fire had exhausted itself. Moscow was in ruins. But by some strange good fortune the Kremlin had in a great measure escaped destruction; and Napoleon after an absence of several days, returned to it again. The place seemed to have exercised a strange fascination over his mind. There was to him an indescribable rapture in dating decrees from the Kremlin, which were to be obeyed alike at Paris, at Naples, at Madrid, and at Vienna. This fascination he seemed almost unable to resist. He therefore very unwisely spent four weeks in this romantic abode; during which time the season advanced, and the horrors of winter rapidly approached. It seems that the policy which the Russian monarch had determined to adopt, consisted of two points. The first was to amuse and delay Napoleon by appearances of negotiation, though never actually to enter into any serious arrangements with him. By this means the retreat of the French would be delayed until winter set in.

The other point was to satiate the deadly vengeance which the Russian army had sworn to execute on the ruthless invaders of their country, by collecting immense armies for the purpose of intercepting the French on their retreat, and destroying them by the combined force of the winter's fury, and the ceaseless and relentless attacks of the troops of the czar. By the treaties which Alexander had recently concluded with the Turks and the king of Sweden, two immense armies, each fifty thousand strong, were released from their services on the northern and southern frontiers of the empire; and were at liberty to march at once upon the line of the retreat of the French army. With these, Witgenstein was hastening from the north toward Polotsk; and Tchichagoff was rapidly approaching Borissow from the south. Other armies, under Kutusoff and Barclay de Tolly—the heroic veterans of Smolensko and Borodino—were passing by a rapid circuitous route in front of the French line of retreat, preparing to intercept them.

Meanwhile, at the Kremlin, Napoleon had made several overtures to the czar, for the purpose of inducing him to treat. They were all in vain. At length, driven to desperation, he dispatched a private letter to Alexander, couched in terms of personal friendship and regard; in which he touchingly referred to their former intimacy, and urged him for the sake of their suffering armies and subjects to agree to negotiate. To this letter, also, he received no answer whatever.

At length, on the 13th of October, the first snow fell; and the sleeping and imprisoned giant was suddenly aroused from his delusive dreams. At the same moment that he received this monition from the great voice of Nature, the news reached him of the fall of Madrid; of the entry of the Englisn army into that capital; and of the deposition and flight of his brother Joseph. Cursing the evil destiny which seemed to attend him, Napoleon at length gave orders to prepare for the retreat, and on the 15th of the month the veterans of Napoleon, who a short month before had first beheld the capital of the czars with such exulting and triumphant joy, now turned their backs in sullen gloom from the spot where Moscow once had stood in stately splendor; and commenced that memorable retreat, surrounded by such unparalleled horrors, which so few of them were ever destined to terminate within the confines of their native land.

The first moment of Napoleon's march was the signal for the commencement of active hostilities on the part of the alert generals and armies of the czar. The retreating troops were encumbered with the richest spoils of Moscow. They carried away with them an immense quantity of gold and silver plate, sumptuous and rich apparel, silks, embroideries, valuable pictures, and other rare works of art of inestimable value. Common soldiers might be seen overloaded with articles of Asiatic luxury and barbaric splendor. Beasts of burden groaned beneath the weight of plundered treasures from a hundred magnificent palaces. Among the rest, by Napoleon's express orders, the great cross of St. Ivan was borne along as his own particular trophy of conquest, together with the standards of eastern climes—of Turkey, of Persia, and China, which had been won by Russian prowess in many a far-distant and bloody field.

When the retreat began, the fair weather which soon returned, the rich spoils which the soldiers bore, and the gay revelry of the forty thousand camp-followers who attended them, among whom were many young Russian women, who had been seduced by the wiles of the pleasing invaders to embrace the opportunity to return with them to Paris—gave the march the joyful air of a triumphant procession. But soon the whole aspect of affairs was changed, and sadly changed, for the worse.

Meanwhile, Kutusoff was hastening with one hundred thousand men, and seven hundred pieces of cannon, toward the town of Wiazma, at which point the Russian commander determined to inflict the first great blow upon the army of the invader. A long journey of seven hundred miles lay before his retreating soldiers in the midst of a hostile and barren country; and it was time to commence the terrific task of crushing and obliterating the host of wearied and overburdened soldiers from whose standards victory had fled.

On the second of November, Platoff, with ten thousand Cossacks, made a furious onslaught on the rear of the army. The whole body of Russian cavalry under Wassiltchikoff attacked the main line of the French retreat, and established themselves on both sides of the Smolensko road, along which the line of retreat lay. The rear guard of Davoust fled before the desultory but furious attack of the Cossacks. The vanguard of the Russians under Kutusoff commenced a cannonade on the corps of Ney; and the division of General Paskiewitz attacked the center of the French posted in the town of Wiazma, and drove them through the streets at the point ot the bayonet.

During this engagement the French lost six thousand men. Before this battle the corps of Davoust alone had lost ten thousand men by fatigue and desertion; and the whole French army had been reduced in proportion. Napoleon had again been vanquished, and as a natural consequence, despondency and a growing disregard for discipline and order pervaded the feelings and marked the conduct of the retreating troops.

It was on the 6th of November that the snow began to

fall, and the rigors of a Russian winter to commence; and from this date commenced the real horrors and unparalleled disasters of the retreat. With the falling snow the wind began to be high and furious, and soon immense drifts obstructed the roads, and rendered it difficult for the wearied and burdened troops to advance. It was not until winter came, that the Russians displayed the real atrocities of the course of retribution which they had determined to inflict upon their invaders. Then it was that the fierce vengeance of the flying clouds of Cossacks began to exhibit itself. Hanging on the outskirts of the wearied and straggling lines of French soldiers, by sudden attacks they slew thousands singly and in small companies, as they struggled through the snow. At the same time hundreds fell upon the way exhausted by the labors of the march. The roads soon became impassable for the artillery, and hundreds of guns were left behind at the base of each rising hill. The soldiers soon became unable to transport their ammunition; and frequent explosions in the rear of their path, and on the outskirts, indicated how frequently the ammunition wagons were sacrificed rather than left to the possession of the pursuers. And soon the road became strewed with the rich and stolen spoils of Moscow, to which, till then, their captors had clung with the same tenacity as they clung to life; even these, the immense toils and perils of the way compelled them to sacrifice.

In one week's time after the commencement of the wintry weather, thirty thousand men had perished. The path of the retreating army was now marked by a long line of deserted cannon, of exploded wagons, and of freezing and dying men and horses. So terrible had the destitution already become, that many of the French soldiers rioted in horse flesh; and even others, it is said, did not abstain from assuaging their horrid pangs by eating human bodies. During the hours of darkness the country became a howling wilderness. Far and wide over the snowy waste, no sign of human habitation, no sound of human sympathy was seen or heard. The driving snowdrifts threatened to bury the wearied soldiers beneath their cold embrace; and when morning dawned, the fragments of the bivouack-fires were surrounded by circles of frozen bodies, which during the night had perished in silence as they lay, from the intensity of the cold.

Napoleon who still remained with his fated army, concentrated all his endeavors toward reaching Smolensko. At this place he had previously ordered immense stores of provisions to be collected, when on his forward march toward Moscow; and he hoped that when his retreating troops reached this spot, he would be able to retrieve a large portion of the disasters of his defeat. He therefore urged on his troops along the Smolensko road, sacrificing everything which impeded their advance. By this time nearly the whole of his baggage and artillery had been left behind; and he now even ordered the great cross of St. Ivan, which had adorned the loftiest pinnacle of the Kremlin, and the Turkish and Persian standards, to be sunken in the waters of an adjoining lake. During all this time the attacks on his troops by the relentless Cossacks continued uninterrupted. Kutusoff with an immense army still hovered around his rear, waiting for a propitious opportunity and favorable ground to bring the exhausted French to another general engagement.

At length, on the 9th of November, Napoleon arrived at Smolensko. The lofty towers and gilded domes of its cathedral, again greeted the eyes of his wearied and famished troops, who, by this time, had been diminished by one half, from the mighty armament which, on the advance toward Moscow, had beheld them. Here from the 9th to the 13th they reposed; and Napoleon put forth prodigious exertions to recruit his shattered forces. His cavalry, which numbered forty thousand men when they first crossed the Niemen, had now been reduced to the pitiful sum of eight hundred; and of all his vast armament with which he entered Russia of five hundred thousand men, but seventy thousand now remained, of whom forty thousand alone were effective troops.

On the 14th of November the French army resumed its mournful retreat. The emperor, with the old and new guard, came first. Next came the division of the viceroy Eugene. Then followed Davoust with the main body of the army; while Ney still continued to conduct the rear. On the 17th of November the Russian general Kutusoff was enabled to bring the French emperor to another general engagement at Krasnoi. His host of wearied soldiers still continued to waste away by hundreds daily; and a stronger hope of a complete triumph now encouraged the mind of Kutusoff, in making another combined attack upon his enemy. Prince Galitzin, with the Russian center, furiously attacked the Young Guard, and succeeded in achieving a result which had never before been accomplished. Sorely pressed on all sides, the guard had formed into squares, and one of these squares Galitzin broke, and absolutely destroyed. Davoust's division was enveloped by an immense cloud of Cossacks, who attacked his division with their accustomed fury, and threw it into confusion. The Russians carried by assault the village of Krasnoi where Napoleon was posted, and compelled him to retire. At the close of the conflict, the harassed, exhausted, and perishing army of the invader had lost six thousand prisoners, forty-five pieces of cannon, two imperial standards, an immense quantity of baggage, and the private archives of Napoleon.

There was a spectacle exhibited during this retreat, comically unique, and yet terrible in its character, which no other warlike movements have ever displayed. For many leagues the whole division of Davoust, now reduced to five thousand men out of seventy thousand, pursued their slow and tedious march completely enveloped on all sides by clouds of flying Cossacks, who kept even pace with their march, and constantly harassed them with their exhausting and desultory attacks.

At length, on the 23d of November, the French army reached the banks of the Beresina. The bridge which crossed this river had been destroyed by Tchichagoff, who had advanced from the south; and this calamity compelled Napoleon to construct another for the passage of his troops. He immediately commanded his engineers to commence the task. A corps of sappers threw themselves into the river up to their necks in the swelling flood, and heroically labored to accomplish the herculean task. The cavalry were commanded to swim over the stream while the process of construction was advancing.

At length the bridge was sufficiently finished for the infantry to pass over. The passage began and continued during the 25th, and 26th, and amid attacks of the Russians on both sides of the river, the French army succeeded with immense difficulty in reaching the opposite bank, with the exception of the division of General Partonneaux, composed of seven thousand men, who were surrounded by the everlasting Cossacks under Platoff, and at length compelled to surrender themselves prisoners of war.

It was during the passage of the rear division of Marshal Victor over the bridge, that one of the most terrible scenes ever witnessed, was presented to view. The Russian artillery under Diebitch was brought to bear directly upon the bridge, ladened with the retreating multitude. A wide semi-circle of cannon swept the whole line of the bridge, with a deluge of fiery shot and shell, carrying death and dismay into the tumultuous crowd, from whose ranks all discipline had long been banished. Terror seemed to fill every mind, and a maddened rush forward to escape impending ruin was seen on all sides. Hundreds were trampled to death beneath the feet of their comrades. The cannon of the Russians ploughed through and through the thick masses of living flesh. Heaps of the dead and dying were piled on the bridge, and began to impede the passage. At this crisis, the cannon balls broke the bridge in the center, and set the two extremities on fire. A scene of horror then ensued which beggars all language. The frantic crowd were compelled to plunge into the half-frozen flood below, and swim for their lives. Thousands of men, women, and horses perished, trampled to death by the struggling multitude, or drowned by the waters of the stream. When the ice dissolved in the ensuing spring, twelve thousand dead bodies were found—the victims of this horrid and memorable passage.

At length, on the 5th of December, Napoleon arrived with the wrecks of his army at Smorgoni. Here he dictated his celebrated 29th bulletin, in which, for the first time, he proclaimed the real horrors of his condition and losses. He placed the supreme command in the hands of Murat, and set off with Caulaincourt and Loban, at ten o'clock at night for, Paris. He had received news of Mallet's conspiracy in the French capital, and he determined to leave his unfortunate army to their impending doom, and make good his own escape beyond the Russian territory. He traveled in a small *britschka*, placed on low runners, made out of rude fir wood. He journeyed night and day with his two companions, closely wrapped up in heavy furs.

Silently and gloomily the fallen monarch traversed, as rapidly as his wearied horses could draw him, the immense and cheerless plains of Poland. How singular must have been his reflections during this sad journey! His insatiable ambition had at length been foiled in its audacious attempt to grasp the scepter of universal sovereignty. He had been the cause of the ruin of a million of his fellow creatures, and the curses loud and deep of myriads of bereaved widows and orphans, over the whole continent, rang in his ears, as the just knell of future and inevitable retribution. Did he care for or feel the ponderous weight of all these curses? It is doubtful! Ambition, when it becomes insatiable, becomes also lost to every dictate of reason, humanity, and justice; and it is probable that in the dark breast of this great, bad man, the only prevalent feeling was chagrin at his own discomfiture, and apprehension as to the future evils which impended over him.

Deserted by their emperor, the French army still continued its retreat; and finally arrived at the banks of the Niemen, the confines of the Russian territory, on the 12th of December. Out of that vast and imposing armament of five hundred thousand men, which in the preceding June had crossed that river, glittering in all the pride, pomp, and majesty of war, twenty thousand enfeebled and exhausted specters alone tottered over it on their return! All the rest had perished, or had been captured during the progress of this memorable expedition—as sacrifices offered upon the altar of the insatiable ambition of one bold and unprincipled but gifted adventurer.

In reflecting on this picture of ruin and unparalleled woe, it is difficult to convey any adequate idea of the real importance and magnitude of the events involved in it. From the day the French army crossed the Niemen till that of its return to its shores, one hundred and twenty-five thousand men had been slain in battle; one hundred and thirty-two thousand had perished of cold, famine, and fatigue; one hundred and ninety thousand had been taken prisoners and subjected afterward to all the horrors of Siberian captivity. In addition to these it should be remembered, that in the various battles fought with the Russians, the latter had also lost an immense number of men. It is computed that the killed and wounded in the

Russian armies amounted at least to one hundred and fifty thousand men during the six months of Napoleon's invasion. What a stupendous and incalculable amount of suffering had this one single daring and prodigious venture of Napoleon, inflicted on a mourning, weeping, and agonizing continent!

At length, on the 20th of December, 1812, Napoleon reached Paris. He arrived unheralded, at midnight. His first care was to convict and punish Mallet and his confederates, who had dared, in his absence, to menace the security of his throne. Soon the pitiful remains of his once "grand army" began to arrive at the French capital; and by their diminished numbers and frightful appearance of suffering and misery, opened the eyes of the astonished Parisians to the full extent of the horrors and losses of the expedition.

The mighty genius of Napoleon never recovered from the disastrous effects of this memorable campaign. An outraged continent soon assembled its armies on the confines of France, determined by one prodigious effort to destroy forever the power of the great curse of modern times. Closer and closer the lines were drawn around the hunted lion, by his determined pursuers; and his prodigious bounds failed to extricate him from their gathering toils. At last, at Leipsic, the memorable battle was fought—fitly called "the battle of the nations"—at which Europe concentrated her energies at one mighty blow to crush the common foe, and the relentless oppressor of all.

Yet, amid these continued disasters, the amazing genius of this extraordinary man remained undismayed. Yielding for the time being to the necessity laid upon him by the voice of destiny, he accepted with a good grace the proffered toy of Elba's diminutive diadem, and retired thither to rest for an interval from his labors; and then once more to come forth and convulse the continent anew with his restless energy and ambition—to enact the memorable drama of Waterloo, and the Hundred Days!

CHAPTER XII.

NAPOLEON DURING THE HUNDRED DAYS.

THE most brilliant assemblage of beauty, celebrity, and fashion, which ever graced a capital with their courtly presence, was the European congress which convened in Vienna in 1815. It was then thought that the formidable hero who for twenty years had agitated the continent with the throes of his ambition, had been safely and permanently caged at Elba; and there had congregated in the palaces of the voluptuous and stately capital of the imperial house of Hapsburg, a galaxy of illustrious statesmen, of skillful diplomatists, of heroic warriors, of powerful monarchs, and of witty, fascinating and accomplished women such the world had never before beheld in one single view. The distracted affairs of Europe were then indeed to be settled; but neither the cares of business nor of ambition in the least degree impeded the more pleasing and attractive pursuits of intrigue, flirtation, and pleasure.

The emperor of Russia, the kings of Prussia, Bavaria, Denmark, and Wurtemberg, and a miscellaneous collection of grand-dukes, margraves, dukes and electors who governed the petty principalities of Germany, were there in person. The British empire was represented by Lord Castlereagh, and the Duke of Wellington; France by the illustrious Talleyrand; Prussia by Hardenberg and Humboldt; and the Austrian sovereign by Metternich, he who alone of European diplomatists had once over-reached and outlied Napoleon himself. The kings of Spain, Portugal, Sweden, and Naples, of Sicily, Bavaria, Saxony and the Netherlands, together with the Swiss and Genoese republics, had all sent their ablest diplomatists to represent them. And while the greatest legislators and soldiers of Europe were assembled there, in those high halls of state, the potency of woman's softer and sweeter charms was fitly represented and exercised by some of the most accomplished and fascinating of the sex, by Madam Grandt, by the countess de Fuchs, and by many other very celebrated belles and beauties, some of stainless and some of easy virtue. Thus the grave deliberations of the congress were agreeably alleviated and diversified by the most brilliant assemblies, by the most sumptuous banquets, by the most delicious *fêtes*, by the most exquisite flirtations, and the most voluptuous excesses which the prolific imagination of man can conceive.

At the very moment when these scenes were gaily progressing at Vienna, another, and a somewhat different one, was being enacted at Elba. The generosity of the allied sovereigns of Europe had placed Napoleon as an independent monarch on this island, which was situated near the Tuscan coast, and within view of the soil of Italy. He was permitted to possess an ample revenue, and an armed force which soon amounted to a thousand men. Three small vessels of war were also at his disposal; and he maintained all the dignities, prerogatives and ceremonies of a court, with the same degree of formality as when he presided at the Tuilleries, or St. Cloud. He was constantly surrounded by many illustrious visitors of both sexes, and the society of his diminutive empire was brilliant and distinguished in the extreme.

On the 26th of February, 1815, the ex-emperor gave a ball in the palace of Porto Ferrajo, his capital, to which all the persons of consequence on the island were invited. Rarely had Parisian elegance and splendor displayed anything more attractive and select than that assemblage. All the foreign ministers were present. The queenly Pauline Bonaparte presided, and threw over the scene that luster which her own peerless grace and beauty alone could impart. Napoleon himself seemed to be in unusually good spirits. He passed around the room and conversed gaily with his numerous guests. To have looked upon that marble brow and those finely chiselled features, then wreathed with smiles, the witchery of which exceeded that of all others' smiles, no one would have imagined that at that very moment Napoleon was about to execute the boldest, the most dangerous, and the most desperate enterprise of his whole life. The hours wore quickly on. The dancing had began. Sweet music and fair forms floated gracefully through that brilliant hall, and while the attention of the assembly was attracted to the amusements which were going forward, the great conqueror drew aside into a remote alcove, one of the most lovely of her sex for a moment's private converse. The person thus highly honored by imperial favor was a Polish lady of rare beauty. She had fascinated Napoleon before the battle of Eylau, and had retained her potent influence over him ever since. Her charms of mind equalled her charms of person; and she seemed not unworthy to be the vanquisher of the vanquisher of Europe. She had followed him to his retreat at Elba; and her society had largely contributed to alleviate the monotony of his residence there. This lady was the celebrated Madam Walewski, the mother of the French diplomatist, who presided over the deliberations of the peace congress at Paris in 1856. With this beautiful and voluptuous woman Napoleon spent a short time in cheerful and witty dalliance unobserved by the gay crowd. To her alone, of all that crowd, he communicated the daring venture he was about to make. He also made an arrangement with her to follow him soon to Paris; and then quietly withdrew, unnoticed, from the ball-room.

At that moment a thousand men were drawn up on the quay of Porto Ferrajo, waiting for the appearance of the emperor. They were under the command of Bertrand, Cambronne and Drouot. Napoleon immediately joined them and gave the instant order to embark. He himself stepped on board the brig Inconstant, which contained four hundred of his veteran guards. His appearance was calm and resolute. He said boldly to those around him: "The die is now cast." The night was serene, and the moon shone brightly upon that adventurous flotilla freighted with the fortunes of one, even greater and more illustrious than Cæsar. He directed the pilots to steer for the coast of Provence. As soon as the soldiers learned that they were on their direct way to France, they displayed the utmost enthusiasm; and then loud shouts of *vive l'empereur*, echoed and reëchoed over the wide surface of the tranquil deep. During the voyage they once came within hail of a French brig. The soldiers lay flat on the deck that they might not be discovered, and the captain of the vessel asked whether they had come from Elba, and how Napoleon was. Napoleon himself replied: *Il se porte a merveille!* In the afternoon of the first of March the flotilla cast anchor in the Gulf of St. Juan, and immediately Napoleon and his adventurous companions disembarked on the soil of their beloved France.

The purpose of Napoleon in making this sudden descent upon the French territory is well known. He designed to regain his lost throne. He intended to make a triumphant progress through the provinces; gathering the augmenting strength and power of an avalanche as he advanced; and thus vested with a new omnipotence to arrive in Paris, to drive Louis XVIII. from the throne, and to resume his forfeited empire. All these brilliant calculations came very near being totally disappointed at their outset. The great hero of Austerlitz and Wagram very narrowly escaped the ignominious penalty which attends in all countries the commission of common treason. Having sent twenty-five of his old guard to seduce the garrison of Antibes in the name of the emperor, the commander of the fortress, General Corsin, ordered them to be arrested. The failure of this first attempt on the part of the desperate adventurer was an evil omen; and indeed it spread very considerable dismay among the soldiers of Napoleon. Even Napoleon himself was astonished, and for a few moments stunned, by this unexpected reverse. He had imagined that the potent magic of his great name would dispel every obstacle; that the soldiers of France would rally in multitudes around his standards;

and that he would have but little difficulty to contend with in his pathway of triumph. Now, however, he saw his very first attempt utterly fail and his future progress might only involve him in further and perhaps fatal perils. But Napoleon's mind had now reached a state of desperation; he had gone too far to recede; and he determined to advance, whatever might be the consequences. Accordingly, at four o'clock the next morning, at the head of his small and insignificant force, he commenced his daring march toward Paris. He entered the mountain defiles of Gap, and took the direct route to Grenoble.

During the first two days Napoleon marched fifty-four miles. At Digne he printed his proclamations which he commenced to distribute along his route. At Grenoble he again very narrowly escaped destruction. The troops which were stationed there were drawn out by their commander to resist and capture him. Before an opportunity however was given for hostilities to commence, Napoleon advanced in front of his own ranks, and addressing the opposite party exclaimed: "Comrades! do you not know me? Do you not recognize me, my children? I am your emperor. Fire on me if you wish, here is my bosom!" At the same moment he bared his breast. The well known person and the familiar voice of their former chieftain proved irresistible to the excited troops, the heroes of many an ensanguined field; and whole companies of them rushed toward him with transport; shouts of *vive l'Empereur* filled the air; and the entire force arrayed themselves immediately among his friends and partisans. Napoleon then entered Grenoble in triumph. He proclaimed some decrees of great importance from that city, in which he announced the downfall of the Bourbons, and his own resumption of the throne. Their burning and rapid eloquence thrilled every breast in France with emotion; and eventually even convulsed many nations of Europe with the throes of revolution and warfare.

While Napoleon was thus advancing toward his capital, with the accumulating power and magnitude of an Alpine avalanche, the court of the Bourbons, and the friends of the ancient monarchy, after a few useless efforts at resistance, fled in dismay in every direction. At first it was thought that some effective show of opposition might be made. Nearly all the celebrated marshals of Napoleon had accepted high posts under Louis XVIII. and their great abilities were immediately put into requisition. Soult, Massena, Mortier, Oudinot, Augereau, Macdonald and Ney, were all engaged in the service of the Bourbons, and were appointed to fill important commands. Ney alone among them however, was enthusiastic in his hopes of success against the strange and magic power of this ancient commander; and as he left the Tuilleries on the 7th of March he exultingly said to the king: "Farewell sire; I will bring back Bonaparte to you in an iron cage!" It was at this moment that the news of Napoleon's departure from Elba reached the gay crowds which were assembled at Vienna. Had a thunderbolt from heaven suddenly fallen in the midst of the ball-room of the imperial palace, it could not have inspired more terror among the numerous and brilliant circle then assembled there, than did that unexpected announcement. The sensation which it produced was prodigious. Sovereigns, ministers, soldiers and statesmen of every grade and character were overcome with mingled amazement and consternation. The congress hurriedly concluded its deliberations; and the assembled monarchs with their advisers immediately began to make arrangements to combat and to conquer this last and desperate effort of the mighty Corsican, to grasp once more the diadem of France, and the supremacy of Europe.

On the 12th of March Napoleon reached the important city of Lyons, and entered it without opposition. It was here that he first came in contact with his veteran comrade in arms, Marshal Ney, the bravest of the brave; and it was here that after considerable deliberation that distinguished hero consummated the unfortunate act of treason, which has forever sullied the luster of many brilliant deeds, and covered his name with infamy. Ney reached Lyons very soon after Napoleon entered it. He came thither for the express purpose of arresting the latter; he left that city the sworn confederate of him whose desperate purpose it was once more to disturb the peace of a distracted continent, and hurl a legitimate monarch from a throne, around which clustered the happiness and security of uncounted millions.

From Lyons to Paris the march of Napoleon resembled more the triumphant progress of a great conqueror, than the perilous return of a banished outlaw. By the fourteenth of March, the growing enthusiasm in favor of the bold adventurer had pervaded the whole of France. The memory of his many mighty deeds still exercised its magic spell over the minds of the most excitable of nations. Though the Corsican had already cost France many millions of valuable lives, it was still true that he held the uppermost place in the nation's favor and admiration. Soon defection spread throughout the whole royal army. Wherever detachments were placed, and wherever fortresses were garrisoned, they successively deserted the standards of the Bourbons, and announced their determination to enlist in the service of Napoleon. By the nineteenth of March the condition of the Bourbons was desperate. All appeals to the honor and integrity of the army of Paris were fruitless. A review of the Royal and National Guards of the capital was ordered on the nineteenth; and nobody appeared. On that day at dinner the king was deserted in the gilded halls of the Tuilleries; and at the midnight which succeeded, the weeping monarch, attended by his family alone, silently departed from the palace of his forefathers and took the road to Blauvais. He pursued his rapid journey through Abbeville and Lille to Ghent; and left the pathway to the throne of France open and free to the adventurous feet of him before whom so many kings in turn had trembled.

At the same hour when Louis XVIII. was leaving Paris, Napoleon was entering Fontainbleau. The perils and uncertainties of the journey were now over; and Napoleon enjoyed a moment's leisure to contemplate the sudden and potentous splendor of his new position. Nor did he attempt to conceal the exulting rapture with which he assumed once more the accustomed reins of empire. His journey, especially the latter portion of it, was the source of infinite pleasure to his ambitious mind; for during its progress he received unanswerable proofs that he still remained after so many misfortunes and vicissitudes, the supreme idol of his beloved France. And as he progressed toward the great capital to whose embellishment and splendor in former years he had contributed so much, he appeared to become buoyant with an unaccustomed glow of rapture and enthusiasm. He seemed to mount on wings of glory to the towering summit of that great and brilliant throne from which he had so long intimidated Europe, and had been the object of the world's mingled awe and admiration.

At nine o'clook on the twentieth of March, Napoleon entered the halls of the Tuilleries. A vast crowd of generals, officers, statesmen and soldiers, filled the spacious apartments, waiting to receive and welcome him. His entrance was the signal for general shouts of enthusiasm. A brilliant crowd of epaulettes immediately surrounded him. They congratulated him with the utmost enthusiasm, and many distinguished ladies of the imperial court crowded their fair forms into the press, reached the emperor, and fervently kissed his hands, his cheeks, and even his clothes. Such transports of joy had never before been seen within the hollow and artificial precincts of a palace. A reception more gratifying to the personal vanity of the great hero could not possibly have been offered him. He retired that night to sleep with sweeter dreams and with brighter reveries of airy and fantastic hope, than his ardent imagination had ever before indulged. If ever there was an hour which was supremely happy and felicitous throughout the tempestuous and chequered life of that extraordinary man, it must have been during the first night of his abode in the Tuilleries, after his dangerous and uncertain journey from Elba. It was happier and more exquisite in its joy, than the hour when he first placed the imperial diadem on his aspiring head; than the hour when he first folded the fair and youthful form of the blushing daughter of many Cæsars in his arms; than the hour when he first imprinted a father's kiss on the infant brow of the apparent heir of such bright hopes, and such a gorgeous destiny as those of the king of Rome; it was happier because his recent humiliation and exile had taught him better to appreciate the splendors of his former position, and to estimate more truly its unequalled grandeur and felicity.

The early dawn of the next morning dissolved at once this empty and delusive dream. Great as seemed the rejoicing at his return, Napoleon found it almost impossible to obtain competent persons who were willing to assume the responsibility of holding the reins of office under him. This ominous fact proved that of the many able men who then surrounded him, none believed in the perpetuity of his supremacy. He immediately summoned to his presence his most able and trusted advisers. They obeyed; but declined to accept the ministries offered them. Cambaceres was offered the ministry of justice; but he refused it. Caulaincourt was offered the portfolio of foreign affairs; but he too declined. Carnot was offered that of the interior, with the same result. Fouché, the most treacherous, unprincipled, and infamous of human beings, alone was willing to resume his ancient functions of minister of police; but even he resumed them only to work the ruin, and to accelerate the downfall, of his master. After very considerable difficulty, and only in consequence of Napoleon's peremptory commands, the government was distributed into the hands of Davoust, Molé, Frochet, Maret, and Caulaincourt.

And now having made these preliminary arrangements, Napoleon had a moment of leisure to look around him, to ascertain his real position, and to estimate the prodigious dangers and difficulties of that position. He sat upon a brilliant but a tottering throne; and a whole continent excited with rage and hostility against him were arming themselves and summoning their utmost resources to precipitate him from his uneasy eminence, and overwhelm him with utter ruin.

On the twenty-fifth of March, 1815, a treaty was concluded at Vienna between the sovereigns of Russia, Prussia, Austria, and Great Britain, by which they bound themselves to combine their forces against Bonaparte and his faction, in order to prevent him from again disturbing the peace of Europe. They each agreed to furnish a hundred and eighty thousand soldiers for the prosecution of the war, and if it were necessary to crush the power of their general foe, to call forth their whole military resources of every description. They also bound themselves by solemn oath never to lay down their arms nor to conclude peace until they had accomplished the complete destruction of Napoleon. Within a fortnight after the ratification of this treaty, all the lesser powers of Europe had signified their accession to it. The contingent forces of the different countries were assessed according to their respective ability; that of Bavaria at sixty thousand men; that of Piedmont at thirty thousand; that of Hanover at twenty-six thousand, and other states at lesser numbers.

It will thus be perceived that all the powers of Europe

were now, for the first time, arrayed against Napoleon. For the first time in the history of the world, a whole continent rose up at once in arms, to crush a single man. The sum total of the military forces which would now be brought to bear against the mighty Corsican, were indeed prodigious, and might have appalled a heart even as heroic and as resolute as his. They amounted very nearly to a million of men. The confederate monarchs resolved to form three great armies. The first composed of two hundred and sixty-five thousand men, under the command of Prince Schwartzenberg, was to assemble on the Upper Rhine. The second, numbering a hundred and fifty-five thousand men, under the order of Marshal Blücher, was to form on the Lower Rhine. The third composed of an equal number of men, were to assemble in Belgium. The military force then at the command of the confederated foes of Napoleon, amounted to more than the six hundred thousand men, which were to be distributed in these three great bodies. There was also a Russian reserve of a hundred and sixty-eight thousand, under the command of Barclay de Tolly, which was rapidly hastening toward the scene of conflict. These swelled the number of veteran soldiers who, within six weeks time after Napoleon's arrival at the Tuilleries, were in motion against him, to very nearly the prodigious multitude of seven hundred and fifty thousand men.* In

* The composition of the principal armies of this immense host was as follows:

I. Army of Upper Rhine, Schwartzenberg, viz.:

Austrians,	150,000	
Bavarians,	65,000	
Wirtemberg,	25,000	
Baden,	16,000	
Hessians, &c.,	8,000	
		264,000

fact "Europe," as Metternich himself declared in the European Observer, "has declared war against Bonaparte." It was not a single power, or even a confederacy of powers; but a whole continent which had arisen in wrath to take vengeance on that haughty and aspiring head, for many previous years of suffering, for the most unparalleled insults and aggressions, for the black despair and ignominy which he had inflicted on them so long, and with such apparent impunity. One of those great decisive crises had now arrived, which determine the fate of the whole world for ages to come. On the issue of the impending struggle, the stability of all the thrones in Europe then depended. If Napoleon was conquered, they and all their innumerable interests and institutions would remain. If he triumphed, his terrific vengeance would sweep away with a fury such as he alone could exhibit, every prop to their thrones, and they would be completely ruined and obliterated.

Napoleon nerved himself to meet this last great struggle, not merely for glory and empire, but even for life and honor, with a degree of energy, resolution and unconquerable heroism, such as has never before or since been displayed in history. He was opposed and menaced by a coalition such as no other man would have dared to confront, or ever did confront. Alexander the Great, when he marched to the conquest of Persia, knew that

II. Army of Lower Rhine, Blucher, Prussians, Saxons, &c.,	155,000
III. Army of Flanders—British, Belgians, Hanoverans, Brunswickers	155,000
IV. Russian Reserve, Barclay de Tolly,	168.000
	743,000

—See PLOTHO, iv., *Appendix*, p. 62; *and* CAPEFIGUE, i., 330, 331,

the vast hordes of Darius were imbecile, luxurious and timid. Cæsar never met so mighty a host, or faced so powerful a foe on the plains of Gaul. We will search in vain in all the annals of ancient or modern heroism for a parallel to this last prodigious struggle of Napoleon to repel the armed and veteran multitudes who, under the command of the most able generals, came swelling up toward France from every quarter of Europe, like the mighty tide of a shoreless ocean, to overwhelm him, and consign him to oblivion. His heroism then became the heroism of desperation; such heroism as induces men to put forth unequalled efforts in the last extremity; the heroism which leads warriors to advance to certain glory and death in the forlorn hope; the heroism which superior spirits alone display when, immediately before they leave the world, they expend all their energies in one final, convulsive, dying throe. The campaign of Napoleon during the hundred days stands forth, unfortunate as was its termination to him, preëminent above all other epochs of military history, and resplendant with unequalled glory and renown.

At that moment the arsenals and fortresses of France were nearly empty in consequence of the immense exhaustion which had taken place during the preceeding years. By the recent treaty at Paris twelve thousand pieces of cannon distributed in fifty-three fortresses, had been ceded to the enemies of France. Yet the genius of Napoleon in this great crisis rose triumphant above every obstacle, and nobly asserted its ancient supremacy. He at once began the reorganization and enlargement of the army. The eagles of the old regiments which had been taken from them by Louis XVIII. were restored; and with them came back the martial spirit and love for Napoleon, which had so often led those veterans to victory and to glory. Three additional battalions were ordered for each regiment. Napoleon invited all the retired veterans of the empire once more to come forward, and join the standards and the fortunes of their ancient leader. Two additional squadrons were ordered to each regiment of cavalry. Thirty new battalions of artillery were raised from the sailors in the fleets in Cherbourg, Brest, and Toulon. Forty battalions in twenty regiments were added to the Young Guard. Two hundred battalions of the National Guards were organized from old and new recruits. All France felt the electric shock communicated by the energy, desperation and enthusiasm of the great conqueror. By these prodigious exertions Napoleon hoped that by the first of September he would have five hundred battalions of troops of the line, and fifty-two of the guards, numbering all together about six hundred thousand men.

It was still more difficult to feed, clothe, and arm so great a multitude in so short a time, than it was to obtain their enlistment. But even this task was not too great for the unconquerable energy of Napoleon. He immediately doubled the number of workmen in all the manufactories of arms throughout the country. He thus obtained twenty thousand muskets per month. The old "bruised arms" were everywhere called into requisition; they were repaired, burnished up, and made fit for use. Additional workmen were employed, and the foundries were everywhere put in active operation for the manufacture of artillery. Innumerable horses were purchased throughout the whole of France. Even draught horses were bought from the wagons of the farmers to draw the guns. The arming of the troops and the equipment of the cannon progressed with extraordinary rapidity. The activity and energy of Napoleon were prodigious. By the beginning of June, 1815, two hundred and twenty thousand men were fully armed and equipped. Many of these were the old retired veterans of the empire, the heroes of Borodino, Jena, and Austerlitz, who had joyfully responded to the call of their illustrious leader, to step forward to his aid in this the hour of his greatest necessity. For all these vast and expensive preparations, payment was made with what ready money the treasury then contained, and with orders on the treasury, redeemable at a future and sometimes a distant period.

Another measure and one more pacific in its nature, it became Napoleon at that crisis to take, in order to secure the full and enthusiastic confidence of the nation. This was the formation and proclamation of a constitution adapted to the then existing state of public feeling, and his own altered and uncertain fortunes. There was then a strong liberal party in the French chambers, the relics of the old Jacobin faction of the revolution, at the head of whom stood Fouché and Carnot; who pretended to insist on a democratic empire or sovereignty, with Napoleon at its head. These must be appeased as well as the other conflicting parties in the state. At length after considerable discussion a constitution was agreed upon, of which the prominent provisions were these. First, the peerage was declared to be hereditary, thus reviving in substance the old feudal nobility. Second, the confiscation of property for political offences was abolished, except for high treason. Third, the family of the Bourbons was forever banished from the soil of France.

After the provisions of this constitution had been agreed on between the emperor and the chambers, the ratification of it by the nation was deemed necessary. To give *eclat* and effect to the ceremony, it was resolved that the ratification should take place on the *Champ de Mai* at Paris, with extraordinary pomp; and that the splendor of the occasion and of its incidents should be such as to impress the nation and the world with the great enthusiasm which was still entertained for the emperor, and of the interest still taken in his fortunes.

Accordingly, for a month previous to the appointed day many thousands of workmen were employed in the necessary preparations. Vast ranges of benches rising in the form of a circular ampitheater, were constructed, capable of accommodating two hundred thousand persons. Preparations were also made for conducting the religious ceremonies, and the political canvass, with the most gorgeous magnificence. When the appointed day arrived the sun rose brightly in the serene heavens, and all nature seemed to assume her most smiling and propitious garb. An innumerable multitude crowded the benches, and presented a spectacle similar to that which the mighty Coliseum at Rome might have displayed, when, in the days of her imperial splendor the inhabitants of the mistress of the world assembled there to witness the performances of Nero on the violin, the deadly combat of trained gladiators, or the destruction of Christian martyrs by savage, wild beasts. The religious ceremony commenced the proceedings. One cardinal, two archbishops, and four bishops took part in the celebration of high mass. Such music as had never before been heard in Paris, save under the lofty vaults of Notre Dame, reverberated through the open heavens, and was wafted afar on the free winds. Napoleon surrounded by his chamberlains, his pages, his marshals and generals, attended by brilliant staffs and retinues and all the pomp and splendor of the old empire, assisted at the ceremonies. Thirty thousand of the National Guards added by their presence to the military grandeur of the imposing scene. Four thousand electors chosen by all the electoral colleges of France, cast their ballots for the new constitution which had been announced. They represented the votes of the fifteen hundred thousand citizens who had thus instructed them, in opposition to five thousand who had given their voices against the proposed constitution, throughout the whole nation. It was on this memorable occasion that Napoleon concluded the august ceremonies with these words: "Emperor, consul, soldier, I owe everything to the people. In prosperity and adversity, in the field of battle, in council, on the throne, in exile, France has even been the only object of my thoughts and actions." The emperor continued for some time to address the vast multitude with an eloquence whose ruggid grandeur and strength rivalled even that of Demosthenes himself; and then closed the imposing pageant with the declaration that "his prosperity, his honor, his glory, could by no possibility be any other than the honor, the prosperity and the glory of France;" a declaration which, false as it was, elicited the loud and long plaudits of that innumerable and enthusiastic multitude.

But more anxious and pressing cares demanded the immediate attention of Napoleon, than that of ministering to the vanity and folly of Frenchmen. All Europe was hastening to descend like an avalanche upon the soil of France, and to overwhelm the throne and empire of Napoleon in one general and eternal ruin. For this great peril the last and deadliest which even the Corsican had ever been called to confront, he now prepared himself; and as the crisis approached nearer and nearer, his efforts became more desperate and herculean.

On the seventh of June, he left Paris to join his army. Previous to his departure he appointed a provisional government, at the head of whom were placed his brothers Joseph and Lucien, Cambacéres, Davoust, Fouché, Carnot, and Caulaincourt. He had fortified Paris so completely as almost to render it impregnable. Intrenchments had been erected to the west of Montmartre, in one direction as far as Clinchy and in the other to Chaventon, in which seven hundred pieces of cannon were mounted. The prodigious energy and animation of Napoleon had filled the whole nation with enthusiasm, and already manned those numerous works with able and experienced gunners. It was Napoleon's intention to operate principally with the main body of his troops, composed of a hundred and twenty-five thousand men, with three hundred and fifty pieces of artillery which were marching under his orders, toward Belgium. Other grand divisions of the army under Souchet and Rapp, were posted in La Vendee, Marseilles and Bordeaux, to overawe the royalists. The fate of Europe depended solely on the great central army under the command of Napoleon himself.

On the 13th of June, the great Corsican joined his camp for the last time. It was situated then at Avesnes, between the Sambre and Philipville, and the returns which were immediately brought him, reported one hundred and twenty-two thousand men then actually present under arms. The arrival of Napoleon filled this vast armament with the utmost enthusiasm; which was increased, if possible, by the proclamation which he issued to his troops. Said he: "Soldiers! this is the anniversary of Marengo and Friedland, of Austerlitz and Wagram. If our enemies dare to enter France they will find in it their tomb. Soldiers! we have forced marches to make, battles to fight, perils to encounter. But with constancy, the victory will be ours. For every Frenchman who has a heart within him, now is the time to conquer or to die!" Once more, and for the last time, the enthusiastic courage, the haughty and confident resolution to triumph, which had characterized the veteran armies, both of the empire, and the consulate, and had rendered them the most formidable warriors that ever marched to battle and to victory; that calm yet heroic spirit was again displayed and felt by those who were now about to contend in mortal conflict for the future supremacy of Europe, under the most able and illustrious of generals. But it was for the last time; and never more was that same spirit destined to pervade a great army, or to cheer a mighty general on to certain triumph.

On the 15th of June, the Prussian army under Blücher

retired on the approach of the French from Charleroi to Fleurus. It was now the chief purpose of Napoleon effectively to separate the British and Prussian forces, and to attack and vanquish them in detail. He sent Marshal Ney, with a detachment of forty-six thousand men to Quartre-Bras, situated on the road to Brussels. At the same time Napoleon marched with seventy-two thousand men toward Fleurus, for the purpose of falling on the Prussians. Blücher retreated from Fleurus to Ligny; and at Ligny the Prussians and French heroes engaged in the first of the three great battles which marked the memorable era of the hundred days.

The position taken by Blücher at Ligny was strong and well chosen. Villages in front of him afforded excellent shelter to his troops, while his artillery, arranged on the summit of a vast semi-circular hill, swept the whole line of the French. At that moment eighty thousand men, among whom were twelve thousand cavalry, marched under the black eagles of Prussia. The large detachment sent under Ney to check the English had weakened Napoleon considerably, and his troops then numbered but seventy-two thousand. The duke of Wellington, deceived by false intelligence which he had received from the traitor Fouché—a traitor to Bonaparte, and to Wellington, both to his country and to his country's foes—was quite unconscious, even until the morning of the 15th of June, that the French army was so near, or that the great struggle impended so soon. Wellington was then at Brussels. Having given orders that all the British troops should immediately assemble at Quartre-Bras, he gaily dressed himself and attended a ball at the palace of the Duchess of Richmond. The assemblage was brilliant in the extreme. The beauty, chivalry, and fashion of Belgium had congregated in those stately halls; while the most distinguished soldiers and generals of the British and allied armies graced the scene with their courtly presence. That company of fair women and brave men presented a singular spectacle. The license of continental manners, the stirring excitement of the tremendous crisis which then existed, the uncertainty of the future, all gave unusual romance to the occasion. Burning words of love and affection were uttered then, which were the more ardent and intense because the impending probabilities of the future rendered their realization so insecure. Many attachments had been formed between the young British officers who had been stationed for some months in Belgium, and the blooming beauties of that land of gorgeous tulips; and now the period had arrived when these proffered contracts of unrealized felicity were soon either to be forever broken by death, or to be happily consummated. Sweet, voluptuous music floated on the midnight air; and many graceful forms then moved in harmony with bewitching melodies, which were destined never again to be heard by them!

> "Soft eyes looked love to eyes which spake again,
> And all went merry as a marriage bell."

That brilliant and chivalrous company were unconsciously treading on a sleeping volcano. A sudden sound was heard which struck terror into every heart and blanched the rosiest cheek. It was the distant booming of the cannon which proclaimed the unexpected approach of the French, and the commencement of the great conflict. The lion whom all Europe dreaded, with one prodigious bound had suddenly leaped among the gay and unsuspecting crowd, spreading the utmost terror and dismay. How truly says the matchless poet:

"Ah! then and there was hurrying to and fro,
And gathering tears, and tremblings of distress,
And cheeks all pale, which but an hour ago
Blush'd at the praise of their own loveliness:
And there were sudden partings, such as press
The life from out young hearts, and choking sighs
Which ne'er might be repeated; who could guess
If ever more should meet those mutual eyes,
Since upon night so sweet such awful morn could rise?

"And there was mounting in hot haste: the steed,
The mustering squadron, and the clattering car,
Went pouring forward with impetuous speed,
And swiftly forming in the ranks of war;
And the deep thunder peal on peal afar;
And near, the beat of the alarming drum
Roused up the soldier ere the morning star;
While throng'd the citizens with terror dumb,
Or whispering, with white lips—'The foe! They come! they come!'"*

The battle of Ligny began by a furious attack of Napoleon on the Prussian right, which was soon driven back with immense slaughter. Blücher quickly sent large detachments to the aid of the assailed point, and thereby sensibly weakened his center. This was precisely what Napoleon had desired and anticipated. He commanded his own center, thirty thousand strong, to cross the streamlet of Ligny, and attack the Prussians.

* Childe Harold, Canto III., xxiv, xxv.

Then the conflict became bloody and furious beyond description, and prodigious exertions were made on both sides. Three times the impetuous assaults of the French took the village of Ligny from the Prussians; and three times were they driven back again by the desperate exertions of the assailed. The Prussians returned to the charge again and again. The combatants fought fiercely hand to hand. Two hundred pieces of artillery thundered into the opposing masses. The houses and streets of the village were filled with multitudes of the dying and the dead; and yet by seven o'clock, after three hours' conflict, the battle remained undecided and one half of the position continued in the possession of the Prussians, and the other half in the possession of the French.

The final issue of the combat would have been doubtful; but at that moment a large detachment from the army of Ney arrived on the field and rendered effectual assistance to Napoleon. He then immediately ordered his old guard to advance to the attack. At the same moment all his artillery were arrayed in the front line. The dense columns of the imperial guard moved forward with steady tread; and in concert with the artillery commenced a charge of prodigious fury upon the opposing masses. Twenty squadrons of cuirassiers, under the command of D'Erlon, also followed up the attack. The Prussian center after a short resistance was completely crushed under the tremendous weight and fury of this great onslaught; and commenced to waver, to fall back, and eventually to retreat. Marshal Blücher fought to the last with the fury of a lion. During the retreat he repeatedly charged the pursuing French. But his horse was shot under him; he fell, and both the Prussian and French cavalry passed over the prostrate body of the marshal, while he lay on the ground entangled beneath his dying horse. The victory of Napoleon was at length complete. His loss was six thousand eight hundred men. That of the Prussians was fifteen thousand men and twenty-one pieces of artillery.

It is worthy of remark that the battle of Ligny was the last in which the aspiring eagles of Napoleon were triumphant. This was the last victory which *he* was destined ever to achieve, whose exploits in many lands, for so many years, had elicited such intense admiration throughout the whole world. On that day the inconstant goddess forever deserted the standards of him whom mankind had once not unaptly termed the favorite child of victory.

While Napoleon was combatting the Prussians at Ligny, Marshal Ney was assailing the English army at Quartre-Bras. The French numbered forty-six thousand men, with a hundred and sixteen cannon. Only the half of this force however was engaged at Quartre-Bras, in consequence of the immense detachment sent by Ney, under General D'Erlon to the aid of Napoleon at Ligny. At the beginning of the conflict the Belgian troops were completely overthrown. But the divisions of Picton and the Duke of Brunswick arrived at that critical moment; and the conflict than began in earnest. There were about twenty thousand men engaged on each side. The French cuirassiers charged upon the English infantry with the utmost ferocity. The artillery of the French ploughed through and through the dense squares into which the

English had been formed. But the steadiness and heroism of the latter remained unshaken; and thus the issue seemed again doubtful between such desperate fortitude on both sides, when the arrival of Wellington on the field with a rëinforcement of ten thousand men, at once changed the aspect of affairs. The battle was still continued with increased fury, but the repeated and desperate charges of the French were as often effectively repulsed, and with immense losses. The day waned and night approached. In vain Marshal Ney put forth his utmost exertions. The greater numbers, the steadiness, and the resolution of the allies, were too much even for the "bravest of the brave." When night fell the battle ceased. The allies were triumphant, and the exhausted troops of the French marshal retired to Frasnes, a mile from the field of battle. The allies slept that night upon the ensanguined plain, and their victory was complete. The French lost four thousand men, the allies lost five thousand; but this unusual disproportion between the conquerors and the conquered resulted from the immense number of French artillery.

All these minor engagements were only preparatory to the greater conflict which was to occur, and which was to be decisive and final in its effects. During the 17th of June the English and French armies were busily converging toward the memorable plain of Waterloo. The day was wet. The water fell in torrents, and the roads were almost impassable. Shivering and dripping with the rain, those vast multitudes silently took up their appointed positions on the field of battle; and at night they laid down to rest in deep mud and large pools of water.

Few even of the bravest slept during the solemn hours of that night. The awful grandeur and importance of the event which was to ensue on the succeeding day impressed even the most thoughtless. To that spot then were directed the hopes and fears of the whole of Europe. Never before, since the beginning of time, had men contended for stakes of such prodigious magnitude. Upon the uncertain issue of the coming battle depended the fate of that mighty hero whose achievements had far transcended the achievements of all other men. A conflict was about to be fought more decisive and important than that of Marathon, of Pharsalia, of Cannæ, or of Blenheim. The destiny of a greater conqueror than either Miltiades, Cæsar, Hannibal, or Marlborough, then hung trembling in the doubtful balance. And now for the first time, the two ablest generals of that age were about to measure their swords together, and the future fate of each entirely depended on the issue. If the British were defeated, retreat even from the battle-field would be impossible. The dense forest of Soignies in their rear would cut off every possibility of escape. If Napoleon was vanquished, his fortunes were ruined forever, and he would become thenceforth either a captive or a fugitive on the earth. And those who were about to engage in this great struggle were fully conscious of the supreme importance of the occasion.

At length the heavy hours of night wore away. The busy sounds of hurried preparation, the confused and multitudinous hum which betokened the near presence of mighty armaments, and which had echoed from both camps during the night, gradually ceased. The morning of the eighteenth of June, 1815, dawned upon the world, and with the light there came that hour pregnant with the fate of so many millions of human beings; the hour to which the events of preceding centuries had long converged; the hour to which many ages yet to come will point as the great decisive epoch which moulded the fate of a continent, and even of mankind. The last grand act in the stupendous drama of Napoleon's career was now about to commence, ere the curtain fell upon it forever.

When the day dawned a hundred and seventy-five thousand men sprang from their dripping beds, and arrayed themselves for the last time for the shock and the carnage of battle. Soon the various regiments of both armies began to deploy into their assigned positions. The battlefield extended two miles in length from the chateau of Hugoumont on the extreme right, to that of La Haye Sainte on the left. Through the center of this line the great high road or *chaussée* from Brussels to Charleroi passed, nearly a mile from the village of Waterloo. Both armies were arrayed on the crest of gentle eminences somewhat semi-circular in form, and parallel to each other, between which a natural slope or glacis intervened. The two armies presented a magnificent appearance. The French numbered eighty thousand, the English and Belgians seventy-two thousand. Like huge serpents the long, dark masses wound around the eminences to the thrilling sound of martial music, and gradually formed into line. Napoleon had two hundred and fifty cannon; the English a hundred and fifty-six. The French troops were formed in three lines, each flanked by dense masses of cavalry. Their brilliant uniforms and dazzling arms presented a gorgeous and imposing spectacle. The English troops were drawn up for the most part in solid squares, supported by cavalry in the rear. In front of their whole position their artillery were skilfully arrayed, directly facing the formidable number of guns displayed by the French. Appearances were certainly in favor of Napoleon before the battle began, both as to the number, the equipment, and the arrangement of his troops. On that great day, each of the opposing commanders had exerted his utmost skill, and had exhausted the whole military art, in the disposition of their respective armies, so as to increase their effectiveness to the fullest degree.

Just as the village clock at Nivelles struck eleven, Napoleon gave the order to commence the combat from the center of his lines. The column of Jerome, six thousand strong, first attacked the English posted in the chateau of Hugoumont. A vigorous contest here took place which resulted in the dislodgment of the English troops, and the conflagration of the edifice. This conflict however was only intended by Napoleon to conceal the main point of attack, which was in the right center. The cannonade had now become general along the whole line. Ney was ordered to attack the British stationed along the hedge, and in the chateau of La Haye Sainte. This was the strongest position held by Wellington. As soon as the latter perceived the large masses of troops which were marching against this portion of his line, he drew up the splendid and powerful regiment of the Scotch Greys, the Enniskillers, and the Queen's Bays in its support. The French columns steadily pressed up the slope till within twenty yards of the British guns. Here a furious conflict ensued. The heroic Picton fell at the head of his regiment as he waved forward his troops with his sword. The Scotch Greys attacked their foes with prodigious energy and effect. The French columns then wavered. The Scotch, shouting "Scotland forever," rushed on to the attack. They carried a battery of twenty guns; charged the second line; routed it; and assailed the third. The third line of the French even began to yield, when Napoleon, perceiving the greatness of the disaster, ordered Milhaud's cuirassiers to charge the advancing foe. In this collision the brave Ponsonby died a heroic death; and so desperate was the conflict that the returning Scotch brought back with them scarcely a fifth part of their original number. As Napoleon gazed from the eminence on which he stood while he surveyed the battle, at the splendid and effective charge of the brave Scotch cavalry he exclaimed: *Ces terribles chevaux gris; comme ils travaillent!* But before the Scotch had completed their charge, they had broken and dispersed a column of five thousand men; had taken two thousand prisoners; and had either captured or spiked eighty pieces of cannon, which comprised the whole of Ney's artillery.

Undismayed by this disaster Napoleon ordered twenty thousand cuirassiers, under the command of Milhaud, to advance to the support of Ney in the center. Soon La Haye Sainte was taken. An entire battalion of Hanoverian troops was almost destroyed by the French, but their tide of conquest was terminated by Wellington ordering up the Life Guards, the Royal Horse Guards, and the 1st Dragoon Guards to the defense. The advance of the French was then stopped; but Napoleon being de termined to carry the important post of La Haye Sainte, brought up his whole body of light cavalry to the attack. Wellington still resisted these furious and repeated onslaughts on his lines, by ordering up to their support his whole reserve, and the Belgian regiments which were stationed in the rear.

Thus for three hours the uncertain conflict raged throughout the whole length of the contending lines, with the most desperate fury. Prodigious acts of heroism were performed by many whose names have long since descended with them to their gory and forgotten graves, on that ensanguined field. The dead and dying lay piled in immense heaps, and the whole of the contending armies were involved in the dense smoke and the thundering uproar of battle. Neither appeared willing to yield. Both seemed determined to conquer or to perish. As evening approached Napoleon saw the necessity of combining his energies, and by one prodigious effort to carry the day. All along the line, two miles in length, the conflict raged with terrific fury; but it was now destined to become more furious, more deadly, more destructive still. Suddenly at half past four o'clock, a dark mass appeared in the distance, moving in the direction of Frischermont. It was a Prussian corps, sixteen thousand strong, who were hastening toward the scene of conflict. Napoleon immediately detached Lobun with seven thousand men to arrest their progress; while he himself determined, at that critical moment to put into execution his last and greatest resource, the one which had rarely failed to win the victory to his standards. and to crush the most powerful, enthusiastic, and formidable foes. This was to bring forward the grand attack of the Old Imperial Guard. It was this veteran corps which had decided the fate of Europe on many great battle fields. It was this corps which had made the best troops of Austria quail and flee at Friedland and Wagram; which had broken the power of the Prussian columns at Jena and Lutzen; which had overwhelmed the Russian lines at Borodino and Austerlitz. Napoleon himself now rode through the ranks of these grim and dauntless warriors, and harangued them with a few words of burning eloquence. He briefly told them that the fate of the day, his own fate, and the fate of France and Europe now depended upon themselves. Loud shouts of *Vive l'Empereur* in reply echoed far and wide over the plain, and drowned for a moment, even the mighty thunder of the cannon. Napoleon accompanied his veteran heroes a considerable way down the slope on their advance; and as each column defiled before him, he addressed them words of stirring eulogy and hope, which revived or increased their courage. They advanced to the final attack of the British center in two great masses, one of which was led by Marshal Ney, the other by General Reille.

Never before, in the memorable annals of warfare, had there been such a shock as that which took place when the Old Guards, having approached with solemn and steady tread within forty feet of the English lines, commenced with their ancient heroism and resolution the task of vanquishing their desperate and powerful foes. The very earth shook beneath that terrific shock. They were met by the English Foot Guards, and the 73d and 30th regiments, with a heroism equal to their own. The eyes of all the combatants were turned toward the spot where that deadly conflict was taking place. Quickly and with desperate energy all the most destructive evolutions of warfare were executed. The combatants seemed determined each to conquer or to perish. Immortal deeds were then achieved, which find no superior in all the blood-stained annals of military glory and ambition. But Wellington had made admirable dispositions to meet this last grand attack of the Old Guard, which had also been anticipated. He had stationed his artillery so as completely to sweep their lines; and as they approached near to his position, his batteries were unmasked, and they poured into the advancing host a prodigious storm of iron hail. The first lines of the Imperial Guards melted like frost-work as they came within range of the terrible guns; and though those in the rear resolutely pressed on to the attack, they made no further advance. They still crumbled away. A dead mass of soldiers rose higher and higher above the earth; but the head of the living column was unable to approach nearer than before, to the object of their attack.

At length the Imperial Guard recoiled. Napoleon who had intently watched their progress, turned deadly pale, when he witnessed their useless heroism and their slow and ignominious retreat. Soon the horrid cry was repeated along the French lines: "*Tout est pardue, la Guarde recuile!*" and the enormous mass, broken and in confusion, fled in headlong retreat down the hill.

At this instant the rest of the Prussian army under Blücher and Ziethen came within range of the field, and opened a battery of a hundred guns upon the tumultuous masses of the French. It was now nearly eight o'clock. Soon the Prussians, thirty-six thousand in number, reached the French lines, and commenced a furious attack upon the exhausted and disordered multitudes. At that moment the star of Napoleon's glory, after having for twenty years shone in unequaled splendor near the very zenith, trembled, flickered, and then descended in ominous gloom, never to rise again. In vain the desperate and ruined adventurer strove to rally his discomfited warriors. In vain he swept on his noble charger over the plain, recalling his faltering troops to return once more to the attack. Terror now pervaded every breast. The retreat became general; and though Napoleon exposed himself in the most dangerous positions, and seemed even to seek for death, in restoring courage and order, all were in vain; and the ruin of his army, his fortunes, and his hopes, was complete and irremediable. At last exclaiming: "All is lost! let us save ourselves!" he turned his horse and fled from the field of battle. The Prussians pursued the helpless fugitives with a rancor which only the memory of the horrors of the battle of Jena, and the unequaled outrages then committed by Napoleon on Prussia, could have excited. Multitudes of the retreating French were slain. The whole of Napoleon's artillery fell into the hands of the pursuers. For miles the earth was completely covered with an innumerable number of broken carriages, wagons, baggage, arms and wrecks of every kind. Forty thousand men only escaped out of that vast and splendid armament of seventy-two thousand, who on the morning of that very day, full of martial pomp and pride, had marched under the French eagles. Nearly forty thousand had either fallen on the battle-field, were wounded, or were taken prisoners. The loss of the allies was sixteen thousand killed and wounded. The loss of the Prussians in the battles on the 16th and 18th of June, amounted to thirty-three thousand.

Thus ended in complete discomfiture all the prodigious efforts of Napoleon, after his return from Elba, to regain his lost throne, and retrieve his fallen fortunes. He had exhausted the whole of France in making these preparations, and now his case was hopeless. If previous to the battle of Waterloo, his heroism had been the heroism of desperation, mingled with hope; it became now the heroism, if indeed it existed at all, of black and unmitigated despair. It remained to be seen whether, after such great reverses, the resolution even of Napoleon could undertake any other expedients to preserve his power, his freedom, or even his existence.

The presence of Marshal Blücher at Waterloo, and the absence of Marshal Grouchy, were the decisive causes of the issue of that eventful day; and the French marshal has been severely censured because of his supposed treachery or dereliction of duty. But these censures are wholly unjust. In accordance with Napoleon's own express orders, Grouchy went in pursuit of the Prussian corps under Theilman at Wavres; and although Grouchy distinctly heard the cannonading at Waterloo from his own position, yet he did not dare to deviate in the least from the instructions which he had received from Napoleon himself. Even on the morning of the 18th Grouchy received a despatch from Soult ordering him still to continue the pursuit; and this fact is clearly indicative of the confidence then entertained by Napoleon as to the certain issue of the impending conflict. Hence the exulting exclamation of Napoleon himself on the morning of the battle of Waterloo, when he beheld the dense columns of the English thrown into squares, and posted in admirable array on those heights which were so soon to be dyed in blood and covered with mountains of the wounded and the slain—"I have these English before me at last. Nine chances out of ten are in our favor!" When too late, Napoleon discovered his error, and the fallacy of his calculations. Then would he have given millions to have recalled his absent legions, and thus decide a moment so pregnant with his unalterable fate. But Grouchy was too far distant either to be reached by a messenger, or to be able to comply before the fate of the day had been determined.

Napoleon was the first to arrive at Paris, and to convey thither the unwelcome news of his terrific disaster. It was soon ascertained throughout France that he had staked his destiny upon the issue of Waterloo; and that he had lost. At four o'clock on the 21st, Napoleon sadly entered the palace of the Elyssée-Bourbons; and his first measure was to propose that the chambers should declare him dictator, as the only means of saving France from impending ruin. But this measure was strongly opposed by Fouché, Lafayette, Dupin, and the leaders of the popular party in that assemblage. The chambers declared its sittings permanent. The prevalent feeling was that, instead of proclaiming Napoleon dictator, he should be requested, and even required, to abdicate, as the only possible means of preserving the country. With great truth Lafayette declared in the assembly that, "for more than ten years three millions of Frenchmen have perished for a man who wishes still to struggle against all Europe. We have done more than enough for him. It is now our duty to preserve our country!" In truth Napoleon had for many years been the real curse not only of Europe but even of France. It is true, he had rendered her name illustrious and preëminent in the annals of warfare. It is true, he had conducted her triumphant eagles into almost every capital in Europe. It is true, he had filled the French capital with the most rare and precious works of art, plundered from every gallery on the continent. It is true, he had made Paris the center of refinement, luxury, and civilization. But these were all hollow and worthless advantages, when compared with the infinite evils which he had inflicted upon his country in return. He had exhausted her finances in supporting his vast projects of ambition. Millions of her bravest and best children had perished on the battle-field in defense of his cause; and their bones were then bleaching in almost every distant clime, in the parched and desert sands of Africa, on the shady banks of the Tagus and the Gaudalquiver, amid the mighty abysmal gorges of the Alps, and on the frozen steppes of Russia. He had kept France for many years in a continual state of restlessness, exhaustion, and revolution, totally incompatible with all real and permanent national prosperity. Nor can we blame the leading statesmen of France that, after the battle and the defeat of Waterloo, they eagerly embraced the opportunity given them to humble and to crush the insatiable and destructive ambition of that desperate adventurer, who had been the messenger of ruin to so many millions of his fellow creatures; who had carried desolation and misery to so many nations; who had even convulsed a whole continent by the prodigious throes of the most grasping and inordinate ambition which ever influenced the breast of any human being.

As soon as the wishes of the chambers were communicated to Napoleon, he became extremely enraged. "Dethrone me!" said he, "they would not dare." "In an hour," answered Fouché, "on the motion of Lafayette, your dethronement will be irrevocably pronounced." Napoleon answered with a bitter smile: "Write to the chambers to keep themselves quiet; that they shall be satisfied." Fouché wrote immediately to the deputies that Napoleon was about to abdicate.

Meanwhile the victorious armies of the allies under Wellington and Blücher were rapidly approaching Paris. The important fortress of Cambroy was surprised and taken on the night of the 24th of June; as was also that of Peronne on the 26th. By the 29th the allied armies reached the forest of Bondy in the suburbs of Paris; and established their right wing at Plessis, their left at St. Cloud, and their reserve at Versailles. Wellington immediately opened communications with the commissioners of the government for the purpose of obtaining the capitulation of the capital. As soon as Napoleon discovered the determination of the chambers to proclaim his dethronement, and being apparently sensible of the hopelessness of his situation, he retired to the private domain of Malmaison, the favorite retreat and the property of Josephine.

This movement on the part of the fallen potentate seems to have been the most unwise perpetrated by him during his whole career. It was a cardinal blunder that he did not remain in Paris; surround himself with the fifty thousand veteran troops who were congregated in the capital; and defend it to the last extremity. Not indeed that he could possibly have been successful in that defense; but a desperate show of resistance at that critical moment would undoubtedly have enabled him to make much better terms with the conquerors than he was actually able to do. He would have probably escaped the ignominious fate which befel him when the allies, having determined not to recognize him as a sovereign, or even as a representative of a party or of a portion of the French nation; and having resolved that he should not on any conditions remain in Europe; they already treated him as an outcast and a wanderer, without the least consideration, influence, or power.

After spending six days at Malmaison, Napoleon collected an immense quantity of valuables and set out for Rochefort, with a large number of carriages ladened with his treasures. He traveled with the pomp of an emperor, and arrived at his destination on the third of July. It was his determination then to sail for America; but the close blockade of the port kept by the English cruisers, convinced him that it was impossible for him to escape their vigilance. Then it was that in an evil hour for himself, but in an hour most propitious to the welfare and peace of Europe and the world, he concluded, as the only resource left him, to throw himself on the hospitality of the British nation, as "the most powerful, the most constant, and the most generous of his enemies." On the 14th of July he embarked on board the Bellerophon, commanded by Captain Maitland; and from that moment he became a prisoner of war, in the keeping of the combined powers of Europe, whom his great talents and his restless ambition had so long filled with terror, apprehension, and despair.

Thus terminated the stirring scenes which so strangely animated and diversified the short but memorable epoch of the hundred days. On the 7th of July, 1815, the allied armies entered Paris. For the first time during four hundred years an English drum was heard reverberating within the walls of the French capital. It was indeed a joyful hour for those brave and war-beaten veterans who had, after so many prodigious struggles and vicissitudes, at length crushed the common enemy and oppressor of all, and restored a lasting peace to Europe. On the 8th of July Louis XVIII. again returned to his capital, escorted by the National Guards, again resumed the reins of government, and ascended once more the brilliant throne of his ancestors.

The most difficult problem which then engrossed the attention of the allied sovereigns and generals was the proper disposition which should be made of Napoleon. Their former misplaced generosity in assigning him the sovereignty of Elba, and the base use which he had made of that generosity, had taught them a valuable lesson of prudence. They were now unanimously resolved that Napoleon should be removed to some remote and lonely island of the ocean, and there, like a chained eagle, be compelled to pass the remainder of his existence. St. Helena was the spot immortalized as the last and abhorred abode of this memorable hero. He first set foot upon its bleak and barren rocks on the 16th of October, 1815, and to the obscure and cheerless heights of Longwood were *his* remaining days consigned who had filled so prominent a place in the world's history. There the mighty conqueror of a hundred battles died in unwelcome obscurity and dependence; and an humble and lonely grave, surrounded by the ocean's everlasting and mournful lullaby, received the remains of him who had once played with scepters and diadems; who had made and unmade kings at his pleasure; who had in turn dethroned the hereditary monarchs of Spain, Naples, Sweden, and Tuscany; who had placed two crowns upon the head of Joseph Bonaparte; who had made Louis king of Holland, Jerome sovereign of Westphalia, Murat king of Naples, Eliza grand-duchess of Tuscany; who had laid low in the very dust the vigorous monarchy of Frederic the Great; who had spanned the Alps with the magnificent Simplon; who had won in marriage the haughty descendant of an imperial race; who had shaken every throne in Europe from Edinburg to Constantinople; and who was conquered and chained at last, only by the combined energies of a whole continent arrayed against him in one final, implacable, and mortal conflict.

CHAPTER XIII.

EXILE OF NAPOLEON AT ST. HELENA.

As the origin of Napoleon's career, its progress, and its culmination of glory, were without a parallel in human history; so also was its melancholy termination. Napoleon at St. Helena presents an unequaled spectacle; for what can be a sublimer sight than that proud imperial eagle, after having soared in triumph over the length and breadth of a vast continent, having been at length vanquished and captured by combined millions in arms, at last being bound, like another Prometheus, with chains stronger than iron, to the lonely and frowning rock of St. Helena, to be preyed upon by the vultures of undying mortification and regret!

It was on the 16th of October, 1815, that Napoleon first beheld, from on board the "Northumberland" man-of-war, the bleak heights which were destined to be his final and detested home, towering in gloomy solitude above the waves.

St. Helena is distant six thousand miles from the coast of France. It rises in lonely and repulsive grandeur in the midst of the Atlantic ocean; and its highest peak is elevated three thousand feet above the level of the sea. It is a volcanic formation, having an uneven and rocky surface, and in no portion of it can sufficient fertility be found to serve the rudest and simplest purposes of husbandry. It is twenty-one miles in circumference. The prospect on every side is cheerless in the extreme—a waste of rude, bleak, and shapeless crags on the one hand, and on the other, an horizon bounded as far as the eye can reach only by the vast unchanging surface of the ocean. At the period of Napoleon's arrival, its inhabitants were five hundred in number, including also a garrison of one hundred and fifty men. The climate is unhealthy, being subject from its exposed position to violent and excessive changes of temperature. Occasionally, tropical storms sweep over the rude surface of the island with sudden and terrific violence, destroying the few shelters which the hand of man may have erected to decorate the waste. James Town, its capital, situated at the base of its towering ridges, was a village of no pretension, chiefly inhabited by the various employees of the British government.

Such was the spot selected by his triumphant foes, as the last residence of the once mighty Corsican. After spending some time at the *Briars*, a pleasant cottage near James Town, inhabited by an English family named Balcome, his removal was ordered to Longwood on the 11th of December, 1815, and then the real importance and interest of Napoleon's exile in St. Helena commenced.

The suite of Napoleon who accompanied him in his exile, was composed of the following persons: Count Las Cases, as his private secretary; a person who twenty-four years before, had emigrated in the suite of the family of the murdered Louis XVI. disguised as a jockey. Count Montholon, Count Bertrand, General Gourgaud and Marchand, his *valet de chambre*—these long tried friends of Napoleon and their families alone were allowed or were willing to share the solitude of their illustrious benefactor.

When Napoleon was about to pass from the Bellerophon, on board the Northumberland, Admiral Keith approached him with a profound bow, and said with subdued emotion holding out his hand: "England demands your sword as a prisoner of war!" Napoleon was quite taken by surprise at this demand; but instantly recovering himself, he placed his hand convulsively on his sword —the sword he had worn at Austerlitz—and a terrible and defiant glance of his eye was his only answer. The aged admiral was astounded. His tall head, white with the frost of years, sunk down, overawed by the fierce expression of the captive; and the latter retained his sword.

Longwood was a small collection of inferior buildings, situated on a bleak and exposed plateau, eighteen hundreed feet above the level of the sea, and near the center of the island. This place was covered with gum trees, which exhibited only a stunted growth, and afforded neither shade nor beauty to the landscape. The main building was a structure of stone, some seventy feet in length, and thirty feet wide, with several additional buildings of much less extent. These were all constructed in the simplest manner without the least pretensions to architectural beauty, and without any of the appliances of luxury, or even of comfort. To this spot was conducted, as to his last and only home on earth, that great potentate who had but recently revelled in the most luxuriant palaces of Europe, and had called the matchless magnificence of Versailles and St. Cloud his own. A close line of sentries had been drawn around the plateau of Longwood by the English governor from the day of the emperor's arrival there; and through these, neither the emperor nor any of his suite could ever pass, except by the special permission of the then commandant of the island. To these, and other indignities, the fallen conqueror submitted in silence. He indeed considered himself deeply outraged by the British government who had placed him in that vile durance. Shortly after his arrival at St. Helena, he addressed a note to the British cabinet, in which he protested that he was not a prisoner of war; that he had voluntarily placed himself under the protection of England, before going on board the Bellerophon; that he could have placed himself under the protection of the Emperor Francis; but that he had reposed full confidence in the honor and hospitality of the British government; that he had been deceived; and that now odious restrictions were imposed upon him, which curtailed his liberty, and were derogatory to his dignity. But these grievances were but trifles compared with those which he was compelled to endure after the arrival of Sir Hudson Lowe, as governor of the island, on the 14th of April, 1816. Then Napoleon began to feel the real ignominy and degradation of his condition.

As this man of mighty will and insatiable ambition reflected, amid the solitude of his ocean home, on his past prodigious career, how singular must have been his emotions! At that very moment a distant continent still shook with the recent shock of his legions, on the ensanguined plain of Waterloo. All the statesmen and sovereigns of that continent still exerted themselves with unceasing industry, to forge yet stronger the chains which bound this formidable giant to his prison. All the inhabitants of that continent, from ocean to ocean, still trembled lest he should once more break loose with invincible power from that distant prison; return again to the capital of his lost empire; wrest his scepter from the hands of those who had just usurped it; and calling around him, as by the omnipotent wand of a magician, a hundred thousand armed followers, again resume his career of conquest; again overturn thrones and dynasties; and once more assume that irresistible supremacy over half a continent, of which he had so recently, and by the merest accident been deprived.

And while all Europe thus trembled with apprehension and whispered with pale lips the possibility of the fulfillment of their fears, behold the exile himself in his distant prison. Surrounded by half a score of his most attached friends, some of whom had been near him when first his rising star began to ascend from obscurity, who had accompanied him ever since, during all the wonderful vicissitudes of his career—he had ample leisure to reflect on the mighty revulsions of fortune and of fate which had overtaken him. Did he commiserate the millions of men, whose bones then were crumbling beneath the earth on a hundred battle-fields, who had been led on to conflict and to death by his own insatiable ambition? Did he then think of the millions of orphans and widows who at that moment from Edinburgh to Cairo, from Madrid to Moscow, were shedding bitter tears over the loss of beloved husbands, brothers, and friends? Did his imagination picture before him the countless hosts of ruined and wounded wretches, who, at that very moment were crawling over the earth, almost from the rising to the setting sun, victims of the horrors of war which his own boundless ambition had inflicted; and who cursed him as the sole cause of their misfortunes?

We doubt, indeed, whether he felt one single compunctious emotion. His memoirs do not give indication of a solitary circumstance which would seem to prove that he experienced any sensation whatever, as the long and cheerless years rolled by, except regret at the discomfiture of his prodigious ambition; hatred and malignity against his cautious and jealous jailors; curses against the mutability of fortune; and defiance of his future fate, whatever the mysterious events of the time to come might develope before him. Napoleon Bonaparte such as he was through his life, amid all its amazing scenes of triumph and glory, of disaster and of wo, the same he remained until he breathed his last sigh of agony at Longwood, unchanged and unchangeable. And the various mortifications, indignities, and insults—the deep despondency and despair—which he was compelled to endure during his captivity, the loss of all domestic ties and sympathies, the exulting joy of his triumphant and implacable foes, and the slow but conscious approach of a painful and premature death—all these things were inflictions which taught his proud spirit to appreciate something of the misery which he had inflicted on millions of his race; and enabled him, unwillingly, to estimate and feel the enormity of his own career, as the cause of infinite suffering on the earth.

Sir Hudson Lowe seemed to have been chosen by the British government, as the jailor of Napoleon, because he was known to possess qualities which would render his authority galling to his captive to the last degree. Nor were their expectations disappointed. As soon as the new governor arrived on the island, he made different and much stricter regulations. The trade's-people were forbidden to sell the emperor's party anything, or to hold any communication with them whatever. All the paths and roads leading up to the heights of Longwood were continually guarded by patrols of soldiers. And when visitors who possessed passports from the governor visited the captive, the guards were to report at what time the visits were made, and how long they continued. Spies were continually lurking around the retreat of the emperor, who reported to Sir Hudson from day to day, everything even to the minutest event which occurred within the reach of their scrutiny. The expenses of Napoleon's household were made the subject of interference and dispute. The quantity and quality of his food and wines were inquired into and objected against. To these and various other annoyances, the fallen despot made but one reply to his persecutor: "You have full power over my body; but my mind is, and will remain, beyond your reach. It is as proud and full of courage on this rock as when I commanded Europe!" We cannot but admire the energy and indomitable firmness of an intellect which remained unyielding and uncrushed by such great disasters, and by such a downfall from so immense an elevation.

In October, 1816, so great had become the terror which agitated the minds of the cabinets of Europe, lest their colossal captive might still escape them, that they imposed new and more stringent restrictions upon him. The articles of the treaty into which England, Austria, Prussia, and Russia had entered, in reference to Napoleon, on the 2d of August, 1815, contained the following provisions:

1. Napoleon Bonaparte is regarded by these powers, as their prisoner of war.

2. His safe-keeping is entrusted to the British government. The choice of his abode and the means necessary to secure his safe retention are reserved to his Britannic majesty.

3. The courts of Austria, Russia, and Prussia shall appoint commissioners to reside at the place of Napoleon's abode, who shall constantly assure themselves of his presence there.

4. The king of England binds himself to fulfill this arrangement with reference to the future secure confinement of Napoleon Bonaparte.

It would seem as if with the progress of time the allied powers became more and more fearful of the escape of their captive. Accordingly in 1816, instructions were sent to Sir Hudson Lowe, that the order should be made known, "that henceforth General Bonaparte is required to abstain from entering any house, and from holding any conversation with the persons whom he may meet, unless in the presence of an English officer." The former allowance made by the British government for the support of the captive's establishment was now also diminished; and Napoleon was compelled to permit the sale of his plate, in order to make up the consequent deficiency. This was not because he did not possess any money for that purpose; but because he wished, by this act, to proclaim to the world that he had been compelled to appropriate some of his private means to the maintenance of one, whom the allied sovereigns had themselves proclaimed to be their prisoner of war, and whom, according to the usages of civilized nations, they were bound adequately to support. During the interviews between Napoleon and Sir Hudson Lowe, the former had uttered sentiments of the bitterest contempt and hostility toward his jailor. Said he, "You never let a day pass without your torturing me by your insults. Where have you ever commanded anything but bandits and deserters? I know the names of all the English generals of distinction; but I never heard of you." Language such as this, naturally filled the narrow mind of Sir Hudson Lowe with the most implacable resentment against his captive; and the various means adopted by him to display his enmity, reminds us of the fable of the prostrate and dying lion assaulted by the audacious jackass.

Napoleon at this period either was or pretended to be poor, and he sent letters to the members of his family in Europe, stating that he was in want of the most necessary comforts. They hastened to offer him the whole, or a large share of, their fortunes. King Joseph placed ten millions of francs subject to his order. Queen Hortense, the beautiful Pauline, and the avaricious mother of the ex-emperor, each offered him the whole of their fortunes; while Eliza wrote to him that she possessed but twenty thousand francs in the world, and the half of these were his. It was chiefly of the liberal offer of his brother Joseph that Napoleon subsequently made use.

The mortifications of the emperor's condition still continued to increase. In October orders were received that, his personal suite should be diminished by the withdrawal of four persons. Soon afterward his private secretary, Las Cases, was arrested; his papers sealed up and removed; and he himself eventually compelled to leave St. Helena, and return to Europe. Sir Hudson occasionally took sudden fits of apprehension lest his prisoner had escaped; and then he would rush up to Longwood, and force himself into the presence of the captive in defiance of all etiquette or even decorum. On one of these occasions Napoleon became incensed beyond endurance. Being informed by his attendant that Sir Hudson was about to enter his apartment thus unannounced, he said: "Tell my jailor that he may exchange his keys for the hatchet of the executioner, but that he shall not enter my apartment except over my corpse. Give me my pistols!" Sir Hudson overheard this threat; and being satisfied that Napoleon had not escaped, he retired. The captive and the jailor never met again. But the latter gave orders to all the sentries that if General Bonaparte himself ever attempted to approach any of them, he should immediately be arrested and confined in the guard-house. An immense iron grating was at last sent for to England, which was placed around the circumference of the plateau of Longwood, several miles in extent. This grating firmly planted in the ground was so high, that it was impossible to scale it, and was guarded by one hundred and thirty sentinels both by day and night. Such were some of the precautions adopted by the British government to secure the detention of the most dangerous, as he was the most able man, in the world. Napoleon, as the crowning act of indignity heaped upon him, saw from his window at

Longwood, the erection of this high railing around the outskirts of his abode; he beheld in it another and clearer proof of the excessive vigilance with which his person and his captivity were watched. And he perceived in these various annoyances and precautions clearer evidence that the possibility of his escape was daily diminishing, and that he was at last destined never more to behold the sunny plains of his beloved France, but to end his cheerless exile, only by his death.

It will readily be supposed that Napoleon's residence at St. Helena, rendered that barren rock the most interesting and observed locality of the whole earth; and that pilgrims from every clime visited it, to gaze upon the fallen conqueror in his low and humbled estate. Such indeed was the fact. The bleak heights of St. Helena became another Mecca, toward which the feet of the curious, the distinguished, and the fair from almost every clime, were continually tending. These offered at the crumbling shrine of the fallen deity, the tributes of their admiration and reverence; and some made propositions to him for the purpose of procuring his release, which indicated that there were hearts which still beat with undying devotion to his cause, and were animated with the belief that he would yet regain his lost empire, and triumph over every foe.

One of these propositions came from the captain of an English merchant vessel returning from the East Indies; who assured him that the whole English nation were outraged at the course pursued toward him by their own cabinet. Another offer came to him from one of the officers of the garrison at St. Helena; who proposed that Napoleon should reach a certain point of the island on the shore, which was but an hour's walk from Longwood; was very remote, obscure, and guarded only by a post of infantry; and that thence row boats would convey him in a few minutes to a vessel which rode at anchor near the spot. A still different offer was made to Napoleon to effect his release by means of submarine vessels, which were to approach a point of the coast which the captive could easily reach, and then hiding himself in a ravine from six o'clock in the evening until the time of departure during the night. Five thousand louis were expended by a friend of Dr. O'Meara, in making experiments in reference to the practicability of this plan.

For some reason or other, Napoleon refused to accept any of these successive propositions. He said to Montholon: "I should not be six months in America without being assassinated by the Count d'Artois' creatures. He sent the *Chouan* Brulard to kill me at Elba. I see in America nothing but assassination or oblivion. I prefer St. Helena to these. *My martyrdom here will restore the crown of France to my dynasty!*" Prophetic words which the progress of time has so truly and so wonderfully confirmed!

It may well be imagined that the monotonous life of the ex-emperor was sufficiently dreary. His only or chief solace was the exercise of dictating his memoirs to some member of his suite. All access to his residence was strictly forbidden, from six o'clock in the evening till six in the morning. This rule enforced a degree of solitude upon him which was in the highest degree irksome. His annoyances continued to increase; and in 1818 the emperor's physician Dr. O'Meara, received orders not to quit the enclosed grounds of Longwood; three months afterward, he was forcibly removed from all intercourse with Napoleon, and soon was compelled to leave the island altogether. During the same year, General Gourgaud, one of his personal suite was induced to return to France, on account of his own sickness.

The year 1819 found the exile still declining in health. In January of this year, he could not quit his bed-room. On the 16th and 17th he became much worse. He was at this time without the advice of any medical attendant, and he was compelled to request the services of a physician who happened then to be on board the "Conqueror," in the harbor of St. Helena. During the year 1820, the fatal disease which was secretly gnawing at his vitals—cancer in the stomach—made rapid progress. The illustrious patient was becoming much attenuated. His once rotund figure was rapidly shrinking to that of a skeleton. He could no longer take his customary rides around the limited domain allowed him. His nights were sleepless, and he received many clear prognostics of the mournful fact that his dissolution was not very far distant.

The exile of Napoleon at St. Helena, is not so remarkable from the fact that he ever *lived* there, as because he *died* there. His life in that remote and obscure quarter of the globe was not particularly worthy of note. It was common-place. He could not display in that humble and circumscribed sphere any of the mighty qualities which have rendered him the most wonderful of men. He would have acted very differently had he spent those years upon the brilliant throne of France. But Napoleon died at St.

Helena, precisely as he would have expired had he closed his career within the gilded chambers of St. Cloud. How that imperial spirit would confront the great King of Terrors *anywhere*, is an inquiry of intense interest; and the incidents which attended that last fearful struggle were in substance the same, whether the conflict occurred on the pinnacle of his glory in France, or amid the glooms of obscurity at St. Helena.

The first symptoms of his approaching dissolution were his vomiting of black matter, proving the presence of ulceration in the stomach, accompanied by an intense pain in his left side. Napoleon was attended during his last illness by Dr. Arnott, an English physician of whose abilities he had received favorable statements. On the 21st of April, 1821, being himself convinced of the nearness of his dissolution, he prepared his will with his own hand, and duly sealed and executed it. He began it by the declaration that "he died in the Apostolical Roman religion, in the bosom of which he had been born!" He also desired that his ashes might repose on the banks of the Seine, among the French people whom he had loved so well. He added that he died prematurely, because he was assassinated by the English cabinet and their deputy.

He then made various bequests to his relatives and most attached followers, amounting to more than a million of dollars. The English government had not confiscated his private property; but had allowed him the full and free disposal of it. Napoleon's plea of poverty, therefore, made publicly during his captivity at St. Helena, was without foundation, and was used merely for the purpose of political effect. His will contained thirty-seven different legacies; among which were many of a hundred thousand francs each to his most attached officers and soldiers, who had remained in France. He made touching allusions in his will to his absent wife, Maria Louisa, and to his son, the ill-fated king of Rome. He also spoke in terms of affection respecting his mother, his brothers, sisters, and the two adopted children of his once loved Josephine—Hortense and Eugene. He forgave his enemies; and desired to leave that world in peace, which he had so long agitated and desolated by his insatiable ambition.

He then prepared himself to die. Not indeed as ordinary mortals would prepare to leave the world; but by composing his mind to a consciousness of the dignity of the occasion; and by so demeaning himself in this last and solemn act of the memorable drama of his life, that it might be said, that the great Napoleon was not unworthy of himself—his genius and his fame—even in the hour which most fearfully tries men's souls.

On the morning of the 26th of April, 1821, the emperor called Montholon to his bedside and said to him: "I have just seen my good Josephine, but she would not embrace me. She disappeared at the moment I was about to take her in my arms. She told me we were about to see each other again, never more to part. Did you see her?" Was this a delusion of that mighty brain, or was it another proof, that denizens of the spirit-land may, and sometimes do, revisit the "glimpses of the moon," and hold intercourse with those they have left behind them?

During the night of the 29th of April, the dying emperor suffered intense agony; and perspired so profusely that his linen was changed seven times. His person had become emaciated to the last degree; but his indomitable mind retained its undiminished energy and power. At four o'clock in the morning, he dictated to Montholon two elaborate projects, which seem, under the circumstances of the case, to be the most remarkable things recorded in history. The dying man, already struggling within the jaws of death, dictated one paper on the "future destination of Versailles," and the other on "the rëorganization of the National Guard of France." Five days before he expired, this wonderful person still interested himself deeply in the internal government and architectural improvement of a country six thousand miles distant from his bedside—a country which he could never by any possibility, again behold!

Conscious of his approaching end, Napoleon during the night of the 1st of May, sent for the Abbe Vignali, his almoner, to administer to him the last succors of religion. It is certainly an incident which serves to show the inherent and divine power of truth, that the greatest intellect which the world has ever seen, did not discard the aid which Christianity is intended to afford, in his last moments. It is worthy of note that he, who all his life, had either been an infidel, a Mahomedan, or a sensualist in the fullest sense of the term, should, when *in extremis*, abandon all other supports, and rely solely on the aid afforded by religion. He who had suppressed the inquisition; who had imprisoned the Pope; who had, more than any other man, broken down the power of priestly arrogance and authority throughout the world; was willing, when the solemn realities of an unknown world were beginning to close around him, to implore the help of a principle and an institution, which he had so fiercely opposed. And yet it illustrates at the same time, the inherent weakness even of the mightiest, that Napoleon desired the utmost secresy to be observed in reference to his acceptance of these last rites; lest forsooth, his conduct might excite the derision of the gay and satirical Parisians!

On the 2d of May, the expiring emperor again dictated to his private secretary two hours in succession During the night of the 3d of May, at two o'clock, he sat up with a convulsive movement; and at length tried to arise from his bed. He was enduring the most intense agony. The deadly cancer in his stomach was gnawing at his vitals, having by a slow yet inevitable process, approached a vital part. "I am burning," said he, "as if my stomach was full of coals of fire." During the succeeding day, for the first time in the history of that mighty intellect, it wandered; and reason for a short time deserted her accustomed throne and became enshrouded in darkness.

At length the 5th of May dawned—the day on which the greatest hero of modern times was destined to leave the world. Toward two o'clock he became delirious. Amid the wild wanderings of that giant mind, an occasional phrase escaped him, which clearly indicated on what favorite themes his last thoughts dwelt:—*France, armée—tête d'armée—Josephine.* Then, at length, as the fatal disease grasped deeper hold of his vitals, and the last pang of agony pierced his frame, he sprang with a convulsive movement from his bed; and though his faithful attendant, Martholon, attempted to resist his rising, so great was the spasmodic strength inspired by that awful torture, that the attendant was thrown down upon the carpet and Napoleon fell with him. By the assistance of Archambaud, he was soon replaced in his bed; and became again tranquil. His pangs of pain and suffering were intense, and yet he bore them with silent and heroic fortitude. At length, an ominous rattling in the throat gave the presage of immediate dissolution, and the last moment had arrived. It was late in the afternoon. A terrific storm had arisen, and the heavens were darkened with heavy and drifting clouds. The ocean had suddenly changed its eternal mellow lullaby to hoarser and louder tones of wrath; and lashed the rock-bound coast with appalling fury. The tempest raged over the rude surface of the island; and blackness and darkness seemed to portend some great calamity to nature. The rude dwelling of the dying hero shook to its foundations with the fury of the storm. But he heeded it not. Within that silent chamber his mighty spirit was dealing then with that dread conqueror who is stronger than the greatest of earthly kings. He who had sent so many myriads of his fellow creatures to a premature grave, was now himself about to descend to its dark and cheerless shadows; and his untamed spirit was soon to appear before the impartial judge of all. At six o'clock in the evening of the 5th of May, 1821, the immortal hero of Friedland and of Austerlitz—the dauntless conqueror on a hundred battle-fields, once the sovereign and dictator of the half of Europe—expired on the lone and barren heights of St. Helena; and left the world to that repose, security, and peace, of which he had so long and so ambitiously deprived it.

The great event was not unanticipated. The whole world awaited with breathless expectation the news which would announce the momentous event; and when that information at length arrived, and spread rapidly from one end of Europe to another—that Napoleon was dead—a whole continent, nay even the civilized world, was convulsed by conflicting emotions—some with joy and exultation that death had at last paralyzed that mighty arm, and some with sorrow, that so glorious a spirit had winged its way from earth, prematurely, in the midst of exile, suffering and obscurity; and that they should never more behold its prodigious feats of heroism and of power.

On the 16th of December, 1840, a singular and imposing spectacle was presented in the ancient and brilliant capital of France. The remains of the great emperor, transported from their lonely bed on the rude heights of St. Helena, had been won back again to France, from their stern janitors; and now, his last ardent wish that his remains might repose on the sunny banks of the Seine, was about to be realized. A procession five miles in length, and funeral solemities unequalled in the memory of man for imposing grandeur and mournful magnificence, were about to commemmorate the event; and to accompany their crumbling dust to its last gorgeous home beneath the dome of the *Invalides*. There his dust now reposes—a shrine to which millions will repair, as to the most impressive and memorable spot on earth—until the end of time; and till that dust, reänimated by omnific power at the last great day, shall arise again to the resurrection of the just or the unjust!

"Yet spirit immortal! the tomb cannot bind thee;
For like thine own eagle that soared to the sun,
Thou springest from bondage, and leavest behind thee,
A name which, beside thee, no mortal hath won.
Though nations may combat, and war's thunders rattle,
No more on thy steed shalt thou sweep o'er the plain;
Thou sle'pst thy last sleep, thou hast fought thy last battle,
No sound can awake thee to glory again!"

In the spring of 1814, after twenty-three years of exile, Louis XVIII. ascended the throne of his ancestors, under the auspices of the armies of the confederate powers of Europe. France underwent a complete transformation. Excepting the short interval of the hundred days, Louis retained possession of an uneasy and insecure throne, until the period of his death in September, 1824. He was succeeded by Charles X. a man of very considerable abilities, and energy of character. This monarch was highly conservative in his principles, and vainly aimed to bring back again the absolute sway of throne and altar, over a people who had read Voltaire and Rousseau, and had heard the thrilling eloquence of Vergniaud and Robespierre. After many obstinate struggles with the spirit and the prejudices of the nation, a revolution broke out on the 27th of July, 1830, in which three thousand persons were killed, and Charles X. was compelled to abdicate. He fled from the country. To him succeeded Louis Phillipe, the representative of the younger branch of the Bourbon dynasty. After eighteen years of dexterous but unprincipled government, Louis Phillipe was also expelled from the throne by a sudden insurrection of the Parisian populace, and a Republic was established in the stead of the banished princes. These events opened the way for the remarkable career of the wise and sagacious statesman, who now governs France, and who has so wonderfully introduced the splendid and prosperous era of the Second Empire.

CHAPTER XIV.

THE CAREER OF LOUIS NAPOLEON EMPEROR OF THE FRENCH.

The elevation of Louis Napoleon to one of the most brilliant and powerful thrones in the world after so many years of exile, persecution, and contempt, presents one of the most remarkable spectacles recorded in history. It was not very singular that, when the elder branch of the great house of Bourbon had proved itself utterly unfit to wield the destinies of France, the prudent and experienced Louis Phillipe should have been substituted in their place, by a nation who were wearied of change, and who desired a permanent government, possessing some considerable elements of popular liberty. Louis Phillipe had won the respect of the whole world, by his natural and acquired gifts, by his prudence and patience in misfortune, and by the talents for government which he had already displayed. But none of these favorable influences operated in behalf of the discomfited hero of Strasburg and Boulogne; and yet, propitious fortune, and his own unexpected displays of genius, have placed in his vigorous hand, a scepter more powerful and despotic than that of Louis Phillipe.

Louis Napoleon Bonaparte was born at Paris on the 20th of April, 1808. He was the son of Louis Bonaparte, the brother of the emperor Napoleon I., and Hortense de Beauharnais, the daughter of Josephine. His birth was celebrated with some enthusiasm, inasmuch as his near relationship to the emperor rendered it not impossible that, at some future period in the absence of more direct heirs, the son of the amiable Hortense might inherit the dominion of the great conqueror. He was baptised at Fontainbleau, and Napoleon and the empress Maria Louisa, officiated as sponsors at the ceremony. All this partiality was based on the supposition, that Louis Napoleon was legitimate; but there were not wanting persons both then, and since, who positively asserted that the father of the present emperor of the French was not the king of Holland, but the Dutch Admiral Verhuel; between whom and Hortense there was known to exist a most intimate and confidential attachment. It is also asserted that Louis Napoleon, the husband of Hortense, was fully aware of this circumstance; that it was not unknown to the rest of the Bonaparte family; that the son of ex-king Jerome used frequently to say, "Napoleon III. is a stranger to our family; he is a Dutchman;" and that the widow of Lucien Bonaparte was accustomed to speak of the prisoner of Ham, only as the "person bearing the false name." Other members of this remarkable family have frequently used in reference to the successful adventurer, an epithet much less charitable or decorous than this.

Louis Napoleon was seven years old when the great disaster of Waterloo prostrated the empire of Napoleon I. in the dust. Immediately afterward his mother retired to Augsburg, in Bavaria, and her son accompanied her. After a considerable period they removed to Arenemberg, Switzerland; and there the studies of Louis Napoleon seriously began. He devoted himself particularly to the *belles-lettres*, and to the exact sciences, as well as to the study of the military art. To improve himself in this latter branch of knowledge, he visited the camp at Thun, and actively engaged in every species of military service.

It was while thus employed that the revolution of 1830 broke out at Paris, which placed Louis Phillipe upon the throne of France. The enmity of this disguised despot to the whole Bonaparte race is well known. Louis Napoleon was in Italy when his elder brother, Charles Bonaparte expired; and he thus became the legitimate heir and representative of the great emperor, inasmuch as the king of Rome was also removed, nearly at the same period, by the fatal artifices and intrigues of Louis Phillipe. Louis Napoleon returned to his retreat in Switzerland, and devoted himself industriously to the pursuit of military knowledge, and of general information. It was at this period that he published a work which exhibits very considerable abilities as an author; his *Considerations militaires sur la Suisse.* This production won for its author no mean reputation; and procured for him from the Swiss cantons, the honorable title and dignity of *Citizen of the Republic.*

During this period, not only Louis Napoleon, but also his mother were very much embarrassed in their circumstances. Of all the vast wealth which the queen of Holland once possessed, nothing then remained to her but one valuable diamond necklace. Driven by necessity, she at length sent word to the Tuilleries, that she was reduced to the deepest misery, and had nothing remaining but that necklace, which she entreated the royal family to purchase from her. In reply she was asked, at what price she would dispose of it? She answered, at four hundred thousand francs. They accepted the sale, and instead of sending her the amount demanded, they gave her the sum of seven hundred thousand. This opportune and generous act on the part of the female portion of the family of Louis Phillipe, preserved the unfortunate Hortense from future want and misery.

But this display of generosity did not prevent Louis Napoleon from feeling it his duty to attempt the overthrow of the "king of the barricades." Feeling dissatisfied with the state of France, and hoping by a revolution to realize his life-long aspiration, and even presentiment, that he should one day occupy the throne of his illustrious uncle, he commenced extensive intrigues with the army. His emmissaries were neither few nor inefficient. Among other officers of distinction, whom he gained over to his interest, was Vaudry, the commandant of the garrison of Strasburg. That officer was active in seducing the soldiers under him; and in holding communications with other commandants throughout France. At length, the conspirators thought that their schemes were ripe, and that the favorable moment for action had arrived. On the 29th of October, 1836, Louis Napoleon crossed the French frontier, and entered Strasburg, in order to meet a secret assemblage of the officers who were disaffected toward the government of Louis Phillipe. The prince addressed them in an animated speech, and strove to excite their enthusiasm. He partially succeeded; the soldiers who had been won over, paraded the streets of the city; the revolution was proclaimed; and an effort made to create a general and favorable excitement throughout the city. The whole movement was premature and abortive. It was easily suppressed, and its precipitate leader, together with his principal supporters, were made prisoners. Louis Napoleon was tried and condemned to death; but on the urgent supplications of his mother, his life was spared, and he was banished to the United States. Little did the family of Louis Phillipe then imagine, that the ruined adventurer whom their generosity had once saved from poverty and starvation, and afterward from death itself, would at a later period, supplant them on their throne; would take the extreme measure of compelling them to dispose at a sacrifice of all their property in France; and would so surround his scepter with every bulwark of power, of popular adulation, and of material defense, that their own return to empire has been made thereby, the most improbable, and the most difficult of all the eventualities which lie hidden in the deep and dark bosom of futurity!

The prince was conducted to Paris under a guard; taken thence to L'Orient, and placed on board the *Andromede.* He arrived safely in New York, and spent the first few weeks of his sojourn in the great republic of the west, in travelling through its most remarkable and interesting regions. At this period of his life, Louis Napoleon was characterized no longer by his ardent love of science, nor by his ambitious longings and intrigues. He had become, partly by the force of circumstances, partly from disappointment and chagrin, and partly from the strong natural bias of his nature, which he no longer suppressed, a reckless debauchee and libertine. His acts of immorality and vice rendered him even notorious. In New York, he became the *habitué* of the most celebrated haunts of infamy and licentiousness. He was equally regardless of all pecuniary liabilities. He outraged public propriety and decency by his extreme excesses. He was even arrested and imprisoned in the common jail, and there herded with the lowest and basest of mankind. Not long prior to his leaving New York, he was arrested for a disgraceful misdemeanor, committed by him in the house of a woman, whose establishment he frequently visited. So notorious had he become at that time, that he received from the French residents of New York the Parisian epithet of *Badenguet;* a term used to designate those debauchees and drunkards who, being hopelessly involved in debt, regularly waste Sundays and Mondays without the barriers, in places of amusement. At this period the prince was reduced to the lowest poverty; and subsisted entirely on the sums loaned and given him by his male and female friends.

He was recalled from this life of degradation and dependence by the sad news of the dangerous illness of his mother. He immediately embarked at New York for Europe, and hastened to the bed-side of the ex-queen of Holland at Arenemberg. She expired; and scarcely had she been interred, when Louis Phillipe demanded from the Swiss cantons, the expulsion of the hero of Strasburg from their territories. He was compelled once more to flee; and on this occasion he took refuge in England.

The life of the Prince Napoleon during his residence in England, very much resembled that which he led, while residing in the United States. His pecuniary necessities compelled him to descend to many ignoble expedients from which doubtless his own sense of propriety would have revolted; while his disappointed ambition and the death of his mother disposed him to indulge still more deeply in the licentiousness and dissipation which had marked his conduct at a previous period. Nor can any one who contemplates the career of this remarkable man, fail to be struck with the amazing extremes of fortune exhibited with reference to his history in England; how, in 1840 he was there an impoverished exile, broken in hope, in fortune, and in character; how, at that time, he was the known and despised frequenter of every haunt of fashionable, and even of ignoble vice; how the smallest municipal office then contented his ambition, and improved his finances; how his condition and his expectations were then looked upon as so hopeless as to be even beneath derision and contempt; and how, in 1854, that same Louis Napoleon was received by the Queen of that vast empire in her stateliest array; how he rode along the same streets which had once witnessed his poverty and abasement, surrounded by the greatest pomp and splendor, by the most brilliant equipages, and by all the grand and imposing display which an opulent and powerful court could throw around him; and how he then retired to be feasted and fetéd with the utmost magnificence in the halls of that palace from whose very portals he would formerly have been repulsed with ignominy!

In 1840 ambition once more gained the mastery over the prudence and the indifference of the prince, and he made his second ill-advised attempt to overthrow the throne of Louis Phillipe. Whatever might have been the extent of the conspiracy which existed in France among the Bonapartists, whatever their resources may have been, it is apparent that they were at that period not sufficiently organized, nor impelled by a spirit properly guided, to secure the remotest prospect of success. In August of 1840, Napoleon embarked on board the *Edinburg Castle*, and landed at Boulogne, with a small number of associates as reckless, as desperate, and as *drunken* as himself. Upon their arrival they attempted to create a ferment in favor of the prince; but all to no purpose.* During the excitement which ensued while Napoleon and his friends were attempting to seduce the garrison of Boulogne from their allegiance, he had an altercation with the commandant in which he discharged his pistol with the intention of shooting him, but missed his aim and killed a private soldier standing quietly in his ranks. This was the extent of his achievements on this occasion. In a very short time the prince was again ar-

* "The captain of the steamer told us that the rebels had drunk sixteen dozen bottles of wine during their passage from London to Wimereux, without counting brandy and liqueurs. The soldiers of the 42nd, who were present at the contest, and whom we have interrogated, have assured us that the rebels were almost all TIPSY." (*Proces de N. L. Bonaparte*, &c., 1 vol. published by Pagnerre, 1840, p. 28.) At length the prefect of Boulogne, M. Launay-Leprevot, says in addition, in his private report:—"L. Bonaparte and suite seem to have landed this morning at about three or four o'clock, at a distance of two miles and a half from the city of Boulogne. During their march towards the town, they stopped *to drink*." (*Proces*, &c., p. 7.) It must be owned that those are not very temperate emperor's nephews. Wine and gold—such constitute all the genius of the modern Augustus. We have not forgotten the libation in the plain of Satory, where the troops were for the first time made to call out: Vive l'Empereur!"

rested; the live eagle which he had brought with him as an emblem of his anticipated success, was decapitated; his companions still reeling with the effects of their debauch, were easily put in durance; and this absurd expedition ended in disappointment and disgrace.

The prince though again guilty of treason, and though he did not even then suffer the penalty which treason deserves, did not escape on such easy terms as before. He was conveyed as a prisoner to the fortress of Ham; and his detention there continued for the period of six years. His sentence was that of imprisonment for life; and it was doubtless the intention of Louis Phillipe to place the restless representative of the Napoleonic dynasty forever beyond the power of again disturbing the security and perpetuity of his throne. It is an evidence of the superiority of mind possessed by this remarkable man, that though a voluptuary when at liberty, when confined within a prison he was capable of, and disposed to, turn his thoughts to dignified subjects of inquiry, and to engage in continuous and careful investigations into the most important questions of political economy, and the wealth and prosperity of nations. In 1842 he published his work entitled, *Analysis of the Questions of Sugars;* which evinced a deep acquaintance with the subject, and a great degree of facility as a writer. This work was followed shortly afterward by another, his *Reflections on Recruiting the Army;* which displayed an equal degree of research and reflection upon a widely different, but equally important department of the public welfare.

In pursuits such as these, six years of captivity

passed away. The prisoner of Ham neither forgot the former impulses of his ambition, nor was he forgotten by the great and powerful party in France of whom he was the representative. On the 2d of May, 1847, he determined to execute his project of escape. The various events which were occurring under the government of Louis Phillipe, clearly indicated to the sagacious mind of Louis Napoleon, that a crisis was approaching, and that he should be prepared to take advantage of it.

The plan of escape projected by the captive was admirably adapted to succeed. Workmen were then passing to and fro through the castle, completing some repairs which had been commenced near the apartment occupied by Louis Napoleon. At the time appointed, he dressed himself in the garb of one of the workmen, throwing a common blouse over the rest of his attire. He shaved off his moustaches. A long pipe adorned his mouth, and a heavy board was laid ready to be elevated to his shoulder in order to complete the deception. There were two relics which the prince valued infinitely, which he was loth to leave behind him; and yet their presence on his person, in case he should afterward be searched, would inevitably condemn him. These relics were so highly prized that for many years Louis Napoleon had uniformly carried them in his bosom. One of them was a letter of his mother filled with expressions of tenderness; and it was the last which he had received from her previous to her death. The other was a letter from the Emperor Napoleon to Hortense, in which he spoke of her son in the following terms: "I hope he will grow up and make himself worthy of the destiny which awaits him." At length, after pondering for some time what he should do with these precious mementoes, he determined to risk the danger of their retention. They are prized until the present hour by their fortunate possessor, as his richest and most invaluable treasures.

Fortune favored the prisoner, and under his strange disguise, he escaped the guards of the castle. He first fled to Brussels, thence to Ostend, and afterward to England. The discontent which existed in France against the government of Louis Phillipe increased, and finally ended in the sudden and mysterious revolution which precipitated him from the throne. Previous to this event, the friends of Louis Napoleon among the French had not been idle. Five departments voted to admit him to citizenship. He published a manifesto in which he ingenously acknowledged his attachment to France, and his honorable ambition to render himself in some prominent way useful to her interests. "My heart tells me," said he, "that I shall be worthy of the confidence of the nation." The dissatisfaction of the people with their rulers increased; the pot-house politicians had at that time assumed considerable importance; and their violence had rendered their influence in the state both decisive and dangerous. On the fall of Louis Phillipe, Louis Napoleon hastened to Paris; but the provisional government, with the imbecile and visionary Lamartine at its head, informed the prince that his presence in the capital embarrassed the new government which then began to rule in France, and requested him to withdraw. He did so; but he was soon elected a deputy to the chambers, and returned to occupy the post thus assigned him by the people. In this position he was not indifferent to the advancement of his personal interests, and to the accomplishment of those more ambitious hopes which had so long and so powerfully animated him.

Lamartine retired from his position as head of the provisional government, after having won for himself the contempt and pity of every intelligent man in France. A new president was about to be elected. *Now* was the great turning point in the destiny of the heir of the Bonaparte dynasty; and his confederates and partisans, fully conscious of the importance of the crisis, were determined to improve it. Their exertions were unremitting throughout France, to secure the election of Louis Napoleon to the presidency. The utmost use was made of the immense and undying popularity of the great Napoleon, among all classes of the French people, in order to excite their sympathy, and to win their votes for his representative. France was filled with innumerable busts, with countless portraits, and with every possible memento of the illustrious Corsican. These exertions and expedients succeeded. Louis Napoleon was elected president of France, by the voices of seven millions of voters. Louis Phillipe may with truth be said to have ensured his own ruin, and the elevation of the rival dynasty, by admitting the remains of the illustrious sleeper of St. Helena to a last resting place on the banks of the Seine which he loved so well, and where he had so ardently desired to rest. From the hour that the conqueror of Austerlitz entered beneath the sublime dome of the *Invalides*, the knell of the house of Orleans struck forever; their future downfall became inevitable; and the accession of a Bonaparte to the throne was an irresistible necessity!

Having thus attained the first step of his ambitious ascent, and having realized the apparently fabulous dream of his youth, and of his manhood, Louis Napoleon began to govern France with an unexpected degree of intelligence, sagacity, firmness, and popularity. All men were astounded at the sudden display of these high and rare qualities which he made. From the very day of his accession to his supreme office, he commenced to win for himself the reputation of being the most able, the most wise, the most successful ruler among the whole herd of European sovereigns; and it seemed almost like a fanciful dream of political romance, or a historical Utopia, that the once dissipated and debauched adventurer who had been the familiar inmate of every haunt of licentiousness in New York and London, should so completely have disrobed himself of his former ignoble qualities, that he should have suddenly assumed the characteristics of the wisest and noblest of the race; and that he should have commenced a life utterly at variance, and indeed incongruous, with all that had preceded. France began to flourish beneath his vigorous and beneficent sway, as she had never flourished before. Public confidence was restored. Commerce and manufactures prospered. Internal faction was broken or at least became impotent and silent. The nation very soon reached a degree of prosperity such as it had never experienced, even under the gigantic scepter of the elder Napoleon.

There was but one impediment in the way of the unlimited progress of France toward national triumph and success. This impediment was found in the legislative body, *the Chambers*, which still possessed very considerable power, which enabled its members to embarrass the president, to impede his operations, and very essentially to mould the measures of the government. The French people soon discovered that while all the plans of Louis Napoleon was characterized by much wise sagacity and benevolent wisdom, he was sorely clogged by the jealousy and obstinacy of the Chambers. The French people began, while their admiration for, and confidence in, the president increased, to conceive a growing contempt for the Chambers. They themselves wondered why the president did not by some sudden *coup* of necessary and salutary violence, rid himself of the useless, and even pernicious weight which harrassed and impeded him. They thought that Louis Napoleon would be perfectly justified in taking some such step; and they were prepared to acquiesce in case his opinion and determination coincided with their own conviction. In truth, his own position was becoming quite untenable. He was frequently loaded with the odium of injurious measures, for the adoption of which he was not in justice responsible; which he even detested; and which he had put forth his utmost endeavors to defeat. In fact affairs had at length come to such a crisis, that either the French Chambers must be suppressed, and the factionists overawed; or Louis Napoleon must descend in ignominy from the high place which he had already proved himself so eminently worthy to fill.

Such was the train of circumstances which brought on the necessity of the celebrated, and sometimes execrated, *coup d'etat* of Louis Napoleon. Under the circumstances of the case, it was a useful, an excusable, even an indispensable, and an unavoidable expedient. It saved France already so often and so sadly torn by internal strife and faction, by the ruinous hostility of parties, and by the frequent change of its forms of government, from the deadly fangs of anarchists, and political desperadoes; and gave it the inestimable blessings of a settled, permanent and vigorous administration of affairs. That some blood must needs be shed in accomplishing this very great and important result, was to be expected. That a very considerable number of raving and selfish fanatics, whose interests and influence were ruined by the triumph of the president, would become frantic in his denunciation, was according to the natural course of things. That even a very few innocent persons might be made to suffer by the casualties incident to the revolution, might also be possible. But that these minor evils were as nothing compared to the vast amount of good which a *coup d'etat* would effect, was unquestionable. The desperate diseases of the state, had evidently rendered the use of the most desperate remedies quite indispensable; and no wise man would blame Louis Napoleon, if he yielded to the existing necessity, and employed such remedies in case his subsequent treatment of the patient was judicious, benevolent and beneficial.

Yielding to considerations such as these, Louis Napoleon determined to accomplish his celebrated *coup d'etat*, which took place on the 2d of December, 1851. The army was first converted to the convictions and purposes of the president. Early on the morning of that day all the most eminent and distinguished opponents of the president were arrested while still in their beds. When the Chambers met, they were expelled from their hall. The streets of Paris were filled with thousands of soldiers, who maintained peace and dispersed the crowds which were disposed to be resistive and riotous. Many were shot down by the military. If there were any unjustifiable acts committed by the agents of Napoleon, it was in the severity with which his troops executed his orders to fire into houses which seemed to contain persons hostile to the success of the movement. No doubt, many persons were injured, and some slain, who were totally innocent of any intention to participate in the events of the day. But even this misfortune, and this injustice, were evils inseperably connected with the accomplishment of the useful and desirable purposes of the movement. A few days of terror and uncertainty were the necessary prelude to the long era of national security, prosperity and happiness, which has since ensued, as the result of the establishment of the power of Louis Napoleon on a permanent basis.

Three days sufficed to accomplish the difficult task of establishing the throne of Louis Napoleon throughout France. When the agitation subsided, some incidents which had occurred called forth the regret of the nation. The imprudence of the military in the execution of their orders was the principal cause of this feeling. Thus for instance, M. Jollevard, a distinguished landscape painter was shot dead while quietly pursuing his artistic labors in his lodgings; and the windows of the houses near him were all broken by the *fusillades* of the troops.* M.

* See "London Times." of December 13th, 1851.

Brandus, another distinguished Parisian, very narrowly escaped death; and a servant of his was shot dead at his side, while standing in the private apartment of his master. Multitudes of dwellings were penetrated by balls in every direction; and for the time being, the lives of their inmates were insecure. One of the most active agents of Louis Napoleon on this occasion, himself admits, that "all obstacles were removed by merely running through them, and those who defended them were passed to the sword."* The public organ of the prince itself admitted that "his troops had not spared one single insurgent."† And yet the inhabitants of Paris had been publicly forewarned of the necessity of their avoiding the public streets during the progress of the movement; and if they chose to incur the risk of the dangers which impended, they were themselves to blame. On the 2d of December, Maupas, the prefect of police published a proclamation in which the events which were about to occur were predicted; and every one was forewarned to avoid them. Said he: "Do not go on the Boulevards, for any gathering together of the people will be dispersed by force of arms, and without previous summons."‡ If, therefore, in the face of premonition so public and so clear as this, a portion of the population of Paris persisted in traversing the streets, and if another portion of them obstinately gratified their curiosity by crowding the windows of sus-

*Report of General Magnare on the affray of December, *Moniteur*, December 9th, 1851.

†*Patrie*, of December 6, 1851.

‡See P. Mager, Histoire due 2 Decembre, page 155. Also Mandnit, Revolution Militaire, &c., p. 248.

pected houses; and if, as a consequence, accidents and injuries ensued, the hero of the *coup d'etat* could scarcely be blamed, when the ends to be accomplished were in general so beneficial to the public welfare.

But while Paris, taken by surprise, and adroitly bound hand and foot, submitted with scarcely any opposition to the will of the usurper, the rest of France was not so amiable, so compliant, or so incapable of resistance. In Marseilles and the adjoining province, the news of the *coup d'etat* in Paris excited considerable indignation. The streets were paraded by hostile and indignant multitudes, who uttered the ancient war-cry of *A bas le tyran! A bas le Dictateur! Vive la Republique!* The people rose in the Basses-Alps, and in the Van, determined to resist and to dethrone the new Robespiere, who had thus grasped the reins of empire, and trodden under his feet the liberties of France. But the whole army had been bought over by Louis Napoleon, and was the subservient instrument of his will. He sent a body of troops into the disaffected provinces and cities, who confronted the numerous bands of insurgents, fiercely attacked them, and put to the sword all who were taken with arms in their hands. The insurrections were thus put down, wherever they occurred throughout France. At Avignon, at Lisle, at Cavaillon, at St. Etienne, at Nievers, desperate conflicts occurred between the insurgents or patriots and the military; and in every case, order and submission were secured by the wholesale massacre of all who refused to yield.* After a few days of commotion and bloodshed,

* Constitutionel of December 16th, 1851. Patríe of the 19th of December. Also, Report of General d'Antist, 7th of December.

the whole of France became tranquil, and submitted to the necessity of obeying the new and irresistible power which had arisen in the state. But that submission, in most cases voluntary, yet in a few instances forced, was not accompanied by apprehensions of the future; for the wisdom, prudence and sagacity which had already been so eminently displayed by the new president, had won the confidence of the nation, both in his abilities, and also in his attachment to the interests, the glory and the prosperity of France.*

The greatest dissatisfaction which existed among the French people against Louis Napoleon, was in reference to the agents whom he had chosen, as his most trusted advisers, and as the most active ministers of his purposes. The most prominent and the most odious of all these, was Marshal de St. Arnaud. This man had spent a turbulent, dissolute, and disgraceful life. At an early age he had espoused the military profession; but he had been expelled from the Gardes du corps for misconduct; and was even fortunate that he then escaped without severer punishment. He was next admitted as a sous-lieutenant

* "They write from Aups, 12th of December: The *rebels* fled across the fields, and the one hundred horsemen who were joined with the infantry, pursued them, AND MADE A GREAT SLAUGHTER OF THEM. On the roads to Lorgues, Salerne, Tourtour, and Aups, the bodies of many *insurgents* were found. The column SHOT ALMOST ALL THE REBELS IT MET WITH. The troops were at a short distance from Aups, when they perceived a man on horseback, who, on seeing them, started off at full gallup. The horsemen rushed after him, overtook him, and discovered him to be an estafet, who was going to announce their arrival to the insurgents. To *take him* and SHOOT HIM, *occupied but an instant.*" (*Moniteur*, 17th December.)

in the legion of Corsica; and from this body he was also soon removed, or turned out for a similar cause. In the year 1824, his situation had become very dependent and abandoned. He had descended to the character of a penniless and dissolute adventurer. He was known as such, in London, in Vienna, and in other capitals of Europe. In 1827, he was imprisoned for debt in St. Pelagie, from which he was at length discharged, only in consequence of the charity of some of his acquaintances. In 1831, he again obtained admission into the army, and shortly afterward, became aide-de-camp to General Bugeaud.

But the conduct of St. Arnaud rendered him repulsive even to the army and to his brother officers. In 1837, he served in Algeria, in the foreign legion; and there, for the first time, he displayed the only redeeming trait of his character—the possession of very considerable military talents. From this period his promotion became rapid. In 1840 he was made chief de bataillon; in 1844, colonel and commandant of the subdivision of Orleansville; in 1847, general of brigade; then marshal of France.*

Meanwhile St. Arnaud lived most extravagantly, at the rate of fifty thousand francs per year. As his fortunes improved his dissoluteness of life increased; and the army

* "Leroy, *alias* de St. Arnaud, no doubt passed off his mischances as an officer, for political disfavors; for, in February, 1831, he obtained his re-entry into the service with the rank of sub-lieutenant, his then constant military *ne plus ultra.* He was placed in the 34th regiment of the line. He was thirty years of age, and although he had spent two or three years within the walls of a prison, he accepted the post of aide-de-camp to General Bugeaud,

in Algeria, not given to excessive virtue or rigor, were scandalized at his excesses. On the termination of that war, St. Arnaud returned to France, and became the intimate friend and associate of Louis Napoleon. The latter, after his elevation to the presidency, promoted St. Arnaud to the post of minister of war. When Napoleon meditated the achievement of his great *coup d'etat*, he selected St. Arnaud as his chief confidant; and concerted with him the measures which were to be adopted, to accomplish the intended result. Louis Napoleon could not have chosen a more capable, a more suitable, or a more unscrupulous assistant. St. Arnaud highly distinguished himself by the sagacity with which his measures were adopted, and by the promptitude, energy, and precision with which they were executed. He thus very materially contributed to the success of the movement; and placed his master under very great obligations to him, for the services rendered on this critical occasion. Nor were those services ever forgotten. The grateful emperor heaped honors, titles, and untold wealth upon his efficient favorite, and elevated him to the highest pinnacle of prosperity and splendor. And last of all, when the war in

when the latter was not ashamed to become the keeper of Madame de Berry. In point of truth, the ex-garde du corps of Louis XVIII. was little better, at Blaye, than a spy upon the daughter-in-law of Charles X.! The Orleanist writers of the *Bulletin Francais* (M. d'Haussonville and M. Thomas) were unwilling to utter the word *spy*, out of deference to M. Bugeaud, the illustrious sword of the Orleanists; but they say that their general-gaoler "considered M. St. Arnaud proper to fulfil at Blaye *some subaltern offices which everybody would not have undertaken.*" See Les Trois Maréchaux, page 6.

the East demanded the presence of a capable and energetic commander to lead the armies of the Allies against the colossal forces and fortresses of the czar of Russia, so honorable and so eminent a position was not considered too great a reward for the distinguished talents and services of St. Arnaud. He died in the Crimea, just before the great conflict under the walls of Sevastopol began, and it is not improbable, that, had he survived, his desperate courage and irresistible energy would have very considerably shortened the struggle which took place for the mastery of that important position.

While such were the character and career of the principle confederate of Louis Napoleon in effecting his *coup d'etat*, the rest of them were not unexceptionable. Veron had been condemned to disgorge one million four hundred thousand francs which he had fraudently obtained from his creditors. Vieyra had been convicted as a fraudulent vendor, and had kept a house of prostitution in Paris. Sercey had been sentenced to five years imprisonment for swindling. Magnan had sold property which did not belong to him, and had appropriated the proceeds.* The fact that these men, and such as these, had taken a prominent part in the accomplishment of the *coup d'etat*, gave to that movement the appearance of the reproach of having been the work of abandoned, desperate and ruined men; who, like Cataline of old, aimed to redeem their own fortunes by the downfall of the republic, and by the elevation to power of one, and he the most desperate of their own notorious associates.

* See Schoelcher: "Alliance with the Men of the coup d'etat," London, 1854.

Thus Louis Napoleon became emperor of the French. Seated on one of the most brilliant thrones in Europe, he has since swayed the perilous rod of empire with extraordinary prudence, sagacity and ability. He has in truth proved himself not unworthy of the exalted hopes which, through all the varied vicissitudes of his life, he ever tenaciously entertained; and not unworthy even of the splendid realization which those hopes have at last secured. Five years of administrative care, energy and vigilance on his part have rendered France more flourishing than she has even been at any previous period. He has surrounded his throne with powerful guarantees of future permanency, by winning the confidence of the nation in his ability and patriotism. He has even added to the other splendors which now encircle his name, those which are reflected from the lurid battle-field, and from the gory triumphs of war. He hated the Czar Nicholas, because the Russian potentate had treated his accession to empire, with poorly-disguised contempt. To be avenged for this inexcusable and inexpiable insult, he sent an ambassador to the Sublime Porte, making such demands on behalf of the Latin or Romish christians in Jerusalem, in reference to the custody of the holy places there, which he knew Nicholas, as the protector of the Greek christians in that city, would oppose, and resent. The war in the east was the ultimate result of that movement on the part of the Emperor Louis Napoleon. War being declared by Russia against the sultan, the French emperor became his ally and adroitly induced England, and the other western powers, to assist him in the task of humbling the czar, under the specious pretext of maintaining the balance of power in the east. Thus Louis Napoleon, to gratify his personal hostility against Nicholas, set all Europe in a blaze; and he has amply avenged himself on his foe. Nicholas, overcome by the cares and the mortifications which attended this memorable conflict, sank into his grave, and now sleeps beyond the reach of war's loud tumult; while on the other hand, Louis Napoleon has earned for himself the reputation of having triumphed over the most powerful, determined and dangerous despot of modern times.

But gentler and brighter memories than these cluster around the recent career of Louis Napoleon. In January 1853, he led to the altar, the fair Eugenie de Montijo, the countess and duchess of Teba. This young lady belonged to the most distinguished family among the Spanish grandees of the first class. Her mother, the countess of Montijo had been for many years at the head of the *haut ton* of Madrid. The family usually spent their summers at Biarritz, a watering place in the south of France; and sometimes, a few months of winter they passed in the French capital. It was thus that Louis Napoleon became acquainted with the accomplished and fair countess of Teba. She was then aged twenty-six years, and was in the blooming prime of her radiant southern loveliness. The heart of the emperor soon felt the power of her peerless charms. It is also said that the attachment was mutual.

When Napoleon first revealed his intended marriage to his council of ministers, they resigned in a body. The princess Matilda remonstrated. But opposition and remonstrance only rendered the emperor more resolute in his determination. He had sought the hand of several princesses of royal houses in Europe, and had sought them in vain. He resolved that he would be repulsed and mortified no more. He loved the graceful and accomplished countess, and he would marry her. Nor has she proved herself unworthy of the exalted eminence to which propitious fortune has elevated her. Before the marriage was celebrated, it was said that Napoleon's marked attentions to her excited the apprehensions of her friends for the safety of her reputation; and before she herself consented to become the bride of the monarch of France she expressly stipulated that Mrs. Howard, the former mistress of Napoleon during many years of good and evil fortune, should be banished permanently from France. Seated now upon the throne of Maria Antoinette, of Josephine, and of Maria Louisa—a throne hung around with so many splendid and mournful memories and associations—the Empress Eugenia gracefully and meekly bears her exalted state; and day by day wins more completely the admiration, the applause, and even the affection of the nation.

And thus, the triumphant drama of Napoleon's career has steadily progressed. He has been welcomed as a visitor by the monarch of England, in the stately halls of the Stuarts and the Plantaganets, and has been received as an honored guest by the greatest capital of the world, with the gift of the freedom of the city, with joyous salvos of artillery, with the acclamations of countless multitudes, with flying banners, with military arrays, and with all the pomp and splendor of the ancient nobility and chivalry of England. And then, Brittannia's Queen and her consort, return the compliment. They visit their recent guest in the land of his birth, and of his triumph. At their coming the gay and brilliant Paris puts on her most resplendent attire to welcome them. Spectacles of beauty, of luxury, and of joy, such as the world had never seen before, surrounded and delighted the strangers, on every side. The most memorable scenes of festivity exhibited during the empire of the great Napoleon, were all thrown into the shade by those which were then witnessed; and strangest of all, the hereditary and once implacable enemies of Pondicherry, of Salamanca, and of Waterloo, exhibited themselves to the world in the amazing attitude of friends, united in a close and an affectionate embrace! And while astonished Europe looks and wonders at the strange and improbable events which have come to pass in these latter days, Napoleon retires to the secrecy of his cabinet, and there laughs at the success with which he has wheedled and won the stern natives of Britain; how he has induced them to honor him in their capital; how he has beguiled their monarch to adulate him in his own more sumptuous palace; and has given him an opportunity of displaying the superiority of Paris and France, to London and England; how he has thrown upon his allies the burden and the expense of a dangerous war, in the issue of which they have not the least particle of real interest; how he has laid the hated Nicholas in his grave; how he makes the ancient monarchies of Austria, Prussia and Sardinia subservient to his crafty policy; and how, since the death of the Russian Czar, he has rendered himself the most remarkable, the most successful, and the most powerful man, of the present time!

On the sixteenth of March, 1856, the long-continued and ardent hopes of Louis Napoleon, that he might be blessed with an heir to his throne were gratified. A son was born to him, who received the title of the Prince of Algeria. As was the case at the birth of the unfortunate King of Rome, forty-five years before, a hundred and one discharges of cannon shook the foundations of the capital, and announced the happy event to the enraptured population. The empress was considered to be in extreme danger for some hours, and she expected that every moment would be her last. The son of the former *accoucheur* of the empress Maria Louisa, Dubois, officiated on this occasion; and the peril of his illustrious patient very considerably increased his own trepidation and nervousness. His father had received ten thousand pounds for his services to the fair daughter of the Hapsburgs. The son, more fortunate than his father receives twenty thousand for his efforts in the service of the more grateful and munificent possessor of the French throne. Louis Napoleon himself was overcome with emotion. Falling upon the neck of his cousin, the prince Napoleon, the former heir presumptive, he exclaimed, amid a burst of tears: "I am sure you will love and protect this child!" He had given to Eugenia on this solemn occasion, that precious reliquary, the letters of Napoleon I. and of his mother Hortense, which, during his whole life he has carried in his bosom, and from which he never parts. It may have exerted no inconsiderable influence on the imagination of the empress during the sufferings of her *accouchement*.

To what high hopes, to what glorious destiny, or to what sad misfortunes and romantic vicissitudes this last representative of the great Napoleonic dynasty may be reserved, are mysteries deeply hidden in the future. But it is a circumstance and a coincidence deserving of special notice, that no prince born in France as heir-apparent to the throne during the last two hundred years, has ever ascended the dizzy and dangerous eminence of his inheritance. Louis XIV. survived both his son, his grandson, and several of his great-grand sons; and was succeeded at last by one of the sons of the Duke of Burgundy. Louis XV. outlived his own son, and was succeeded by his grandson Louis XVI. The unfortunate child of the latter, the dauphin, perished miserably as we have seen, in the dark and filthy dungeon to which the ferocious and blood-thirsty fanatics of the revolution had consigned him. The King of Rome, the heir-apparent of a mightier dynasty, died in reality a states' prisoner at Vienna, the victim of the combined intrigues of Metternich and ballet-dancers. The Duke de Berry, the representative of the restored race of the Bourbons, was assassinated before he reached the purple; and the Duke de Bordeaux, the son of Charles X. and the Count of Paris, are fugitives and exiles from the land of their forefathers. Whether the Prince of Algiers who, in his turn now represents the hopes of the resuscitated power and splendor of the Napoleonic race, shall be happier and more fortunate than preceding princes, time by its slow yet steady flight alone can demonstrate.

But for the present, the birth of this prince is a propitious circumstance for the prospects of Louis Napoleon. It confirms his possession of the throne. It establishes a great dynasty. It renders that dynasty at once powerful in legitimacy, and in the voluntary affections of the French nation. And it invests the future fate of France and of the Napoleons, whatever that fate may be, with a deeper, intenser, and more tragical interest during all coming time.

The Prince of Algiers was born at a propitious moment. He may fitly be termed the harbinger of peace to a distracted continent. At the period of his birth the plenipotentiaries of great and belligerent powers were assembled together, through the skilfull management of Louis Napoleon, in the same capital in which the imperial infant first saw the light, in order to lull the fierce and bloody genius of war to repose, to bind him fast with chains, which all wise and good men hoped would prove eternal, and to diffuse the blessings of peace and concord over many afflicted and desolated lands. The coincidence of his birth, and the establishment of a European truce may be the happy presage of a more glorious futurity; and this last *Memorable Scene in French history* may be one of the most fortunate and propitious which has occurred in that vexed land of revolutions and convulsions, during the progress of several troubled centuries. Since the downfall of the great Corsican, the most dangerous foe to the repose of Europe has been the aggressive policy and the insatiable ambition of the Czar Nicholas of Russia. He had resolved to insert the gem of Constantinople's crown among the brilliant jewels of his own diadem; and to make the ancient inheritance of the false prophet an appendage to his own stupendous empire. Nor would even these mighty aspirations, had they been realized, have been the probable *terminus* to his encroachments on the integrity and the rights of Europe and nations; and it is impossible to predict where the mighty surges of his proud and arrogant ambition would at last have been stayed. But the haughty autocrat now sleeps in a trance so profound that there is no fear of his waking! The silent though stately tomb covers the mouldering form once so instinct with fierce and despotic energy; and the sultan no longer trembles on his throne at the approach of the Muscovite legions. Nor is it probable that any of the successors of Nicholas I. after the severe lesson which they have received by the events of the Crimean war, will ever again venture to reassert his aggressive and oppressive principles, in reference to the prerogatives and the territories of neighboring countries. And it is but just to Louis Napoleon to say, that *he* first ventured to excite the immediate hostility of the great czar; that he first defied his gigantic power; that he was the soul of the coalition which dared to meet his innumerable legions in the field, and to assail them on the battlements; that he manfully upheld the spirit and energy of the members of that coalition, when they were about to fail; that he carried on the conflict resolutely till victory had been nobly won; that he, in the appropriate moment of triumph proposed the assembling of plenipotentiaries for the arrangement of a peace between the belligerents; that he aided these plenipotentiaries in not a few important crises in their deliberations, to overcome great difficulties, and eventually to harmonize upon equitable terms of settlement; and that to him are chiefly due the present humiliation of Russia, the premature decease of the turbulent Nicholas, the European concord which at present prevails, the unequaled prosperity which now adorns the land over which he rules, and in some measure the greater glory and felicity, which the future may yet reveal to Europe and to the world!

Even the premature death of this remarkable man would not necessarily undermine the stability or terminate the duration of the government which he has inaugurated; for the *Council of Regime* which he has appointed to take charge of the empire during the time which might elapse between his death and his son's majority, would secure the perpetuity of the empire. In June, 1857, elections took place throughout France for the members of the *Corps Legislatif;* and the result of the contest showed conclusively that the power of the factions hostile to the Imperial government was broken; and the approving voice of the nation clearly indicated that they were still content to live beneath the rigid yet satisfactory operation of the Second Empire.

THE END.

A Curious and Interesting Work.

THE LIFE, TRAVELS, LABORS AND WRITINGS

OF

LORENZO DOW;

INCLUDING HIS SINGULAR AND ERRATIC

WANDERINGS IN EUROPE AND AMERICA.

TO WHICH IS ADDED HIS

CHAIN JOURNEY FROM BABYLON TO JERUSALEM; DIALOGUE BETWEEN CURIOUS AND SINGULAR; HINTS ON THE FULFILLMENT OF PROPHECY, ETC.; AND THE VICISSITUDES OR JOURNEY OF LIFE, AND SUPPLEMENTAL REFLECTIONS,

BY PEGGY DOW.

Complete in One Volume, 507 pp. 8vo. Price, Stamped Cloth, $1 75; Embossed Morocco, $2 00.

Since the days of George Whitfield, it has not fallen to the lot of another minister of the gospel to enjoy so great and wide-spread a celebrity as that of the late Lorenzo Dow. In England and Ireland, in the United States and the Canadas, there are probably few persons now living who have reached adult age, to whom his name is not familiar. There is not a state in our Union that he has not visited, and there is scarcely a town in the older States in which he has not been listened to by hundreds, if not thousands, of the present generation.

It is hardly possible that one who attracted so much of the public attention during his life should soon cease to be an object of interest. Many among those who have listened to his public teachings, as well as those who know him only by reputation, would doubtless be gratified to possess the means of forming a true estimate of the character of the man—the causes of his singularities, the secret of his influence, and the peculiar bent and power of his mind. It is to gratify this desire that the present edition of his collected works is given to the public. His Journal, which comprises the history of his life to his fortieth year, will suggest to an attentive reader a clew to the enigma which his apparently mysterious conduct often presented.

The intellectual endowments of Lorenzo Dow were far from contemptible. He had great natural shrewdness, great firmness, and invincible energy and perseverance. His advantages of early education were small, and he seems never to have attained the power of treating a subject methodically, or of pursuing a course of consecutive reasoning. Still there are many valuable observations for the conduct of life in his writings, and a vein of homely good sense and sound morality pervades them all. He considered the press next to the pulpit for usefulness and therefore, as he says, he "collected the quintessence" of his writings for the benefit of posterity.

MILLER, ORTON & CO., Publishers,

25 Park Row, New York, and 107 Genesee-st., Auburn.

DR. KANE'S ARCTIC EXPLORATIONS

IN SEARCH OF SIR JOHN FRANKLIN,

DURING THE YEARS 1853, '54, 55:

BEING A

PERSONAL NARRATIVE,

AND CONTAINING AN ACCOUNT OF HIS

IMPORTANT DISCOVERIES,

THE PERILOUS ADVENTURES OF HIS PARTY,

AND THE

THRILLING INCIDENTS CONNECTED THEREWITH.

FULLY AND ELABORATELY ILLUSTRATED BY

Several Hundred Wood Cuts and Steel Engravings,

INCLUDING PORTRAITS OF

Dr. Kane and Mr. Grinnell,

THE DRAWINGS AND PAINTINGS BY THE DISTINGUISHED ARTIST,

JAMES HAMILTON, ESQ.

FROM SKETCHES BY DR. KANE.

THE STEEL PLATES EXECUTED UNDER THE SUPERINTENDENCE OF J. M. BUTLER, OF PHILADELPHIA. THE WOOD ENGRAVINGS BY VAN INGEN AND SNYDER.

TWO VOLUMES, OCTAVO. PRICE, $5 00.

THIS BEAUTIFULLY EXECUTED AND INTENSELY INTERESTING WORK SHOULD BE OWNED AND READ BY EVERY ONE.

PUBLISHED BY

CHILDS & PETERSON,

124 Arch Street, Philadelphia,

MILLER, ORTON & CO.,

25 Park Row, New York, and 107 Genesee-st., Auburn.

The Trade and Agents Supplied.

☞ **Single Copies sent by Mail or Express, *prepaid*, on receipt of $5 00.** ☜

HENRY VIII. AND HIS SIX WIVES.

A New and Interesting Work

BY H. W. HERBERT,

COMPRISING BIOGRAPHIES OF

HENRY THE EIGHTH OF ENGLAND,

Katherine of Arragon,
Married, 1509; Repudiated, 1533.

Anne Boleyn,
Married, 1533; Beheaded, 1536.

Jane Seymour,
Married, 1536; Died, 1537.

Anne of Cleves,
Married, 1540; Repudiated, 1540.

Katherine Howard,
Married, 1540; Beheaded, 1541.

Katherine Parr,
Married 1543; Died, 1548.

PORTRAITS of HENRY VIII. AND EACH OF HIS WIVES
441, pp, 12mo. PRICE $1 25.

NOTICES OF THE PRESS.

This is a lively and highly entertaining historical narrative of the reign of one of the most marked of all the British Sovereigns.—*Detroit Inquirer.*

Grand, gloomy, tender, picturesque, exciting, sad, and true to fact, as well as true to human nature.—*Sunday Courier.*

The life and times of Henry VIII. are subjects of more interest and importance, not only to the people of England, but to all men everywhere, than perhaps any other portion of British History —*People's Organ.*

A happy medium betwixt the stately dignity of history and the extravagance of romance. Strict historic truth is gilded with the graces of fancy.—*Detroit Free Press*

TALENTS, HEROISM, PASSION!

STRIKING INCIDENTS! NOVEL ADVENTURES!

CATHERINE II. OF RUSSIA!

AND HER SUCCESSORS.

Comprising Incidents in Russian History to the Fall of Sebastopol. By SAMUEL M SMUCKER. Steel Portrait, 338 pages. 12mo. Price $1.

MILLER, ORTON & CO., Publishers,
25 Park Row, New York, and 107 Genesee-st., Auburn.

MAGNIFICENT WORK OF HISTORY.

A Whole Library in Itself!

Cost $11,000—1207 Pages—70 Maps—700 Engravings.

A

HISTORY OF ALL NATIONS,

FROM THE EARLIEST PERIOD TO THE PRESENT TIME;

OR,

UNIVERSAL HISTORY;

IN WHICH THE

HISTORY OF EVERY NATION, ANCIENT AND MODERN,

IS SEPARATELY GIVEN.

BY S. G. GOODRICH,

Consul to Paris, and Author of several Works of History, Parley's Tales, etc.

It contains 1207 pages, royal octavo, and is illustrated by 70 Maps and 700 Engravings; bound in imitation Turkey morocco.

Invariable retail price, $6,00 in one volume; $8,00 in two volumes.
The same, full gilt edge and sides, $8,00 in one volume; $10,00 in two vols.

***** It is believed that the above work, by Mr. Goodrich, will be very acceptable to the American public. It is the result of years of toil and labor, assisted in his researches by several scholars of known ability, and has been gotten up at a great expense by the proprietors. No pains have been spared in the execution of the Illustrations and Maps, which are entirely new, and prepared by the distinguished author *expressly* for the work. Indeed, all the other historical writings of Mr. Goodrich sink into insignificance, when compared with this, the result of his riper and maturer years. It is admitted that *One Hundred Dollars* could not purchase the same matter in any other shape: and the publishers confidently expect that, in consideration of the great literary value of the work, the large sum expended in preparing it for the press, and the exceedingly moderate price at which it is offered, that it will be favorably received by every lover of good books.**

MILLER, ORTON & CO., Publishers,
25 Park Row, New York, and 107 Genesee-st., Auburn.

New Work, Unrivaled for Interest, Value and Instruction.

The Book of the Age!

RECOLLECTIONS OF A LIFETIME,

OR

MEN AND THINGS I HAVE SEEN IN EUROPE AND AMERICA.

BY S. G. GOODRICH,

The veritable "Peter Parley," author of "The History of All Nations," &c. &c.

In two volumes, 1105 pp. large 12mo., 25 Original Engravings, including an accurate Steel Portrait of the Author. Price, Black or Scarlet Cloth, $3 00; Scarlet Cloth, Gilt Edges, $4 00; Half Calf, Marble Edges, $5 00; Full Calf, Gilt Edges, $7 00.

This work embraces the prominent public events of the last half century, both at home and abroad; a complete Autobiography of the author—his early days, education, and literary career; and an amount of original curious, and valuable Personal Incident, Anecdote, and Description, seldom, if ever, met with in a single work. It is the AUTHOR'S LIFE-LONG WORK, and nothing superior, if anything equal to it, in blended amusement and instruction, has ever been published. Mr. Goodrich is the author and editor of **170 Volumes,** of which over **seven millions** of copies have been sold! and this, the great work of his life, embodies the condensed substance of his *ample Literary and Practical Experience; the War with England in* 1812–14, in which Mr. Goodrich was a private soldier; the *Hartford Convention,* whose operations took place under his immediate observation, and with most of the members of which he was personally acquainted. Embracing curious and interesting details respecting *Old Jeffersonian Democracy, Old Federalism, and Connecticut Blue Lights;* curious and marvellous events connected with the rise and progress of RELIGIOUS SECTS in the United States; with descriptions of the *French Revolution of* 1848, *and Louis Napoleon's Coup d Etat,* both of which the author witnessed. Also, a full account of the "PETER PARLEY'S TALES," of which Four Millions have been sold.

In the course of the work will be found a *Gallery of* PEN AND INK PORTRAITS of *over Two Hundred Celebrated Persons*—Presidents, Vice-Presidents, Kings, Queens, Emperors, Soldiers, Poets, Wits, Enthusiasts, Physicians, Preachers, Lawyers, Politicians, Diplomatists, &c.—all described from personal acquaintance or observation—among whom are the following:

George IV.	Lamartine,	Henry Clay,	Duke of Wellington,	Benjamin West,
William IV.	Victor Hugo,	Dan'l Webster,	Lord Brougham,	Fenimore Cooper,
Prince Albert,	Alex. Dumas,	M. Van Buren,	Sir J. Mackintosh,	Percival,
Queen Victoria	Mad. Catalini,	M. Fillmore,	King Rhio Rhio, or	Brainerd,
Sir W. Scott,	Mad. Malibran,	J. C. Fremont,	Dog of Dogs,	Willis,
Lord Jeffrey,	Pasta,	General Scott,	Louis Phillippe,	Hawthorne,
J. G. Lockhart,	Talma,	Prof. Silliman,	Louis Napoleon,	Mrs. Sigourney,
W. Blackwood	Mlle. Mars,	Eli Whitney,	Thos. A. Emmett,	Miss Sedgwick,
Hannah More,	Rachel,	Judge Kent,	Bishop Seabury,	Mrs. Child,
Dr. Chalmers,	Ristori,	Geo. Cabot,	Bishop Wainwright,	Charles Sprague,
Edw. Irving,	Pope Pius IX.	H. G. Otis,	Dr. Mason,	Longfellow,
Thos. Hood,	Pres't Monroe,	Jas. Hillhouse,	Dr. Romeyn,	Pierpont,
Louis XVIII.	J. Q. Adams,	Uriah Tracy,	Archibald Gracie,	T. Buchanan Reed,
Charles X.	Dr. Dwight,	Nath'l Smith,	Minot Sherman,	Jacob Perkins.

To all which is added, the Author's recent

ANECDOTES OF TRAVEL,

In England, Scotland, Ireland, France and Italy, together with a COMPLETE CATALOGUE OF THE AUTHOR'S WORKS, now for the first time published; with curious commentaries on the COUNTERFEIT PARLEY BOOKS, got up in London.

☞ The Publishers will send this work, Postage Paid, to any Post-Office in the United States, on receipt of price as above.

MILLER, ORTON & CO., Publishers,
25 Park Row, New York, and 107 Genesee-st., Auburn.

The Latest and Best—A New Book for Housewives.

PRACTICAL AMERICAN COOKERY
AND
DOMESTIC ECONOMY.

BY MISS E. M. HALL.

One Volume, 436pp. 12mo. Price, $1 00.

This work has been prepared with much care and well directed attention. It contains the results of experience, and will be found on inspection to be all that is essential, either for the most simply or elaborately furnished table. The Recipes are carefully prepared and conveniently classified and arranged.

The ***Cookery*** contains **973** Recipes, relating to every department of the subject, and is illustrated with **44** appropriate Engravings.

The ***Domestic Economy*** contains **363** Recipes and recent important information relating to the Garden, the Orchard, the Wardrobe, the Laundry, and to all those household and domestic affairs upon which instruction is sought by the thoughtful and caretaking mistress. This department of the book, so seldom to be found in works of the kind—we deem a convenient and important feature. A Cook-book has become a household hand-book, and as such is frequently consulted. By embracing in the same volume the most important information relating to the general subject and to the details of household management, the publishers feel that they have supplied a want which will be appreciated by American housewives.

OPINIONS OF REVIEWERS.

This is the latest, as it is also one of the best and most complete books of practical domestic cookery that has ever been published in this country. It contains over 1,300 recipes, relating to every department, and illustrated with about fifty instructive engravings. The work has been prepared with great industry, care, and judgment; the recipes are for the most part simple, easy, and of great variety. To housekeepers this work will be an invaluable *vade mecum*, including as it does important instructions for the management of the garden, the orchard, the wardrobe, the laundry, and every variety of domestic affairs.—*Boston Atlas.*

This work will prove an invaluable aid to young housekeepers, and in fact old ones may glean some excellent hints from it. Instructions for the behavior of guest, host, and servant—rules for carving and serving, besides recipes for cooking all kinds of dishes. In this fast age, when young ladies are educated for the drawing-room instead of the kitchen, when housekeeping has become a vulgar employment, and economy and care are obsolete words, such a book is greatly needed.—*Geneva Courier.*

Here is another book for housewives, and we should think it a very good one. The recipes have been selected and arranged with much care, and what is better still, are the results of experience.—*Olive Branch.*

True economy should induce every good housewife to purchase this work.—*Boston Transcript.*

This is a valuable and truly useful work, comprising everything needful to be known in the domestic economy, essential to the comfort, convenience, and enjoyment of a family. No female should be without a copy.—*Oswego Palladium.*

It is an *American* book, and this fact alone is enough to commend it to the good sense of every American woman, in preference to the garlic-scented French style of cookery. Everything in the shape of cooking, from a roast turkey down to the most delicate preserve, may be learned from Miss Hall's book.—*Chris. Secretary.*

In fullness of material, in happy and simple arrangement, and in profuseness of illustration, we have as yet seen no book for housewives which claims to be equal to Miss Hall's book in interest and value.—*American Spectator.*

We scorn all bribes, but admit we should like to dine with Miss Hall, or any one of her proficient pupils. Her book has effected us even to tears; had we been hungry as erst we have been, it would have been overpowering. In all candor, we believe this to be a very good book. It contains directions for carving, preparation of beverages, medicinal and other, and a great variety of very useful information.—*N. Y. Criterion.*

MILLER, ORTON & CO., Publishers,

25 Park Row, New York, and 107 Genesee-st., Auburn.

www.ingramcontent.com/pod-product-compliance
Lightning Source LLC
LaVergne TN
LVHW020118110826
845151LV00001B/197

* 9 7 8 1 4 2 5 5 4 2 5 1 1 *